MW00607952

Jefferson Davis's Mexican War Regiment

Jefferson Davis's Mexican War Regiment

JOSEPH E. CHANCE

UNIVERSITY PRESS OF MISSISSIPPI
Jackson & London

Manufactured in the United States of America

94 93 92 91 4 3 2 1

The paper in this book meets the guidelines for permanence and durability of the Committee on Production Guidelines for Book Longevity of the Council on Library Resources.

Library of Congress Cataloging-in-Publication Data

Chance, Joseph E., 1940–
Jefferson Davis's Mexican War regiment / by Joseph E. Chance.
p. cm.
Includes bibliographical references (p.) and index.
ISBN 0-87805-504-5
1. United States. Army. Mississippi Infantry Regiment, 1st (1846–1848)—History. 2. United States—History—War with Mexico, 1845–1848—Regimental histories. 3. Davis, Jefferson, 1808–1889—Military leadership. I. Title.
E409.5.M56C47 1991
973.6'2—dc20 91-17625
CIP

British Library Cataloging-in-Publication data available

To the memory of Harold B. Simpson,
my friend and inspiration,
this work is humbly dedicated.

CONTENTS

ACKNOWLEDGMENTS

Many people have helped me find the information that I needed to put this book together. I wish to thank George Gause, Virginia Haynie, Nicole McKelvy, and Dian Cook from the University of Texas–Pan American Library for their untiring efforts.

My thanks also go to Tom Fort from the Hidalgo County Museum in Edinburg, Texas, for his help on the history of the steamboats that plied the Rio Grande during the Mexican War era. Laurier McDonald of Edinburg, Texas, supplied me with a great deal of firsthand information about the battle site of Buena Vista, which we visited in 1987. Jon Harrison of McAllen, Texas, furnished me with information concerning the armaments and uniforms of the Mexican War. Dr. Ed LeMaster, William Shockley, and Norman Burandt of UT–Pan American supplied advice on technical matters associated with computers and printers.

Dr. Robert Spurlin, of Victoria College in Victoria, Texas, shared his knowledge of the Mexican War and the efforts of his historical research freely with me. Jeffrey Mauck of UT–Pan American pointed out several new sources for information on the Mexican War, and was always eager to engage me in lively and informative discussions.

The Papers of Jefferson Davis at Rice University were especially helpful to me in the preparation of this manuscript. The officials at Rice kindly shared many documents, microfilms of Mississippi newspapers, and microfilms of the combined service records of the Mississippi Regiment. *The Papers of Jefferson Davis,* volumes 2 and 3, were a priceless resource to me in the development of this manuscript. The editors of these volumes deserve special thanks for their exhaustive scholarship. These volumes are important works for all students of the history and culture of the American South. I would especially like to thank Lynda L. Crist, editor, and Mary S. Dix, associate editor, for all the many kindnesses they showed me.

The Department of Archives and History of the State of Mississippi was especially helpful, and I wish to acknowledge the services of Hank Holmes of that department. The State Historical Museum of the State of Mississippi was also very attentive to my many requests. I owe thanks to Mary Lohrenz, curator of this collection, for the many services she rendered.

Special thanks are given to JoAnne Prichard and the staff of University Press of Mississippi for their help and encouragement on this book. Dr. Grady McWhiney kindly read the original manuscript and offered many valuable suggestions. Dr. Nancy Prince drew the maps that appear in this book.

Finally, I wish to single out for particular praise my wife, Carolyn Louise, who encouraged me to continue working on this project until it was complete. She edited the draft versions and offered many useful suggestions on how to improve the style and substance.

Thanks to you all.

October 4, 1989 J.E.C.

INTRODUCTION

On May 13, 1846, the United States declared war on the Republic of Mexico. This was to have a different character from any others fought by the United States before or since: It was a war of conquest. American soldiers were to invade and conquer the territories of Mexico. To carry out this mandate from the Administration of President James K. Polk, it was necessary to have a large army. However, the United States military forces at this time amounted to no more than eight regiments of infantry, two regiments of cavalry, and four regiments of artillery: a total of 7,200 men. Thus, to prosecute the war, it was necessary to levy an army of volunteer soldiers from each state in the Union. This book is a history of one of these volunteer regiments of citizen-soldiers: the 1st Mississippi Volunteer Regiment—generally known as the Mississippi Rifles because of its distinctive arms. The Rifles fought with distinction, participating principally in the capture of Monterrey and the crucial Battle of Buena Vista. At Buena Vista, the courage and daring of this volunteer regiment literally saved the American army from encirclement.

An analysis of the Rifles is important because the Mississippians offer a prime example of what can be accomplished with the American volunteer soldier. This study examines the elements that made the Mississippi Regiment a successful fighting force at a time when other volunteer regiments failed.

The valor of the Rifles in Mexico threw a spotlight on their leader, Jefferson Davis, and drew him from regional fame in Mississippi into a national limelight. On February 23, 1847, we find Davis leading his 370 men against more than 4,000 Mexicans on the North Plateau. All eyes are on Davis and his red-shirted volunteers, as Gen. Zachary Taylor calls out, "Steady, boys! Steady for the honor of old Mississippi." The men who saw Davis in action that day would carry the picture in their memories, and his name thereafter was always mentioned whenever veterans assembled to reminisce about Saltillo. And that was far from the only such incident.

Jefferson Davis made both friends and enemies during his service in Mexico, and these persons influenced many of his later decisions. His disagreement with Gen. Winfield Scott over arming the Mississippi Regiment with percussion-cap rifles was only a precursor to many later acrimonious disagreements, especially during his tenure as Secretary of War in the Pierce Administration. Both men had strong personalities, but their dislike for one another could probably be traced back to a disagreement over suitable arms for the Mississippians.

The friendship between Jefferson Davis and Albert Sidney Johnston, classmates at Translyvania University and West Point, was cemented by their actions together during the attack on Monterrey. Davis had ample opportunity to see Johnston in action. Outside Monterrey, Johnston's cool commands had organized a possible rout of volunteers by the Mexican lancers into a determined resistance, which ultimately drove off the lancers' attack. Indeed, these actions must have contributed to Davis's choice of Albert Sidney Johnston as commander of the Confederate Army of the West. Even after reversals of the Confederate Army at Forts Henry and Donelson, Davis came to the rescue of his beleaguered friend with his much-quoted statement: "If Albert Sidney Johnston is no general, then I have no generals." His thoughts must surely have wandered back to that sunlit day outside Monterrey.

In Mexico Davis had also seen firsthand the bravery and leadership qualities of Braxton Bragg. Twice during the attack on Monterrey Captain Bragg had brought artillery through the narrow twisting and turning streets of the city to the aid of the American attackers. The mutual respect between Bragg and Davis was strong, and after Johnston's death at Shiloh, President Davis appointed Bragg as Johnston's successor. Davis' confidence in Bragg never faltered, even in the wake of Bragg's disastrous campaigns in

Kentucky and Tennessee. Only Bragg's own resignation of his command after the Battle of Missionary Ridge removed him from the Army of the West.

However, the major purpose for this study is to honor the memory of the men of the famous Mississippi Rifles, who vied for the honor to fight for their country and gallantly carried out this obligation. All hail their memory.

Jefferson Davis's Mexican War Regiment

ONE

Mississippi on the Eve of the Mexican War

> To arms—to arms!!!—Mississippians!!!
> Your country now demands your services . . .
> Yazoo is already in the field! anxious for the conflict!
> —*Yazoo City* Whig, *May 29, 1846*

In the spring of 1846, the attention of Mississippians was focused on events then occurring in south Texas. The newly annexed state of Texas was engaged in a dispute over its southern boundary with the Republic of Mexico. The Mexican government claimed the area south of the Nueces River (near present day Corpus Christi), while Texans maintained that the southern boundary of their state extended to the Rio Grande (present day Brownsville). To protect American interests, Gen. Zachary Taylor and his "Army of Occupation" had been ordered by Pres. James K. Polk from camp along the Nueces River into the disputed area. Taylor's army took up positions across the Rio Grande north of the Mexican city of Matamoros, in close proximity to the Mexican Army of Gen. Francisco Mejia. The Mexican Government responded to this act by reinforcing the garrison at Matamoros and replaced General Mejia with the more militant Gen. Mariano Arista.

Tensions between the two armies grew day-by-day, and on April 25, a patrol of sixty-three American dragoons was attacked and captured by a large force of Mexican soldiers operating north of the Rio Grande. This was all the pretext President Polk needed to propose to Congress a declaration of war. Taylor, not waiting for an official declaration, attacked superior Mexican forces at Palo Alto and Resaca de la Palma and defeated them, May 8 and 9. On May 11, Congress declared war.[1]

The people of the state of Mississippi, long sympathetic to Anglo settlers in Texas, had aided and abetted the Texas Revolution of 1836 with supplies and volunteer soldiers. Texas had always been viewed by Mississippians as a potential state, and moreover, a Southern state whose votes would be important in maintaining a national balance of power between slave and free states. Strong cultural ties existed as well, since many new Texans had either been born in Mississippi, or else had kin in that state.

The news of war with Mexico brought the immediate mobilization of volunteer soldiers throughout Mississippi. Maj. Gen. John A. Quitman of the Mississippi militia estimated, in a letter written to Congress on May 1846, that 5,000 Mississippians could be readied immediately for service in the army.[2] By June 1 the number of volunteers congregating at Vicksburg was estimated to be as large as 17,000.[3] Mississippi's Gov. Albert Gallatin Brown, anticipating a request from the Federal Government for at least 2,500 men, conditionally accepted twenty-eight companies, which were organized under his orders of May 9, 1846.[4] However, the state quota for Mississippi volunteers levied by Secretary of War William L. Marcy was limited in the first call to a single regiment of infantry or riflemen for twelve months' service. The public was bitterly disappointed:

> We learn . . . that only one thousand men will be called from this state for the service against Mexico. There are now many more than that number ready for the field, and much dissatisfaction will exist if a greater number than that is not suffered to enter the service.[5]

Governor Brown, blamed by the public for this restriction, wrote feverishly to Washington to request an expansion of the quota. The Vicksburg *Intelligencer* of May 25 published this cynical salute to the governor: "Were he to come among us, not a cannon would be fired, as that would horrify him with the idea of a battle wherein some of his fellow citizens . . . might get hurt."[6] The governor countered his critics in a letter to Secretary of War Marcy by proposing that Mississippi be allowed to fill the quotas of delinquent states,

> which hesitated because they feared an extension of slavery. Mississippi entertains no such scruples and she will with great pleasure cross the line or do whatever else the Administration may ask in the vigorous prosecution of this just and righteous war.[7]

In a further entreaty to Marcy, Governor Brown stated, "The truth is you have not given Mississippi a 'fair shake'."[8] Even with the governor's pleadings, the quota remained in force, and many volunteer companies were to be sorely disappointed by not being selected to serve. The Jefferson County Volunteers were so frustrated that they penned this verse:

THE REQUIEM OF GOVERNOR BROWN

Our Gov'ner has betrayed his trust,
He has disgraced our name.
And for his treacherous act we have
Condemned him to the flame.

We found him in a humble sphere,
And honored him with trust;
But he has faithless proved, and we
Consign him to the dust.

Alas! let this thereafter be
A warning to the rest.
We love a brave and valiant man,
A coward we detest.[9]

In 1846, the state of Mississippi already possessed a well-organized militia, armed, outfitted, and regularly drilled. This volunteer state militia was the centerpiece of a rank-conscious society that was thrilled by uniforms and martial airs. Military titles of rank were awarded rather indiscriminately to the general citizenry. Thomas McMackin, a well-known Vicksburg innkeeper of this era, had developed a practical rule for addressing his customers:

> Every guest is titled; every man under 25 is a colonel; from 25 to 30 they are judges; above 30 they are generals.[10]

For the young man, service in the militia offered many advantages. It allowed him to escape—temporarily—the monotony of farm and plantation life; it gave him a handsome uniform, guaranteed to catch the eye of the young ladies, and a brilliant social life. *The Southron* of January 21, 1846, published in Jackson, Mississippi, allows us a glimpse of what it meant to be a volunteer:

> THE MILITARY BALL
>
> Our city was enlivened on Friday last by the arrival in the cars of the two military companies of Vicksburg, the "Volunteers" and "Southrons", who came here by the invitation of our own gallant little corps, the "State Fencibles", commanded by Capt. C. W. Clifton, to partake of the festivities of the night. The stranger companies, . . . with two fine bands, discoursing most martial music, made a brilliant display as they passed along the thronged streets to their quarters, where they were received by Gen. Duffield and staff.
>
> At half past 3 o'clock they partook of a collation at Gen. McMackin's hotel, and listened to a most spirit stirring address from Gen. Duffield.
>
> The ball commenced about 8 o'clock. At half past 8 the military entered, escorting the commander-in chief and his staff. . . . As they entered, the scene was most imposing; the pit of the theatre being boarded over, presented with the stage a uniform floor, on which were assembled some 300 ladies and gentlemen; the house was brilliantly lighted, and the scenery so arranged at the sides of the stage as to give the effect of a beautiful salon, lighted with chandeliers hanging from the centre. As the military—about 120 in number, filed around the whole area, to the music of the orchestra, the view from the boxes was glorious beyond description. The glitter of gold; the mingled glow of colors; the brilliancy of jewels and the airy gracefulness of plumes, made a scene of such surpassing splendor, that it absolutely oppressed the mind as it dazzled the vision. The ladies looked beautiful in the extreme. . . .
>
> The supper was prepared in Monsieur Savalle's best style, and appeared to give general satisfaction. Dancing did not cease until an early period of the morning.

This social event must have been only one of many held throughout the state. However, the major purpose of this gathering was not lost in the social events of the previous evening.

> The next day, the military were reviewed by Gen. Duffield on market square, where they performed a number of evolutions, and proceeded from thence to capitol square, where they fired by companies. The firing of the Southrons was beyond all praise; the men were steady, attentive to the command, and discharged their pieces like one gun. That of the Volunteers was very good, but not equal to the Southrons. The State Fencibles made one horrible failure, which they afterwards redeemed by some very capital fires. The three companies then proceeded to the depot, where they embarked on the cars prepared for them. . . .

The state militia of Mississippi was trained and ready long before word came that General Taylor and his forces were under attack on the Rio Grande. It's small wonder that Governor Brown found himself with 17,000 men when the Federal Government had asked for a mere 1,000.

TWO

On to Mexico, Hurrah for the Volunteer!

ATTENTION!

The number for the Jackson City Volunteer Company being now complete, a meeting of the members will be held in the theatre, this day (Wednesday) at four o'clock, P.M., for the purpose of organizing the Company—by electing officers, and selecting a name and uniform—Punctual attendance of every member is requested.

—The Mississippian, *Jackson, Mississippi, June 10, 1846*

Taylor's victories at Palo Alto and Resaca de la Palma caused a sense of urgency in the volunteers. They wanted to get into the fight before it was over. In the words of William E. Estes, a young volunteer from Brandon, Mississippi: "Turn us loose on that country."[1]

The streets of Vicksburg must have been a beehive of activity by June 10, as twenty-two companies of warlike volunteers descended upon that peaceful city. Under orders from Governor Brown, these militia units, had assembled to select the ten companies that would constitute the regiment. Governor Brown had certified the following companies as candidates for selection:

Vicksburg Southrons	Capt. Willis
State Fencibles	Capt. McManus
Raymond Fencibles	Capt. Downing
Yazoo Volunteers	Capt. Sharpe
Carroll Volunteers	Capt. Howard
Natchez Fencibles	Capt. Clay
Claiborne Volunteers	Capt. Poore
Tombigbee Volunteers	Capt. McClung
Marshall Volunteers	Capt. A. B. Bradford
Pontotoc Volunteers	Capt. J. D. Bradford
Lexington Volunteers	Capt. Arnyx
Grenada Hornets	Capt. Judson
Woodville Volunteers	Capt. Cooper
De Soto Volunteers	Capt. Labauve
Vicksburg Volunteers	Capt. Crump
Lafayette Guards	Capt. Delay
Lawrence Volunteers	Capt. Williams
Quitman Riflemen	Capt. Parkenson
Copiah Volunteers	Capt. King
Lauderdale Volunteers	Capt. Daniel
Tippah Volunteers	Capt. Jackson
Attala Guards	Capt. McWillie[2]

Competition was keen among the volunteer units to be chosen by the Vicksburg receiving officer. *The Southron* recounted the woes of the Natchez Fencibles, rejected for being undermanned (only ninety-two men were present to answer roll call, whereas the minimum was mandated by state law as ninety-three). Captain Clay was mortified to discover that several of his men had left the premise to "partake of some refreshment." The Fencibles were given fifteen minutes to assemble the correct number of men, but Clay could not meet the deadline, and the Fencibles were turned down in favor of the Vicksburg Volunteers. An outcry of foul play against the Fencibles was trumpeted by the Jackson newspaper; but the receiving officer, in his own defense, later stated that the count of Natchez Fencibles had had to be further reduced by two, because two members of that unit were under the minimum age of eighteen.[3]

The disappointed company of young men from Natchez

chartered a special train to Jackson to discuss the matter with the governor in person. The party arrived late in the evening to find that Governor Brown had "become suddenly indisposed," had taken to bed, and could not be disturbed. Captain Clay vowed that his company would be selected for service by *someone*:

> It was the intention of the company to proceed to Louisiana and tender themselves to the Governor of that State, and if not received, to march to Gen. Taylor and tender him their services at head quarters. He [Clay] said that the State of Mississippi had Repudiated him, and he would seek an asylum of honor and glory elsewhere. The company left for Vicksburg, by the same train, at 12 o'clock at night.[4]

Clay seems to have carried out his threat, for the Natchez Fencibles may have served in one of the regiments of Louisiana militia illegally called into federal service by Gen. Edmund P. Gaines. These regiments were mustered in for three months' service in the military—just about enough time to reach south Texas and draw a few days' rations.

The Claiborne Volunteers, also not chosen for the 1st Mississippi, traveled to Galveston at their own expense, and on June 20, 1846, were mustered in as Company K of the 1st Regiment of Texas Foot Rifles. The regiment had a brief stay at Point Isabel, where they reported killing a rattlesnake 13 feet 4 inches long and weighing 35 pounds. After many adventures, which included a boiler explosion on the steamboat that was carrying them to Camargo, Mexico, they arrived on August 28. As three-month volunteers, the regiment's term of enlistment had expired, and to their colonel's amazement (Albert Sidney Johnston), most of the men refused to reenlist. The remaining eighty-two volunteers quickly assembled under Capt. William Shivors and asked to be mustered in as an independent company. General Taylor was delighted by the look of these men, and readily assented, reporting that he would accept them even if they "all had consumption."

Meanwhile, for those who had been tapped for the Rifles, barracks had already been erected southeast of Vicksburg, in an area that became known as "Camp Independence."[5] Selection of the militia companies was completed by June 16, and the 1st Mississippi Regiment was certified as ready for federal service. The volunteer companies and their officers were as follows:

Company A (Yazoo Guards): captain, John M. Sharp; first lieutenant, Phillip J. Burrus; second lieutenants, Amos B. Corwine, Thomas P. Slade

Company B (Wilkinson Guards): captain, Douglas H. Cooper; first lieutenant, Carnot Posey; second lieutenants, James Colhoun, Samuel R. Harrison

Company C (Vicksburg Southrons): captain, John Willis; first lieutenant, Henry F. Cook; second lieutenants, Richard Griffith, Rufus K. Arthur

Company D (Carroll County Guards): captain, Bainbridge D. Howard; first lieutenant, Daniel R. Russell; second lieutenants, Lewis T. Howard, Benjamin L. Hodge

Company E (State, or Jackson Fencibles): captain, John L. McManus; first lieutenant, Crawford Fletcher; second lieutenants, James H. Hughes, Charles M. Bradford

Company F (Lafayette Guards): captain, William Delay; first lieutenant, William N. Brown; second lieutenants, Frederick J. Malone, Josephus J. Tatum

Company G (Raymond Fencibles): captain, Reuben N. Downing; first lieutenant, Stephen A. D. Greaves; second lieutenants, William H. Hampton, Francis McNulty

Company H (Vicksburg Volunteers): captain, George Crump; first lieutenant, Robert L. Moore; second lieutenants, John Bobb, John S. Clendenin

Company I (Holly Springs Guards): captain, Alexander B. Bradford; first lieutenant, Christopher H. Mott; second lieutenants, Samuel H. Dill, William Epps

Company K (Tombigbee Guards): captain, Alexander Keith McClung; first lieutenant, William H. H. Patterson; second lieutenants, William P. Townsend, William B. Wade[6]

The companies consisted of at least ninety-three men, rank and file, with most of the enlisted men unmarried and some below the legal age of eighteen years. The aggregate strength of the regiment was 936 officers and men.

The first and most important order of business was the election of field officers, that is, colonel, lieutenant colonel, and major.

For the post of colonel, the following names were placed in nomination: Jefferson Davis, Congressman from Mississippi who was at that time in Washington, D.C.; Gen. John M. Duffield, major general of the Mississippi militia; Alexander B. Bradford, a Seminole War veteran and major general of the Mississippi militia; Reuben N. Downing, captain of the Raymond Fencibles; Gen. W. L. Brandon; and Gen. A. G. Bennett. The results of the first ballot were Davis 300, Bradford 350, Downing 135, Brandon 91, and Bennett 37. Under Mississippi law Alexander Bradford had been duly elected. But Bradford expressed the opinion that any man leading this regiment should be elected by a majority and not a plurality and immediately resigned his newly elected position. On the second ballot, voters consolidated behind Jefferson Davis and elected him to the post of colonel by a 147-vote majority. For the post of lieutenant colonel, the nominees were Alexander Keith McClung, former federal marshal of the Northern District of Mississippi, Duffield, Bradford, Downing, and Douglas H. Cooper, captain of the Wilkinson Guards. A strongly contested election ensued, with McClung the victor by a majority vote on the second ballot. Numerous nominees were proposed for the post of major, and after many ballots Alexander B. Bradford was elected by majority vote to this position.

To fill the captain's posts vacated by the election of McClung and Bradford, companies I and K elected as their captains James H. R. Taylor and William P. Rogers respectively.[7]

The following regimental positions were filled by appointments made mostly from the Vicksburg companies: Richard Griffith, adjutant, Seymour Halsey, surgeon, John Thompson and James D. Caulfield, assistant surgeons, Thomas P. Slade, quartermaster, Kemp Holland, assistant commissary of subsistence, Humphrey Marshall, sergeant major, and S. Dodd, drum major.

From some of the bitterest experiences suffered during the Mexican War, it was found that the success of a volunteer regiment depended, to a large degree, on the competence of its officers. Many volunteer regiments, whose ranks were filled with first-rate men, failed in Mexico simply because they had elected unqualified officers. Ambitious local politicans with no military experience and few scruples often campaigned for senior ranks. Brilliant stump speeches filled with promises often persuaded naive young volunteers to vote for men who were unqualified to lead.

One volunteer, who enlisted in an Alton, Illinois, unit, described such a stump speech in his memoirs:

> Our company, the Alton Guards elected our own officers . . . a staff officer called the meeting to order, when a large red-faced man mounted the bar and delivered the following speech. "Fellow citizens! I am Peter Goff, the Butcher of Middletown! I am! I am the man that shot that sneaking, white livered Yankee abolitionist s—n of a b——h, Lovejoy. I did! I want to be your Captain, I do; and will serve the yellow bellied Mexicans the same. I will! I have treated you to fifty dollars worth of whiskey, I have, and when elected Captain I will spend fifty more, I will!" It is needless to state that he was elected almost unanimously.[8]

Many of the newly elected volunteer colonels could not handle even the simplest of military formations. However, the Mississippi volunteers had selected for post of leadership three men of unusual talent and ability. It will be important in our understanding of this regiment to know something of the background of these men and why their fellow volunteers felt them qualified to command.

Much has been said and written about Jefferson Davis, and many excellent biographies exist, so the remarks written here will consider only that portion of his life that relates directly to the history of the regiment. Davis was born on June 3, 1808, in Christian County (now Todd County), Kentucky, the son of a Revolutionary War veteran. He grew up in Wilkinson County, Mississippi, and attended the county academy there. He entered Transylvania University in Louisville at the age of thirteen but later transferred to West Point, from which he was commissioned a second lieutenant in 1828. Davis fought in the Black Hawk War, being stationed at Forts Howard and Crawford in Wisconsin.

While stationed at Fort Crawford, under the command of Col. Zachary Taylor, Davis took an active interest in the commandant's daughter, Knox, and the two soon fell in love. When Maj. Stephen W. Kearny approached the commandant to plead in behalf of Davis for Knox's hand in marriage, Col. Taylor rejected Davis's suit, offering the following reason: "I will be damned if another daughter of mine shall marry into the Army. I know enough of the family life of officers. I scarcely know my own children, or they me."[9] Other sources hint that Colonel Taylor had a second reason, that he was "slightly prejudiced against Lt. Davis on account of a trifling incident in military life. . . ."[10] In any event, Davis was forbidden by Colonel Taylor to call upon Knox at the Taylor home, so the couple were restricted to seeing each other at the homes of mutual friends.

In 1835 Davis resigned from the military, because chances for advancement in rank were rare in a peacetime army. Since Knox was still determined to marry Jefferson, even if the couple had to elope, Colonel and Mrs. Taylor finally gave a "reluctant consent."[11] Knox and Jefferson were married on June 17, 1835, at the home of Zachary Taylor's sister in Kentucky. Davis moved his new bride to Mississippi and began to construct a plantation on the Mississippi River below Vicksburg, the famous Brierfield.

But the "star-crossed lovers" were not to live together for long. Within weeks of their arrival in Mississippi, both came down with malarial fever. Davis managed to recover slowly, but Knox grew progressively weaker and died on September 15, 1835. A grief-stricken Davis retired to Brierfield and shunned social life, spending his free hours in his library reading and studying.

Davis's efforts as a planter were rewarded with more success, and he prospered. An interest in politics caused him to emerge again into society and seek the congressional seat from his district of Mississippi as a Democrat, to which he won election in 1845. Meanwhile he had met and won the hand of the lovely Varina Howell, and he was married for the second time on February 26, 1845. Davis and his new bride had scarcely settled in Washington when the Mexican War broke out. Congressman Davis, who had privately expressed a desire to lead a volunteer regiment to Mexico, was elected to command the First Mississippi while still in Washington.

He accepted the new military assignment, but did not resign his seat in Congress, believing that the war would not last very long. However, on July 13, 1846, he did make a promise to his constituents:

> Unless the government of Mexico shall very soon take such steps as to give full assurance of a speedy peace, so that I may resume my duties as your Representative at the beginning of the next

> session of Congress, my resignation will be offered at an early day, that full time may be allowed to select a successor.[12]

Lieut. Col. Alexander Keith McClung was a man of mystery, excitement, and an accomplished duelist, according to the accounts of his contemporaries. He was born in either Fauquier County, Virginia, in 1811, or Mason County, Kentucky, in 1812, depending upon which source is quoted.[13,14] His mother was a sister of John Marshall, Chief Justice of the United States Supreme Court, and his father was related to the Breckenridges of Kentucky. In 1828, young McClung joined the United States Navy as a midshipman, but the close life of a sailor did not set well with the tempestuous redhead. Extremely sensitive, he was quick to resent wrongs against his person, and on his first voyage, before the ship docked at Montevideo, McClung had been in several altercations with his shipmates. While ashore at Montevideo, McClung fought a duel with another midshipman named Hinton, resulting in the loss of a thumb to Hinton and an arm wound to McClung. McClung was ordered off the ship at Rio de Janeiro with orders to return to the United States on the next available ship and to resign his naval commission, which he did.

McClung moved to Kentucky to study for a legal career, but controversy quickly found him again. In 1829 near Frankfort, in an affair of honor, he slew his maternal cousin, James W. Marshall. McClung moved to Mississippi in 1832, resided in Columbus for three years, and finally settled in Vicksburg. Always a man of mystery, McClung was regarded in Mississippi as "an exceedingly handsome young gentleman of twenty-three years with aristocratic tastes, but no real financial resources, it being understood that he had run through with his patrimony."[15] Trouble was not long in finding McClung at his new address, for in 1839 he became embroiled in another affair of honor with John Menifee. Menifee, from Vicksburg, was an officer in the Vicksburg Rifles and considered to be a marksman with dueling pistols. The two antagonists met at dawn on Dueling Island, in the Mississippi River, to exchange shots from sixty paces. An air of unconcern was assumed by McClung, who continued to puff on his pipe as he stepped off the required distance. When the two turned to face each other, Menifee appeared slightly shaken by the nonchalance of his opponent and fired quickly, missing McClung. Tossing aside his pipe and taking careful aim, McClung fired and killed Menifee. It was rumored that McClung also killed six of Menifee's brothers in duels, as they challenged him one by one in an attempt to avenge their slain brother.

McClung was an outspoken Whig, who believed that "the devil was the first Democrat."[16] He established a Whig newspaper in Jackson in 1840, the *True Issue*, a paper devoted to the election of William Henry Harrison to the Presidency.[17] Under McClung's editorship, "Argument, satire, and the most withering ridicule, filled by turns the editorial columns." This vituperation forced him into yet another duel, which he won. But since he was felt to be responsible for the Whig majority of electoral votes cast for Harrison, McClung was awarded with the appointment as federal marshal for the Northern District of Mississippi.

In Jackson, another opponent faced him through the sights of a dueling pistol. General Allen, an impetuous young man, had long feuded with McClung, who withstood his taunts with more reserve than he usually showed, but finally Allen overstepped the bounds. He approached McClung one day on the grounds of the State Capitol and struck him across the face with an open-handed slap. Both men were armed, a pair of dueling pistols and a Bowie knife each. The distance was set at eighty paces, the understanding being that the two parties were to pace off the required distance, then advance firing. If honor was not satisfied with the discharge of both pistols, they would resort to the Bowie knives.

They paced off the required distance and turned to face one another. Allen fired the first shot, which missed McClung. McClung, not eager to kill the young man, called out, "Are you content, Sir, now that honor is satisfied?" Allen cast aside his pistol and drew another, advancing to within a hundred feet of McClung for a second shot. From this range, McClung discharged a single shot, which struck young Allen in the mouth, shattered several teeth, severed his tongue, and finally lodged in his spine. Allen lived only a short while longer and expired in great agony while en route to a physician.

McClung resigned his federal commission in 1844 to publish a newspaper, *The True Issue*, which advocated the election of Henry

Clay to the Presidency. The distinguished Mississippian Henry S. Foote wrote that McClung was "a man of high literary culture, and might be called the ablest and most polished writer among Mississippians."[18] However, even McClung's efforts were not enough to elect Henry Clay. McClung ran for the state legislature in 1845 on the Whig platform, but was defeated in his bid for office by James Whitfield, who later became governor of the state. When war with Mexico became imminent, McClung organized the Tombigbee Guards and was elected its captain.

Maj. Alexander B. Bradford was an attorney residing in Holly Springs, Mississippi, and considered one of the coming men in Mississippi politics.[19] He was the oldest man in the regiment, a veteran of the War of 1812 and the Seminole War, and held the rank of major general in the Mississippi militia.[20] In the Seminole war Bradford had made his name with his daring charge at the Withlacoochee River. His courage, sometimes bordering on the foolhardy, was to become a byword of the regiment. This possibly apocryphal account of an incident from the Seminole War indicates the flamboyant side to his nature:

> During the Florida War, he was a Colonel of a regiment of volunteers from Tennessee. At a certain time it was expected to have a battle with the Indians. Just before the expected battle, Gen. B. was taken sick. Some of the volunteers thought and perhaps hinted, that it was very convenient to be indisposed just then. He was aware of the surmise of some of his men, and of course felt unpleasant under the circumstance. However, in a few weeks a battle was fought. When Gen. Bradford had formed his regiment in line of battle, he determined to draw the enemy's fire. For this purpose he ordered a company to advance; but a moment's reflection determined him to sacrifice his own life instead of those of the company. Without saying a word he waved his hand to the company thus ordered out, to retire into line again, and drawing his sword, he galloped out in front of the enemy's line, and brandishing his sword high over his head, bade them defiance. In a moment, hundreds of rifles were levelled upon him and fired. He fortunately, and almost miraculously, escaped unhurt. He then deliberately returned to his regiment who had watched with intense anxiety his movement; and then from one end of the extended line to the other, arose a shout of acclamation. . . .[21]

With the benefit of Davis's experience and McClung and Bradford's brashness, the regiment was potentially an effective military force. But much still had to be done to prepare the Mississippians for service in Mexico.

Col. Jefferson Davis lost no time in attending to the needs of his troops. While still in Washington finishing the First Session of the 29th Congress, he had a brief meeting with Cadmus Wilcox, a young plebe from West Point. Wilcox later remembered the occasion:

> I remarked to Mr. Davis that I had seen in the newspapers references made to his having been elected colonel of a regiment of volunteers from his State, and asked if it was true and if he would accept. He replied it was true he had been elected colonel and that he would accept if he could have the men armed with rifles. On being asked why his acceptance should be contingent upon the weapon with which the regiment might be armed, he remarked if armed with the ordinary infantry musket it would be but one of many regiments similarly armed; but with the rifle, besides being more effective, there would probably be no other body of men so armed, and it would be known and referred to as the Mississippi Rifles and, consequently, would be more conspicuous.[22]

Davis was well aware of the defects of the current standard issue weapon for the American soldier, the model 1822 flintlock. The weapon was a smoothbore, caliber .69, 57 inches in length with a barrel length of 42 inches.[23] The cartridges were of paper and contained a single round lead ball, several lead buck shot, and a charge of powder. Loaded from the muzzle with a rammer, the powder was discharged by a flintlock. Such muskets were not considered accurate beyond fifty yards, and in the words of young Lieut. Ulysses S. Grant, "At a distance of a few hundred yards a man might fire at you all day without your finding out."[24] However, the weapon was not designed for individual accuracy but to be fired by a mass of close formation troops in volley. The standard infantry tactic of the day for an attack, as proposed by Gen. Winfield Scott, was a volley delivered at close quarters followed by a charge with bayonets.

Davis wished instead to arm his troops with the United States rifle, model 1841. A professional soldier, he must have known that

Taylor's quick victory at Palo Alto over forces more than twice as large as his own were the result of superior artillery pieces. Better weapons would give infantry an edge, too. The model 1841 was a rifle, caliber .54, 48 inches in length, barrel length 33 inches. The paper cartridge contained only powder, and the ball was inserted in a greased patch, which was used to seat the ball tightly into the riflings in the barrel. The ball and greased patch were inserted into the muzzle with a rammer. The black powder charge was ignited by a percussion cap, and the expanding gases forced the ball out through the riflings, causing it to spin as it emerged. This imparted aerodynamic stability and resulted in highly accurate individual fire. A good rifleman could hit man-sized targets consistently at 300 to 400 yards.

The standard armament for a regiment of the period consisted of eight companies with muskets, two with rifles, the rifle companies being used primarily as skirmishers and sharpshooters. Naturally, Davis's novel proposal to arm the entire regiment with percussion-cap rifles met with considerable opposition from official quarters. His principal critic, General Scott, noted that the model 1841 could not be fitted with a bayonet and was slower to load than the more conventional musket. Davis, speaking of the controversy in 1889, remembered:

> Gen. Scott . . . objected particularly to percussion arms as not having been sufficiently tested for the use of troops in the field. Knowing that the Mississippians would have no confidence in the old flint-lock muskets, I insisted on their being armed with the kind of rifle then recently made at New Haven, Conn., the Whitney rifle.[25]

Davis prevailed over his critics, and a thousand rifles, hereafter to be known by the name "Mississippi Rifle" were purchased from Eli Whitney, Inc., for use in Mexico. These firearms were the first mass-produced rifles with interchangeable parts to be adopted by the United States Government. To substitute for the missing bayonet, Davis authorized his troops to carry short artillery swords, Bowie knives, pistols, and the new Colt five-shooter revolvers for action at close quarters.

Early regimental parades must have been a colorful sight, with each of the volunteer companies clad in its own distinctive uniform.

However, at some early date a standard regimental uniform was selected, which consisted of "a red shirt worn outside their white duck pants, and black slouch hats."[26]

Davis had not yet joined the regiment, but the men were set to work immediately with drill and training under the supervision of McClung and Bradford. Standards of discipline were high for these volunteers, and the unit was popular with the people of Vicksburg. William E. Estes from Brandon, remembering his stay in Vicksburg, wrote:

> It was a noticeable fact, at the time that during our stay near Vicksburg, of more than a month, not one member of the regiment was arrested. One of the boys threw a soda bottle [there were no beer bottles in those days] through Genella's window and came near demolishing his china shop, but Genella refused to have him arrested.[27]

About the first week in July 1846, the Mississippians were moved down the river from Vicksburg to New Orleans on steamboats. Estes remembers that his company and two others "took passage on the *Old Magnolia*." Other companies of the regiment traveled aboard the *M. B. Hamer*.[28] The regiment camped at the Chalmette Plantation, about three miles below the city, the site of the Battle of New Orleans in 1815. Other volunteer regiments were already there, awaiting passage to south Texas. The setting was less than ideal. "Our volunteers were turned out to the open fields, knee deep in mud and water, and compelled to sleep on wet clothes for three or four days," noted an observer.[29] Sanitary conditions were uniformly bad, and camp hygiene was neglected. Young men who had been reared in an isolated rural setting soon found themselves easy prey to communicable diseases, to which they had not previously been exposed. The sick list began to lengthen.

Davis arrived to take command on July 17, and immediately moved his regiment to some empty cotton sheds on the outskirts of the town.[30] But the damage had already been done, and many of the diseases contracted in New Orleans would later result in high death and discharge rates in south Texas.

Volunteers had not been allowed access to the vacant military barracks in New Orleans during this time, these barracks having been designated for the exclusive use of the regular army.[31] The editor of the *Vicksburg Whig* was furious at what he regarded as an act of duplicity and gouged the officials in New Orleans with the sharp end of his quill:

> A Lieut. Wetmore, attempts to justify himself for not permitting the Mississippi Volunteers to occupy the Barracks, and seems to sneer at the Jeffersonian [a New Orleans newspaper] for intimating that the regiment was composed of gentlemen. We suppose that many of Uncle Sam's upstarts—dressed in little brief authority—who lord it over the regulars as if they were slaves, cannot imagine how any cotton planter can be a private in the ranks, and yet, strange as it may seem to them . . . there are privates in the regiment of better families, better education, better feelings, and more talent, than many of the Government upstarts who hold the offices. . . .[32]

After delays due in part to an inadequate supply of troop transports, the regiment was finally embarked for Brazos Island, a barrier island off the coast of south Texas. Companies F, G, and I, led by A. K. McClung, boarded the privately owned charter steamer *New York* on July 22; companies A, D, E, and K, led by A. B. Bradford, boarded the screw steamer *Massachusetts* on July 23. Both of these ships had arrived off Brazos Island by July 27, while the remainder of the regiment under the command of Davis left New Orleans on board the *Alabama* on July 26.[33]

THREE

Army Life on the Rio Grande

All plants here have thorns, all animals stings or horns, and all men carry weapons.
—*Lt. Adolph Engelmann, 2d Rgt., Illinois Foot Volunteers*

The sea voyage from New Orleans to Brazos Island was a great adventure to most of the men of the 1st Mississippi, and they were blessed with a calm passage. Letters back home described vast schools of flying fish and the many porpoises that seemed to play tag with the ships. However, sharks also followed the vessel and looked huge to the youthful Mississippians, but all agreed that the sunsets at sea were the most beautiful they had ever seen.[1]

The Rifles went ashore in south Texas at Brazos Santiago (Brazos Island), on July 28, 1846. A shallow bar of 6 to 7 feet blocked the pass leading to Point Isabel, so troops and equipment were brought ashore on lighters. Rufus K. Arthur reported that the harbor contained "50 to 60 vessels" of every class from "ship down to sloops." The pass and the beach were littered with shipwrecks of all sizes. The wreck of the *Col. Harney* was visible on the bar in the pass, as well as the remains of a small sloop.[2] Shortly after his arrival, Arthur reported seeing the schooners *Cora* and *John Francis* become stuck on the bar, and sink under the relentless pounding of the surf.[3]

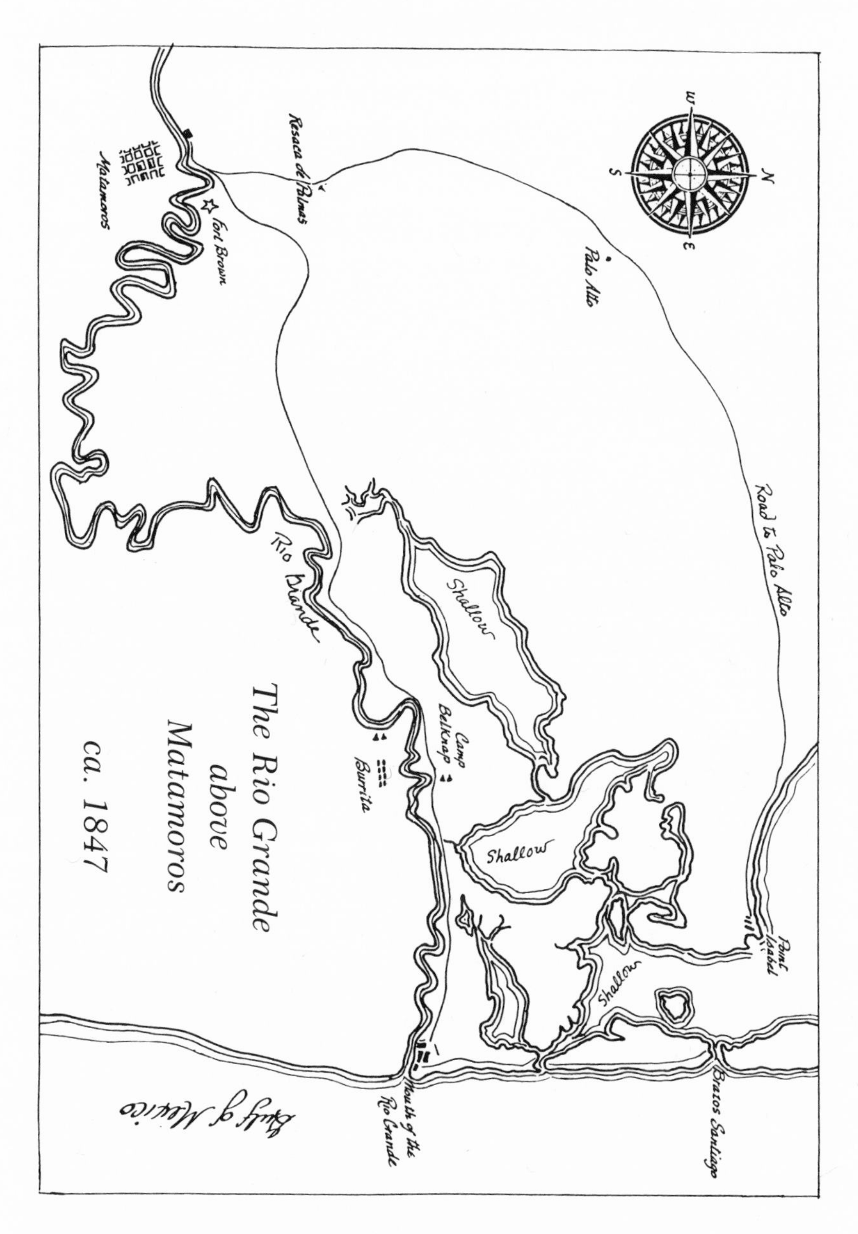

The Rio Grande above Matamoros. Map drawn by Nancy Moyers, University of Texas-Pan American

Brazos island was a treeless barrier island, about three to four miles long and about two miles wide. It had no source of fresh water, and the regiment had arrived in the summer. Capt. William P. Rogers characterized the island as a "lone and desolate sand beach."[4] Under a merciless summer sun, the Rifles suffered greatly.

Colonel Davis arrived with the first companies of the regiment, accompanied by his body servant Jim Green, and his Arabian mount Tartar. (Many soldiers in the Mississippi regiment were aided in their camp chores by their servants, who had accompanied them on the campaign.)[5] Davis quickly set to work to shape the Mississippians into a military unit. The men considered that their new Colonel had a "courteous and pleasant manner," but were also quick to add that he was a "strict disciplinarian." Before tents could be pitched, Davis had issued orders that the men were to be drilled regularly and that he would commence the next day at sunrise to drill the officers.

The regiment was issued Army regulation muskets, since their Whitney rifles had not yet arrived. Colonel Davis fumed over the delay. He wrote to Robert J. Walker on July 22, a fellow Mississippian and Secretary of Treasury in the Polk Administration, asking him to "make some inquiry concerning this matter."[6]

On August 3, Colonel Davis received a note from General Taylor:

Matamoros, Mexico Aug, 3d, 1846

My Dear Col,
[I] very much regret I cannot at once order you with your Comd, to Camargo, where the greater portion of the army will be concentrated, which is impracticable at the present time, but will do so as soon as possible with our limited means of transportation; . . . I propose bringing up the Regts, from their encampments on the banks of the Rio Grande, where I flatter myself they will be pleasantly situated, as regard pure air, health, wood & water, pretty much in the order in which they arrived in the country, . . . I can assure you I am more than anxious to take you by the hand, & to have you & your command with or near me,—I expect [to] leave by the first boat which reaches here [Matamoros] from below on her way to Camargo, & should have

been highly gratified could I have seen you before [my departure]
for that place, . . .
I remain Truly & Sincerely Your Friend

Z. Taylor[7]

From the friendly tone of the letter, it can be surmised that personal hostilities had ceased between Taylor and Davis. One biographer of Davis reported that the misunderstandings between the two had been settled by a chance meeting on a steamboat passage down the Mississippi River on February 1845.[8] Certainly Taylor knew Davis's background and qualifications, and only two months earlier in the halls of Congress Davis had made a stirring speech in praise of Taylor's qualifications for leadership.[9]

The Army had been idle now for more than three months after its impressive victories at Palo Alto and Resaca de la Palma. The terms of service for the volunteer regiments ranged from three months to one year, and that time was beginning to expire. Many regiments transported to south Texas and provisioned by the government were to be mustered out of federal service before they had an opportunity to perform any type of useful service. Taylor was partly to blame for the delay, because his first plans for the capture of Monterrey had envisioned an overland march from Matamoros by way of Linares, a city some seventy-five miles southeast of Monterrey. However, scouting reports by the Texas Rangers indicated an insufficient supply of water along that route,[10] so Taylor settled on a water route up the Rio Grande to Camargo, followed by an overland march to Monterrey along the valley of the Rio San Juan. To complete the water leg of the journey and later to ship supplies, shallow-draft steamboats were needed, and government agents were at this time feverishly scouring the Mississippi Valley to locate and purchase such craft.[11]

Taylor left his headquarters at Matamoros to take the field and arrived at Camargo on August 5, aboard the steam *Whitesville*.[12] In his letter to Davis, Taylor had proposed to transport the volunteers to Camargo in the order in which they had arrived in south Texas. However, orders had already been issued for the Mississippians to leave ahead of seven earlier-arriving regiments.[13] On August 3, they were moved to the mouth of the Rio Grande to await transportation.[14]

Camp life at the mouth of the river, as described by Rufus Arthur, had by this time degenerated to a stoic struggle for survival:

> Our pretty regular bill of fare is hard bread, broken by an axe; mess pork, with the fat 4 inches thick and the lean one-sixteenth part of an inch, and coffee when we can get it . . . occasionally . . . the Comissary gets a few beans, and then we indulge in the luxury of bean soup. Our sleeping is not much better. We lie on the sands and the strong winds keep it whirling about and over us . . . it fills our hair, mouth, nose, whiskers, moustaches, . . . and mixes with our victuals, so that I am afraid we should wear out our teeth, had we to stay here. During the heat of the day, . . . we keep to our tents, reading or sleeping, whenever we can drive away the swarms of flies that infest this region. We complain at home of a few flies and mosquitoes, but I do not think any man in this army will be heard to say one word about flies when he returns. . . .[15]

Morale became very low at this camp, and Capt. William Rogers reflected the feeling of many others when he wrote:

> I am at the mouth of the Rio Grande I am not well and am low in spirits. I dreamed of home last night and of cool refreshing water. The volunteers of the regiment have much to endure—poor fellows some are already dead and others must soon go no doubt. As to myself I will endure God willing and never give up. . . .[16]

At the Rio Grande, Davis continued the drill he had begun at Brazos and to instill the discipline and training that the regiment needed to be successful as a military unit. Young James Browning complained in his diary about the "regular mounting and relieving [of the] guard," and that, "strict Military Discipline has been Rigidly enforced." In marked contrast, many of the volunteer regiments failed even to post guards around their camps while on the Rio Grande, and discipline was lax. Consequently, a rowdy element was set free to wander about the countryside to rob, rape, and murder Mexican civilians without fear of punishment.

The health of the Mississippi Regiment was not good; by the end of August, 108 volunteers had been discharged for health reasons with an additional seventy listed as sick.[17] The lowly amoeba was to fell many more volunteers in Mexico than Mexican muskets or cannon balls. The drinking water was described as "bad," and by

August 10, about half of the regiment was "afflicted with an affection of the bowels." Davis, concerned with the health of his troops, wrote, "Our Regt. have suffered much from disease, had transportation been furnished promptly we would [have] gone with a full Regt. and what is more important with [men] full of zeal, and vigor; into the Campaign."[18] An observer wrote of the Mississippians that "our Regiment will not exceed 500 stout healthy men." The number of men discharged for health problems at the "mouth of the Rio Grande" reinforced this grim judgment (see Appendix A).

On August 19, the first shipment of Whitney rifles arrived and were distributed among the troops. The men of the regiment were very pleased with their new rifles, and one wrote home, "We have named our rifles after our damsels—and you know they will not kick."[19]

By this time Davis had lost patience with the supply system of the Army, and he wrote angrily to Robert J. Walker:

> We have met delay and detention at every turn, the quar[ter] masters at New orleans have behaved eith[er] most incompetently or maliciously, and I am now but two days in possession of the Rifle[s] ordered forward before I left Washington. But don't give the quarter master's Dept. credit for that, my acknowledgements for having them now are due to your Naval Militia—Maj. Roach despairing of the q.M. Dept. applied to Capt Webster of the revenue service who placed the arms on the cutters "Ewing" and "Legare" and brought them to the Brazos Santiago. The ammunition and accountrements sent from Baton Rouge to be forwarded by the quarter Master have not arrived and the ordnance stores [on the frontier] above, have a very insufficient supply of Rifle ammunition. All this arises from having a bundle of papers and prejudices against Volunteers charged with the duties of quarter Master at New Orleans—Viz. Lt. Col. & Asst. Qr. Master Hunt of the U. S. Army.[20]

Davis had to act quickly to find percussion caps and dashed off a hurried message to John S. McNutt, who commanded the ordnance depot at Point Isabel: "Maj. Bradford of the 1st Mi. Vol. will hand you this, I have sent to your post to request you if possible to send me some rifle ammunition and percussion caps, we may get on without the ammunition having a small allowance of that furnished to the two rifle companies as originally armed but now that the percussion rifles have arrived the caps are indispensable and we have none."[21] A response to this message was not recorded, but it is probably safe to assume that Davis's request was honored.

Another problem existed with regard to the use of the Whitney rifle: No manual of arms existed. The step-by-step commands given to load this rifle obviously could not include one for priming the pan, as firing pans did not exist on the new percussion-cap rifles. For the use of the regiment, Davis developed his own manual exclusively for the use of arms that employed a percussion-cap ignition system.[22] Unfortunately, no records of this manual of arms are known to exist;[23] it would be of some interest to compare the approach taken by Davis with some of the later manuals developed for the same type of firearm.

At last, the day after the rifles arrived, orders came to ship out, and the Mississippians began their passage up the Rio Grande to Camargo. Some fifteen or twenty steamboats were constantly navigating the river between the mouth and Camargo. Nearly all of them were either owned or chartered by the federal government.[24] Company G and a portion of Company C boarded the *Exchange* on August 20, while Companies A, E, H, and squads from Companies B and C embarked on the *Virginian* on August 24, followed by the remainder of the regiment aboard the *Col. Cross,* which departed two days later.[25]

Life on board the *Col. Cross* during the trip to Camargo was anything but pleasant, as can be seen from the August 31 diary entry of Capt. Franklin Smith, quartermaster of the Mississippi Rifles:

> Everybody dissatisfied, unhappy, the boat fetid & stinking, & many, very many, sick. I was suffering dreadfully with the universal complaint, Diarrhea, so hot, such a dreadful stench from the necessities [privies], biscuit half cooked, no place to poke one's head in where a moment's comfort could be found, night or day. The sick strewed about, some delirious & crying out for their friends. I became so weak that I could scarcely walk.[26]

The *Col. Cross* arrived in Camargo on September 4, bringing the last portion of the regiment to reach this destination, after a trip marred by several accidents.[27] The Mississippians fresh from the United States and the isolated beach camp on Brazos Santiago were about to be treated to their first views of a Mexican village and its inhabitants. Camargo was located on the right bank of the Rio San Juan, about three miles from where that river empties into the Rio Grande. The village, with a prewar population of about 4,000, contained three principal plazas, each of which was surrounded by adobe brick buildings. These buildings were mostly in need of repair because of a late spring overflow of the Rio San Juan, which had inundated most of the city except for the church and main plaza. The daily temperatures at Camargo in August rose to well over 100 degrees, hot enough in the opinion of one observer from the volunteer army to "burn the hair off dogs and scortches wollen blankets."[28] Col. S. R. Curtis, stationed at Camargo, wrote to his brother that he found the main plaza a storehouse for "pork, beans, hard bread, soap and candles, . . . the whole town is covered with a dense cloud of dust, and so far as comfort is concerned one could hardly imagine a more desolate place if he has never encamped at Brasos (Island) . . . in August."[29] The Army camped outside town, and white tent cities lined both sides of the Rio San Juan south of Camargo for several miles. The army camp sites were plagued by all manner of poisonous reptiles and stinging creatures, especially scorpions, tarantulas, and ants.

Taylor's army at Camargo had swollen to 15,000 men by late August. The tropical climate and the unsanitary practices of the camps combined to create wholesale disease and death among the ranks of the American troops. Dysentery, yellow fever, and other communicable diseases were diagnosed by army surgeons. The death toll in Camargo rose to around 1,500 before the end of hostilities.[30] Burials were so common that the supply of lumber brought to Camargo by the army was used up in the construction of coffins. The dead were then wrapped in a blanket as final preparation for "a soldiers grave." A Tennessee volunteer reported from Camargo that, "Hour after hour was heard the mournful, melancholy sound of the dead march, and the slow, heavy step of the detail that bore some shroudless, coffinless corpse to its long home."[31]

Capt. Franklin Smith, appointed to the regiment after it had been originally organized, delirious with fever and heavily dosed with laudanum, described in his journal the commonplace sight of the sick and dying soldier in Camargo:

> The soldiers are dying—But who thinks of a private a volunteer private He dies & is buried uncoffined! The only announcement *not of his death* but that a man one of the genus homo is dead is the firing of a half dozen guns—The shooters trying to fire to gether & trying at nothing else & thinking of nothing else—The firing announces that homo is dead—Black Thompson Smith Jones Clay Polk Mason Brown Peterson whatever his name or lineage it boots not to say nor is it said or known except to the man *detailed to give him rice water & close his eyes—Barem* go the guns—homo is dead! That is all that is known. . . .[32]

By early August, supplies for the planned attack on Monterrey were arriving almost daily by steamboat from the mouth of the Rio Grande. But the American army was plagued by a continuing shortage of wagons needed to transport supplies and provisions on the overland leg of the invasion. General Taylor had despaired of promises from the quartermaster corps and had sent agents throughout the Mexican countryside to purchase wagons and pack mules from the Mexican citizenry. Few good wagons were found but army purchasing agents soon recruited a swelling remuda of "Mexican canaries" (burros) complete with their skillful Mexican handlers. American soldiers quickly found that the loading of a Mexican burro required a combination of very special skills and patience possessed only by the Mexican handler.

On August 17, the regulars at Camargo, totaling eight regiments of infantry and two batteries of artillery, were paraded in a dress review. The line of troops extended for over three fourths of a mile.[33] American volunteer soldiers lined the parade route and were in awe at this vast assemblage of smart uniforms, the precision of the marching formations, and the polished brass barrels of the cannon in the field artillery batteries. The regulars were impressed too. For these professional soldiers, whose career had consisted chiefly of manning isolated frontier posts at no more than company or battalion strength, this review may have been the largest assemblage of United States Army soldiers they had ever seen. In fact, with volunteers included, the 15,000 men at Camargo probably constituted the largest army that the United States Government had ever assembled in one place in its entire history.

While the parades and planning continued at Camargo, American soldiers were availing themselves of the opportunity to observe the Mexicans for the first time at close range. Their response to the Mexican life-style was what modern jargon calls culture shock. One young Mississippian wrote that, "We have seen many things which are novelties to us backwoods boys, such as Mexicans and horned toads, white lizards and hairless dogs. . . ."[34] Being young for the most part, American soldiers quite naturally concentrated on the habits and attitudes of young Mexican women. Both senoras and senoritas had the habit of gathering in groups each day along the river banks to bathe in the nude, a practice that seemed wildly uninhibited to young men fresh off the farm—or at least to their families back home. Lieutenant Napoleon Jackson Tecumseh Dana, of the 7th Infantry Regiment, wrote his wife on October 5, "So you had a dispute with your uncle about my looking at the naked girls of Camargo. Everybody looked at them, dearest one, and no one could go to the river without seeing them. If men were in swimming, the women would not mind it but would come right in too. They think nothing of such things. . . ." A week later, he wrote her, "Captain Backus tells a story: whilst he was riding near the river at Reynosa one day, a woman came up to him out of the water, perfectly naked, stood and talked with him and had not even the decency to put her hand before it."[35]

Of course, what was said of Mexican customs in letters depended on the intended audience. John P. Brock, a Virginia volunteer, wrote to his parents that the Mexican ladies from Camargo were "hansom and dress quite costly. Tho they are too dark their coller is much like that of our little negroes." However, when writing to a pal several months later—a letter that Mama and Papa probably did not see—young Brock presented a slightly different viewpoint:

> I should like to have you with me to visit the Cenoretis [senoritas]. Oh my friend here is the beauty of the trip. I wish to heaven I could have you with me at one fandango. I no you would not give it for all the balls you ever seen in the states. Then to see them bathing by fiftys in the cristal stream of the Cordileras.

> Then to visit them at their own private dwellings, where you will find evry accomodation that you could request. If this is not true happiness where shall we find it.[36]

This brings us to the meaning of the word "fandango," which could be very roughly translated "dance," except that in northern Mexico it meant much more. Capt. Franklin Smith attended a fandango held at Guardado Abajo, a small village near Camargo, which he described in his diary:

> An old Mexican was the fiddler—his the only instrument. I was surprised to hear so many tunes familiar to me among others was Fisher's horn-pipe. The waltz is their greatest dance—they are fondest of it . . . when they waltzed the Mexican youth generally got a show—but few of the voluntarios could go the waltz—the women were dressed principally in silk—with gold beads around the neck On the N. E. corner of the yard near one of the lights heavy gambling was going on at Monte—at the S. E. corner an old woman had a large table loaded with oranges pecans & dried figs—I noticed the girls giving back to the old woman the presents of fruits which the vols. gave them—I remarked this & was told that it was a regular perquisite of the old Crone.[37]

Americans were amazed to see Mexican women constantly smoking cigarettes, usually of the variety rolled with corn husks. They smoked even while dancing, commented one volunteer, "puffing away like a *steamboat*."[38]

Many of the customs of the American soldier likewise amused the citizens of northern Mexico, especially the high esteem given to women of all classes by the Yankees, even women of the street. An Ohio lieutenant related that the "boys" were appalled to see peon women carrying heavy loads while their husbands walked alongside, unencumbered. "I have many times seen our boys stop them, and take the loads from the women and put them on the backs of the men, and tell them that that was the way we do in the United States."[39]

While camped at Camargo, many of the volunteers caught their first glimpse of Gen. Zachary Taylor. Capt. William P. Rogers of the Mississippi Rifles expressed an almost unanimous opinion: "I have seen General Taylor and he is a rough looking man and I do not think he has the appearance of a great man."[40] Other volunteers found Old Rough and Ready "a plain old farmer-looking man—no particular indications of smartness or intellect," "an ordinary looking old man . . . a keen eye and a large nose," "short and very heavy, with pronounced face lines and gray hair, wears an old oil coat [cloth?] cap, a dusty green coat, a frightful pair of trousers and on horseback looks like a toad." Taylor, a living example that "clothes do not make the man," was an anomaly. In an age that stressed military smartness and glittering uniforms, he set a style for casual dress that horrified his junior officers.[41] However, beneath this rough exterior was a true son of frontier America, a man nurtured in pragmatism and populism. His frontier military training had been received far away from the military establishment of Washington and the parade grounds of West Point. To survive as a soldier and to care for the needs of his troops, he had learned to cast aside those rules and practices that were common back east but did not apply to the American frontier. His young subordinates, many fresh from the parade grounds of West Point, were very critical of his manner of dress, his simple life-style, and his affable standards of discipline for his troops. Their initial criticism turned to almost unanimous praise as they began to understand Taylor's true nature. Beneath Zachary Taylor's simple exterior resided a very shrewd and capable soldier. Taylor's understanding of his men and this harsh country in which they had been placed was to constitute one of the main assets of the American army in the upcoming campaign in northern Mexico.

Tom Owen offered this anecdote about Taylor, which illustrated his innate sense of shrewdness:

> During our war with the Seminoles, the army was frequently supplied with corn which had become damaged by exposure to damp air. General Taylor had a horse which was called "Claybank," a very good animal, but he did not particularly fancy Uncle Sam's musty rations. The general used to partake of the same fare as the soldiers under him, and so did Claybank, so far as the corn was concerned, but he was a little dainty. The general was very fond of hominy, and musty corn made any thing but a pleasant diet. He would not lay himself liable to the suspicion of "picking" to the prejudice of the soldiers, so old Claybank would be let loose among the sacks of corn, and after smelling very carefully, the sagacious animal would commence gnawing a hole

> into one which pleased him. The general would watch the maneuever until he saw Claybank had made a choice, then, calling his servant, would direct him to have Claybank stabled immediately, for fear he might do mischief: he would say, "As the animal has gnawed a hole into the bag, take out a quart or so of the corn and make a dish of hominy." The trick was played several times, but by-and-by it became known, that whenever Claybank gnawed into a sack, sweet corn was to be found. . . .[42]

Owing to the reduced amounts of equipment and supplies that could be transported by pack animals, General Taylor decided to limit his invasion force to 6,000 men. He himself selected the volunteer regiments that would accompany the regulars to Monterrey, after a last visit to the volunteer camps. Rufus Arthur reported that army officers, looking over the Mississippi Regiment, were pleased "with the discipline, arms, and appearance of the men. . . . The General expressed himself delighted with our rifles—he says they are beautiful arms."

The 6,000-man invasion army was to be divided into four divisions, two divisions each of regulars and volunteers. The disposition of regular troops was as follows:

1st Division: 1st, 2d, 3d, and 4th U.S. Infantry, the 2d U.S. Dragoons, and the artillery batteries of Bragg and Ridgley, commanded by Brig. Gen. David E. Twiggs.

2d Division: 5th, 7th, and 8th U.S. Infantry, an artillery battalion serving as infantry, Duncan's artillery battery, and Captain Blanchard's Louisiana volunteers, all under the leadership of Gen. William E. Worth.

The two divisions of volunteers were organized as follows:

3rd Division: the 1st and 2nd Brigades, commanded respectively by Thomas L. Hamer and John A. Quitman. Hamer's brigade consisted of the regiments from Ohio and Kentucky, while Quitman, a Mississippian, was to lead the 1st Tennessee Regiment and the Mississippi Rifles. The division was commanded by Gen. William O. Butler.

4th Division: Texas volunteers, under the command of Texas Gov. James Pinckney Henderson.[43]

The remaining regiments of volunteers, mostly untrained green recruits, were placed under the command of Gen. Robert Patterson and left to guard the supply route that would soon extend from the mouth of the Rio Grande to Monterrey. The left-behinds howled with disappointment, but there was no help for it.

The 2d division had left Camargo while the Rifles were still downriver, crossing the Rio San Juan on August 19, over a bridge built of planks laid across the decks of steamboats. The destination of the first leg of the march was the ancient Mexican city of Cerralvo. At Cerralvo the American army would concentrate for the final leg of the march to Monterrey.

With such limited means for transportation, General Taylor was reluctantly forced to exclude all tents and a great deal of personal gear from the supply train. The soldiers were required to carry a part of the stores in their packs and haversacks. Siege artillery taken to Monterrey was limited to two 24-pounder howitzers and one 10-inch mortar. Taylor was to be criticized later for not bringing more of his siege artillery from Camargo to attack the extensive permanent masonry fortifications of Monterrey.

The Mississippians left Camargo on September 7, 1846, and vanished into a harsh desert environment filled with dense chaparral brush. Marching feet stirred up thick clouds of white caliche dust under a merciless tropical sun. With daytime temperatures hovering at 100 degrees, the heavily laden soldiers quickly emptied their canteens, only to find that few streams and waterholes existed in this part of the country. The ordinary foot soldier, according to Z. K. Judd, a volunteer soldier on this march, carried the following equipment on his person:

> a large cartridge box with heavy leather belt two and one fourth inches wide to carry over the left shoulder, a similar belt with bayonet and scabbard attached to carry over the right shoulder, and then a waist belt correspondingly wide and heavy old white leather, and [also] a knap-sack in which [we] carry our clothing, and any other little necessities. It was so arranged that a strap came in front of each shoulder and under the arm with a long strap to reach around our bedding. With all these traps in front and the filled knap-sack behind, we were nearly covered from neck to waist. . . . We were required to carry all these fixtures, our clothing and bedding and a few rounds of ammunition and then a canteen in which would hold three pints of water, and then a small cotton sack called a hover-sack [sic], in which to

> carry our dinner and sometimes a day or two['s] rations. They also were made to swing over our shoulder.[44]

The Mississippians reached Cerralvo, located sixty miles southwest of Camargo, after a six-day march. Camps were made at the villages of Guardado Abajo, Mier, Chicarrones, and Puntiagudo (now named General Trevino). From Puntiagudo south to Cerralvo, the road rose in elevation, and the fierce summer temperatures began to moderate in intensity. Captain Rogers remarked on the change in scenery: "The mountains all the time in the distance, Oh beautiful! How beautiful!"[45]

"Seralio [Cerralvo] is a handsome town built of stone and did contain about 2 or 3000 inhabitants but most of them have left now, . . ." wrote Captain Rogers. Other Americans were also enthralled by the charming sights of this handsome city. Benjamin Franklin Scribner remembered:

> We pitched our tents near the old Spanish town of Cerralvo, which bears the impress of an antiquated fortress, and reminds one of the dilapidated castles we read of in romances. The houses are built of gray stone, with loopholes for windows. Through the centre of the town runs a beautiful clear stream, spanned by bridges and arches. There is also a large cathedral with chimes and a towering steeple. It is said to be 166 years old.[46]

A large spring south of Cerralvo furnished irrigation water to a network of canals that interlaced the city. The patios of the private residences in Cerralvo abounded with flowery gardens, which contained large pecan trees and all manner of citrus, grapes, and avocados. Taylor's army camped at the spring south of the city to rest from the effects of a grueling march and make final preparations for the assault on the fortified city of Monterrey.

FOUR

The Capture of Monterrey

"Hot work Captain—I'll not let the old man talk to me about his deeds at the battle of New Orleans again—it could'nt hold a candle to this fight"
—*Samuel Lane, as quoted in a letter from Capt. J. L. McManus to* The Southron, *Jackson, Mississippi, January 1, 1847*

From the American camp at San Francisco, about fifteen miles north of Monterrey, officers and men speculated as to whether or not the Mexicans would attempt to defend the city.[1] This idle talk was silenced the next day, September 19, when the Americans approached within range of the defenses of Monterrey. The advance units, led by General Taylor, passed through the haciendas of San Domingo and Muscatel and topped a rise in the road. Before them in the distance lay the city of Monterrey nestled in a valley. Mexican defenders were quick to spot the invaders, now within range of the northern fort, and three cannon shots were fired in rapid succession.[2] The first shot passed within 10 feet of Taylor and his advance party, and the other two passed through the mounted Texas regiments without damage.

The Americans were moved back half a mile out of range and ordered to camp at the beautiful park known locally as San Domin-

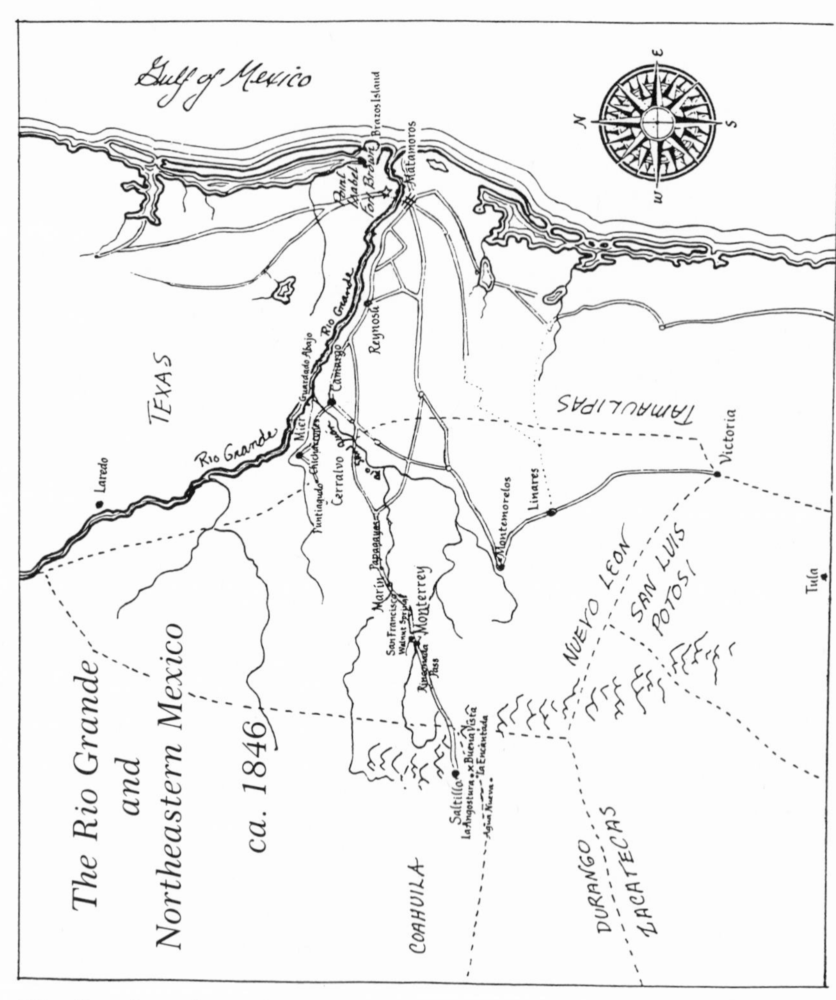

The Rio Grande and Northeastern Mexico. Map drawn by Nancy Moyers, University of Texas-Pan American

go. The grounds of this park were covered with pecan and walnut trees watered by a large spring, which bubbled forth cold, crystal-clear water. This camp became known to American soldiers as Walnut Springs.

Taylor immediately ordered forth parties of engineers to report on the defenses of the city. The resulting observations painted a grim picture: Monterrey was heavily protected by structures constructed of thick stonework. Against such solid defenses American field artillery batteries were ineffective. The meager train of siege guns brought forward from Camargo, two 24-pounder howitzers and a 10-inch mortar, were insufficient to mount a large-scale attack. Maj. Philip Barbour of the 3d U.S. Infantry quickly recognized what must be done: "The city *has to be carried* and [since] there are no guns in our train of sufficient caliber to batter, the bayonet will probably have to do the work."[3]

Monterrey was indeed a well-fortified city. Situated in a valley bounded on three sides by the Sierra Madre Oriental, the city guarded the principal pass through these mountains connecting northern Mexico with the central highlands. The eastern and southern sides of the city were protected by the Santa Catarina River, a rapid but shallow stream running in a course directly adjacent to the eastern edge of the mountains. The western boundary of Monterrey was protected by strategically placed fortifications on Loma de Independencia and Loma de Federación, hills of about a thousand feet in elevation, which straddled the main road through the mountain pass from Monterrey to Saltillo. The major fortress atop Loma de Independencia was known as La Obispada, built from the deserted ruins of a bishop's palace. An army attacking Monterrey from the southwest along the Saltillo road must first capture these two fortified hills.

Dominating all northern approaches to the city was a sizable fortress known as the Citadel. Built from hewn black rock and surrounded by a dry ditch, the Citadel was designed to be a redoubt with bastions.[4] Its walls formed a square about 270 yards on a side, which enclosed an unfinished cathedral. Referred to by the Americans as the Black Fort, this fortification was armed with eight cannons[5] and garrisoned by five hundred men, which included a detachment of Mexican cavalry.

Within cannon range of the Black Fort and slightly to the northeast of the city, a series of redoubts and breastworks had been constructed. The largest of these redoubts, located in the most advanced position to the northeast of Monterrey, was an earthen lunette built atop a fortified stone building, and since the building had been used as a leather tannery, the Mexicans called this redoubt La Tenería.[6] Tenería was armed with two 8-pounders, a 4-pounder, and a mountain howitzer, and its garrison of 350 was commanded by Col. José Maria Carrasco. The landscape around Tenería was dotted with abandoned stone quarries, and the many adjacent fields were covered with tall cornstalks and sugarcane that the Mexican defenders had neglected to burn.

South of Tenería was a large two-story stone building with a flat-topped roof, which housed a distillery. The roof had been sandbagged and holes bored in the walls to make firing embrasures.

Immediately behind the distillery ran a deep ravine containing a creek, which flowed from an ojo de agua (spring) in the middle of the city easterly to join the Santa Catarina River at a point northeast of the city. Lining the steep south bank of this ravine was a complex of breastworks, an extensive brush abatis, and another earthen fortification with the forbidding name "El Rincón del Diablo" (the devil's corner)—Americans called it Fort Diablo—armed with two cannon. Farther up the creek toward the city was located La Purisima, an ornately designed bridge adorned by a statue of the Virgin Mary. The northern end of the bridge was fortified with a strong *tête-de-pont* with three mounted cannon surrounded by breastworks for infantry.

Houses within the city had stone and adobe walls drilled for loopholes, from which infantry could direct fire into the streets, and the *azoteas* (flat roofs surrounded by parapets three or four feet high) were sandbagged to form an elevated firing platform for defenders.[7] The streets of the city were extensively barricaded, and many of the barricades were fitted with embrasures for cannon.

Manning these excellent defenses was a Mexican army under the command of Gen. Pedro Ampudia, whose size was estimated at 10,000 men[8]—7,000 regular troops and 3,000 volunteers. This army consisted of the following regular units:

6th Regiment
2nd, 3rd, and 4th Regiments of Light Infantry
3rd, 4th, and 10th of the Line, and two companies of the 6th of the Line
The Actives of Mexico, The Actives of Morelia, and the
Active Battallions of Aguas Calientes, Queretaro, and San Luis Potosi
7th, 8th, and the Light Cavalry Regiments
3rd Cavalry Regiments of Guanajuato, San Luis Potosi, and Jalisco.[9]

The morale of the Mexican Army, shattered by the defeats of Palo Alto and Resaca de la Palma, had been slowly improving. On September 18, Mexico City had sent $28,000 to be distributed among the troops, and on the evening of September 19, an additional $8,000 had been received from Saltillo. The citizens of Monterrey helped to stimulate patriotism, especially the pretty young ladies. Señorita Dosamantes of the city donned a captain's uniform and rode among the troops, who responded with enthusiasm.[10] Señorita Dona Maria Josefa Zozaya, noted for her beauty and acts of kindness, a great favorite of the Mexican soldiers, appeared to speak of patriotism.[11]

Late on the evening of September 19, Maj. Joseph F. K. Mansfield returned to the American camp after an armed reconnaissance of the southwestern portion of the city. Mansfield reported to Taylor that it was possible to circle Monterrey from the west side of the city and block the road to Saltillo. Such a movement would isolate the city from reinforcements, cut off lines of communication, and deny an important escape route from the city to the defenders. Major Mansfield further reported that emplacements on Loma de Federación and Loma de Independencia were vulnerable to assault. Their capture would leave the southern portion of Monterrey, with few other defensive positions, open to direct attack.

On the basis of this scouting report, a plan was developed for the capture of Monterrey. Taylor divided his small army, sending Worth's 2d Division and the Texas Rangers to attack Monterrey from the southwest. The remainder of the American forces were to create a diversion by feigning an attack against the forts along the northeastern boundary of the city. The diversion was crucial to the success of the plan of attack; Taylor must convince Ampudia that the major American thrust was to be struck on the northeast suburb.

At two o'clock on the afternoon of September 20, the 2d Division left Camp Walnut Springs on a march to circle Monterrey from the west. The soldiers who remained in camp prepared themselves, each in his own way, for the upcoming battle. Maj. Philip Barbour wrote in his diary the following entry for September 20:

> I feel as calm and collected as if I were in the Astor House, having long since made up my mind that, during a time of war, my life is the rightful property of my country, and cannot be taken from me, or preserved, except by the fiat of the great God who gave it. And to His will, whatever it be, I am perfectly resigned.[12]

This was the final entry in his diary. Major Barbour was struck down by a musket ball on September 21, trying in vain to lead the troops of the 3d Infantry to safety through the tangled maze of streets in the northeastern suburbs of Monterrey. Capt. William P. Rogers of the 1st Mississippi wrote, "It is supposed that we will have a battle tomorrow or the next day, will I come through unscathed and alive—God grant I pray. Am I prepared to die—I fear not, and yet I hope I am."[13] Correspondingly, while many soldiers in the command prayed for their redemption, others were tending to more practical matters. Brig. Gen. David Twiggs, a veteran of the army, was imbibing a large dose of a cathartic—in fact too large a dose. Twiggs had a theory on visceral wounds: Bullets entering the abdomen would not puncture an intestine if the "patient had loose bowels."[14]

By eight o'clock on the morning of September 21, the 1st Division of regulars and the volunteer divisions were formed in a line of battle. The formation fronted a slight depression from which the two 24-pounders and the mortar were set up to fire upon the Black Fort from a range of about 1,500 yards. General Twiggs, who led the 1st Division was conspicuously absent; the overdose of purgative had rendered the veteran officer hors de combat. Lieut. Col. John Garland was to command the division. Taylor ordered the 1st Division to advance on the northeastern suburbs, rendezvous there with a reconnaissance party led by Major Mansfield, and to attack Fort Tenería if in the major's opinion those works could be carried.[15]

While approaching his objective through fields of tall corn and sugarcane, Garland's path veered, and he entered an open field more than 200 yards west of the rendezvous point. The 1st Division was now spotted by the Mexican defenders, and a murderous crossfire commenced between the artillery in the Black Fort on one side and the emplacements in Forts Tenería and Diablo on the other. Garland's forces rushed into the city to find cover from the artillery and became lost in a maze of narrow, winding, and often dead-end streets. The advancing American troops moved into range of the *tête-de pont* with disastrous results, as reported by Lieut. Robert Henry:

> We rushed into the streets. Unfortunately, we did not turn soon enough to the left, and had advanced but a short distance when we came suddenly upon an unknown battery, which opened its deadly fire upon us. From all its embrasures, from every house, from every yard, showers of balls were hurled upon us. Being in utter ignorance of our locality, we had to stand and take it; our men, covering themselves as well as they could, dealt death and destruction on every side; there was no resisting the deadly, concealed fire, which appeared to come from every direction. On every side we were shot down.[16]

In the midst of this confusion, Capt. Electus Backus led his company of the 1st U.S. Infantry into a tanyard about 150 yards to the west of Fort Tenería. From atop the flat roof of a building in the tanyard, Backus was able to see into the rear of Fort Tenería and directly observe Mexican soldiers servicing the fort's artillery. He quickly stationed his men on the *azotea* of this building and commenced a hot musket fire into Tenería.[17]

From outside the city, General Taylor was able to hear the intense fire of the attack, and readied the volunteers of Mississippi, Tennessee, and Ohio to advance into Monterrey to the aid of the regulars. The planned diversion had become a battle, and the beleaguered soldiers of the 1st Division appeared to be trapped, unable either to gain a foothold in the city or extricate themselves from their precarious position in the narrow streets. The Kentucky Regiment was held in reserve, to protect the siege artillery.

Col. William B. Campbell of the 1st Tennessee, anticipating the order to march, prematurely had his troops load their weapons. Seeing this, Col. Jefferson Davis muttered impatiently, "They are getting the start of us."[18] Sure enough, when the word was passed to move forward, the other volunteers were busily loading their weapons, and the Tennesseeans were able to seize the lead position of the advance. Davis and the Mississippians followed the Tennesseeans in file, and the Ohioans brought up the rear. The Black Fort quickly spotted the volunteers, and an 18-pounder solid shot was sent whistling through the ranks of the Tennesseeans, horribly mutilating seven men.[19]

Rufus K. Arthur, younger brother of the editor of the *Vicksburg Whig,* received his baptism of fire with this shot and reported:

> I regarded every thing passing around us as a frolic until we came to the fort and found some eight or ten men lying in our path, horribly mangled by a cannon ball, and uttering the most distressing groans and shrieks—some with their legs or arms off, and others crawling on the ground and dragging their entrails after them.[20]

The Volunteer Division, moving at the double-quick, soon came into the range of the cannon in Forts Tenería and Diablo, their objectives. They were greeted by a steady fire of copper solid shot and musket balls, which whined and shrieked through the ranks. The advancing Mississippians stumbled onto a group of American soldiers, who had lain hidden in the tall sugarcane to escape Mexican cannon fire.[21] These troops were probably the ragged remnants of the regulars, bloodied in the earlier attack.

At a range of about 300 yards from Fort Tenería, the volunteers deployed in lines. The Tennessee Regiment faced the north wall of the fort, in front of which was a deep ditch dug by the Mexicans for defensive purposes. The Mississippi troops were positioned to face the northwest wall, which was not protected by a moat.

The lines were ordered to open fire, and soon the rattle of musketry broke out. The line of fire of the right companies of the Mississippians was obstructed by a "small body of troops in the undress of our 'regulars'," who had interposed themselves between the volunteers and the fort,[22] so Davis requested and received permission to position his men slightly to the left of his first position and closer to the fort than the line of Tennesseeans.

The Mississippi Rifles commenced firing on targets within the fort, keeping up a rapid and ragged individual fire. The company captains attempted to synchronize the firing, but there were no targets vulnerable to volleys, so the men ignored orders and continued to aim at whatever moved. A hail of copper grape and solid shot was poured on the Mississippians from Fort Tenería, but the men held their positions and returned the fire with spirit. Morale remained high. Pvt. Edward M. Cohea of the Mississippi Regiment quipped to his comrades that, "with plenty of powder I could never get out of ammunition—I could hold up my cap, and catch it full of bullets in a minute."[23]

Davis was unhappy with the extreme range at which his riflemen were forced to operate and commented to Lt. Daniel R. Russell, "Damn it, why do not the men get nearer to the fort? Why waste ammunition at such distance?"[24] The Mississippi line was advanced to 180 yards from the fort, but just then the cannon fire from the fort mysteriously slackened off. This sudden lull was quite likely the result of Captain Backus's troops pouring a deadly fire into Fort Tenería from their rooftops. The Mexican gunners in Fort Tenería had ceased to serve their cannon and were crouched behind cover.

Outside the front wall of Fort Tenería, Davis, the trained military man, was fussing and fuming for orders to storm the fort: "Now is the time! Great God, if I had thirty men with knives I could take that fort."[25] While Davis, the professional, awaited orders from General Quitman, another officer of the regiment sensed the same opportunity and acted. Leaping in front of Company K, which he had formerly commanded, Lieutenant Colonel McClung drew his saber and brandished it in the direction of Fort Tenería. "Charge! Charge! Tombigbee volunteers follow me!"[26] At a more rational moment, the Mississippi Rifles would have realized that McClung was issuing an illegal order, but Company K knew him by reputation and answered the command with a shout. With McClung in the lead Company K raced to take Fort Tenería. Other Mississippi companies saw the movement and broke ranks without orders to join the charge.

Davis, sensing the futility of trying to recall the regiment, echoed the McClung command. Pvt. Joseph Heatron, wounded by a Mexican musket ball, rose to his knees and cheered the regiment on.

General Quitman had not planned to use the Mississippians in hand-to-hand combat since their Whitney rifles were not equipped with bayonets. But it was now too late for such niceties, so Quitman quickly signaled Colonel Campbell to advance the Tennessee regiment, which moved toward the fort with fixed bayonets.

Many Mexican soldiers, harrassed by Backus's fire, abandoned their posts and crossed the creek to enter Fort Diablo. Those soldiers that remained in La Tenería retreated to the fortified distillery. McClung entered La Tenería through an embrasure followed by Lieutenants Patterson, Townsend, and Wade, Captains Rogers and Gregory, and Privates Kerr and Bell.[27] McClung stepped up on to the rampart of the fort and signaled his oncoming comrades with a waving saber. A Mexican soldier drew a bead on the redheaded nearby Colonel, but Lieutenant Patterson shot the man and saved McClung's life.

Davis galloped up on Tartar, dismounted, and dived through the sally port into the fort. Tartar was alarmed by the sights, sounds, and smells of battle, but he continued to remain near Davis—a display of terrified loyalty that made the horse a favorite of the American troops at Monterrey.[28]

Other Mississippians now streamed into the fort, and the bayonets of the Tennessee regiment were seen just outside the walls. Davis ordered Lieutenant Townsend to gather all prisoners and collect the muskets and other small arms from about the fort. Musket balls were still whizzing into the fort, as some of the excited Tennessee volunteers continued to pour fire into Fort Tenería from the outside. Capt. Reuben Downing and Lt. Daniel Russell shouted to the Tennesseeans to cease firing, and the Tennessee flag bearer unfurled the regimental flag to signal the American capture of the fort. All eyes were caught by this event. Mexican defenders inside the city of Monterrey reported seeing the flag of the 1st Tennessee, "a blue flag with the American eagle and stars."[29]

A final discharge of musketry from the roof of the distillery was poured onto the American volunteers standing about Fort Tenería. Mexican officers quickly signaled their men to cease firing and offered their swords to surrender the stone tower. A. K. McClung was struck by one of the balls from this last volley and fell to the floor of Fort Tenería writhing in pain.

A large caliber ball had struck his left hand as it rested on the scabbard of his sword, tearing away a portion of the hand and passing into the left hip. The ball exited from McClung's back near the spine, creating a jagged wound.[30] The lieutenant colonel's wounds were hastily dressed, but his lips turned blue as he faded into shock. He was wrapped in a blanket and hidden in the deep ditch on the north face of Fort Tenería. American wounded could not be attended to by surgeons or removed from the field until nightfall, since the Black Fort and Fort Diablo continued to fire on all targets.

Plans for the attack on the north eastern side of Monterrey had been ill-conceived. Soldiers were now scattered about Fort Tenería, awaiting orders from their field commanders who had none to give. The terrain of this "diversionary" area had not been carefully reconnoitered, so no one was sure how the land lay. Mississippi company officers reported questioning Colonel Davis,[31] and he himself attempted to find out from General Quitman what the next objective would be, but the brigade commander was also unsure of how to proceed and reluctant to issue orders on his own initiative.

Thus, the American volunteers waited idly and lost the momentum generated by the success of their attack. The 1st Mississippi had attained its objective, the capture of Fort Tenería, but would not function as a cohesive unit for the remainder of the day.

Davis did organize a squad of men, Mississippians and Tennesseeans, and crossed the creek south of Fort Tenería to attack Fort Diablo. The remainder of the Mississippians either remained in Fort Tenería and fired on Diablo from there, or else moved into a lane paralleling the creek, where a stone wall gave the riflemen some shelter. Fort Diablo was situated on a slight elevation and could not depress its cannon far enough to reach Davis and the men, but the Mexicans poured in a fierce fire of small arms. Corporal Grisham was killed by two musket balls, dying "calmly, silently, with his eye upon the foe."[32] Capt. Reuben Downing was struck by a musket ball in the arm and retired from the field. Gen. Twiggs, slightly drawn and haggard, finally made his appearance on the battlefield, and was heard to cry feebly to the men, "Go on! Go on! Secure your victory."

Davis, attempting to organize an attack on Diablo from his forward position south of the stream, was thwarted by an order to withdraw. In the words of Lt. Daniel R. Russell:

> I first saw you beyond the creek fifty men in view & about you. You told me on asking for orders, that we could take that fort. pointing to the 2nd fort, in five minutes, & ordered me to form my men. I asked you where? you said where we stood.—While I was engaged executing your command I again met you . . . you were cursing bitterly you ordered me to retire from my position to recross the creek & form in the lane, you said you had been ordered to withdraw your men, & repeated you would have taken the fort in five minutes if you had been allowed to proceed. . . .[33]

The confusion due to the lack of reconnaissance, and the slow flow of information from the battlefield confounded the best attempts to move the army forward. Colonel Garland had reported to General Taylor the failure of the first attack by the regulars and had recommended withdrawal of troops from the city—just as the volunteers were gaining some success. Taylor issued orders to implement this recommendation, and these orders were the very ones that recalled the Mississippians from in front of Diablo. As this withdrawal was being executed by American troops, a messenger rushed breathlessly to the old general with word of the American capture of Fort Tenería. The messenger was especially proud of the capture of the distillery, which he reported to be filled with newly processed social liquids. Taylor replied drily, "No doubt of it, I thought it was by the way you fought to get into it."[34] Taylor then issued orders to have the distillery emptied immediately, lest his troops be tempted.

Bolstered by these reports of success, Taylor quickly countermanded his earlier orders for retreat, and sent General Butler into the city to supervise the attack on Diablo and the Purisima Bridge.[35] General Butler hastened into the city and was in the act of organizing the attack when he was struck down by a musket ball. Command of the Volunteer Division was passed to General

Hamer, with instructions to attack Diablo from the right flank. American regulars had penetrated the city to the *tête-de pont* at the end of Purisima Bridge, but were driven back by heavy Mexican fire. Davis, with a portion of his regiment, had been halted east of the *tête-de pont,* in a lane that paralleled the creek and was ordered to await reinforcements for an attack on La Purisima. General Hamer suddenly appeared and relayed the latest confused order from General Taylor for all American forces to retire from the city. Led by the Ohio regiment, with Davis's Mississippians forming the rear guard, the weary column of volunteers straggled from the suburbs of Monterrey in a long and disorganized line.

From the Citadel, now visible to the retreating Americans, a detachment of cavalry was dispatched to attack the disorganized stragglers. This unit was the 3d and 7th Lancers, under the command of Gen. Garcia Conde. The Lancers were an elite unit of cavalry, whose riders carried as their principal weapon a distinctive lance, usually nine feet in length and tipped with a long metal point. These weapons were not particularly effective against seasoned troops, but were greatly feared by the young volunteers. Rumors abounded in the army that the lance points were poisoned and that any wound from them resulted in a fatality.

The Lancers thundered down upon the bedraggled American column, spearing those soldiers nearest the point of attack. Luther Giddings of the Ohio Regiment reported that large parties of lancers left their ranks and

> murdered indiscriminantly all the wounded Americans in that part of the field. The surgeons and their assistants, flying from the fate of their patients, were hotly pursued by the enemy. . . .[36]

A wave of panic overcame some of the volunteers, who threw down their arms and rushed into a nearby cornfield to hide from the approaching enemy.[37] It is quite possible that General Hamer, an Ohio politician untrained in the military formations necessary to defeat such an attack, simply panicked when he saw the thundering horsemen.[38] Albert Sidney Johnston, who had been serving under General Butler as a volunteer aide-de-camp, knew what to do. He rode among the frightened troops and urged them to turn and form a line of battle along a nearby chaparral fence. His quick appeal to common sense rallied the men in the advance of the column, and a line of battle was formed facing north. Capt. Joseph Hooker who had seen the lancer attack, commented that, "It was through [Johnston's] agency, mainly, that our division was saved from a cruel slaughter. . . . The coolness and magnificent presence [that he] displayed on this field . . . left an impression on my mind that I have never forgotten."[39]

The party of lancers divided into two wings to attack, and Davis, noting this move, hastily organized his Mississippians into a second line, facing south, to receive the second wing of attackers.

> The left of their line [the Ohio Regiment] was fifty yards or more to our right, we abandened the muskets [mesquites?] & prepared our little band to receive the lancers. They came up gallantly, their fiery little chargers prancing & rearing, handsomely. We now saw about fifty of them had passed around our left flank & were approaching through the corn upon our rear, Two of the enemy rode up to within about 60 or 70 yds, of us, just to the edge of the corn, They were both brought from their saddles by shots from our rifles.[40]

The cool actions of Albert Sidney Johnston and Jefferson Davis had enabled the men in their command to rally, and drive off the lancers. An orderly withdrawal then commenced as the cautious volunteers, forgetting their fatigue, moved off smartly in tight formations back to camp.

As twilight signaled the end of a very long day, Colonel Davis called for volunteers to complete one more trip into the city: Alex McClung must be brought from the battlefield back to camp. Lieutenant Patterson stepped forward, selecting Edward Gregory, Argyle Kerr, Jack King, and Thomas Broom to complete the detail.[41] Constructing a rude litter, they turn their weary steps back toward Monterrey, and returned several hours later with McClung, alive but weak from loss of blood. The first day's actions in Monterrey had cost the Mississippians seven dead and forty-seven wounded.

On the morning of September 22, the Mississippians and the Tennesseeans were sent from camp to relieve a force that had guarded the captured Fort Tenería during the night. This relief column took a circuitous route to Tenería through the high corn and sugarcane fields, hoping to avoid the guns from the Citadel.

They managed that successfully but Fort Diablo spotted the advance and directed a heavy cannon fire at the Americans, which killed Private Dubois and wounded Private Gregg.[42]

The arrival at Fort Tenería was greeted by the sight of distant smoke encircling Loma de Independencia, where General Worth's 2d Division and the Texas Volunteers were still battling to capture the Bishop's Palace on the west side of the city. Before the day was out, the American flag was seen waving from La Obispada.

Meanwhile, the east side of Monterrey was almost completely quiet. The volunteers from Mississippi accepted philosophically "Such Shots at the lower Fort which was in Our possession as the enemy thought proper to send at us."[43]

A norther blew through Monterrey in late afternoon, and the resulting temperature drop caused a heavy rainfall on the exposed troops in Fort Tenería. Davis had ordered his quartermaster to bring blankets and food to supply the troops stationed at Fort Tenería but nothing arrived. The quartermaster had been unable to obtain an escort for his supply wagon, which would have been vulnerable to the Mexican cavalry stationed in the Citadel. Nightfall brought cold temperatures, and the volunteers' teeth chattered as they stood watch in breastworks filled with water.[44] Signal rockets were fired from the Mexican forts throughout the night at regular intervals, and Fort Tenería heard a great deal of activity and movement inside the Mexican lines. The Tennesseeans and Mississippians braced themselves for a possible attempt to retake the fort.

But the sounds of Mexican movements were not a prelude to attack, but rather a signal to abandon the key Mexican forts and defensive positions on the northeastern side of Monterrey. Mexican. Gen. Pedro Ampudia had become alarmed by the successes of General Worth on the west side of the city and decided to consolidate his remaining forces in the center of Monterrey. Ampudia feared that rapid American advances into the outskirts of the city would isolate the many small Mexican garrisons from reinforcement.

By dawn of September 23, sentries in Fort Tenería reported to Davis that only a few heads were visible above the walls of Fort Diablo. Davis responded to the news by leading a patrol to the fort to investigate. To their surprise, the Mississippians found that Diablo had been stripped of its armaments and contained only one man, who claimed to be a noncombatant. The patrol, which consisted of Companies B, D, and H of the Mississippi Rifles and one company of the Tennessee regiment, continued moving to the east and found more deserted fortifications and empty houses. Approximately fifteen prisoners were captured during this sweep, and under questioning they revealed that the Mexican defenders had been withdrawn to the Main Plaza. On the move again, the patrol met its first strong resistance at a large stone hospital, from the roof of which the Mexicans poured a heavy fire. Pvt. John M. Tyree was struck by a musket ball and died.

The patrol sought cover and awaited the arrival of reinforcements, and quickly the rest of the regiment, under Major Bradford, arrived, accompanied by a portion of the 2d Texas Mounted Volunteers, on foot for the day.[45] A plan of attack was rapidly developed.

On the basis of information supplied by captured Mexican soldiers, the Main Plaza was thought to be one block west of the Cathedral, a structure that dominated the skyline of Monterrey. The force decided to push westward along a street one block north of the heavily fortified hospital. This street turned out to be lined with fortified houses and walled gardens, and the glint of Mexican bayonets could be seen from the rooftop parapets. The street was blocked by a barricade manned by Mexican soldiers.

This street was a death trap—a type of defense that had been successful for the Mexicans in earlier actions. Some of their barricades were even provided with cannon. The Mississippians were not accustomed to street fighting, but the Texans had had experience with this kind of thing, and the Rifles quickly adopted the techniques of their comrades-in-arms.[46] Grabbing up axes and crowbars, the Americans literally tunneled through the doors and adobe common walls of the houses, killing the armed occupants as they found them and mounting to the roofs by inside stairs. The *azoteas* of the captured houses then became vantage points from which to fire on other Mexican strongholds. The fine Whitney rifles in the hands of Mississippi marksmen began to take a heavy toll on the Mexican defenders.

General Taylor had evidently realized that slow communications from the battlefield were the cause of many of the problems during the attack of September 21. On this day he rode into Monterrey and took immediate command of the troops fighting on the eastern side of the city, boldly directing his troops in the house-to-house fighting, without regard for his personal safety. The sight of Taylor sharing their dangers gave the men a strong boost in morale.

As the Main Plaza was approached, resistance became fierce, and Braxton Bragg was summoned to bring a field artillery piece into the city to clear the barricades in the streets. Lt. Stephen A. D. Greaves, a Mississippian fighting in the streets of Monterrey, reported:

> Lt. Bragg entered the city, late in the evening, with his train of Flying Artillery, & commenced firing along the streets, & driving the enemy back upon the Plaza, That end of the city [the western] was then in the possession of the Americans, who were in almost every house firing upon the enemy, As soon as our troops saw him enter the streets of Monterey, galloping, fearlessly, at the head of his Artillery, they commenced cheering, & seemed to enter into the fight with more spirit and enthusiasm. Just after him Came Ex. President Lamar of Texas, on horse back. at full speed, with his sword drawn, cheering on the men & urging them to battle nobly for Texas & the U. States.[47]

Bragg's display of nonchalant courage could not fail to catch the eye of Jefferson Davis, and must surely have strengthened his opinion about the abilities of Braxton Bragg. The entrance into Monterrey of Mirabeau B. Lamar also remained in Davis's fond memory. In a speech delivered more than three decades later, he said:

> At Monterey, with a bright red vest, heedless of danger, [Lamar] rushed into the thickest of the fray, and, with the cry of "Brave boys, Americans are never afraid!" at the head of the gallant Second regiment, charged home to victory. He was an ideal Texan—a man of rare genius and tender affection.[48]

By nightfall the American eastern attacking force had advanced from Fort Tenería on the outskirts of the city to the edge of the Main Plaza in the very heart of Monterrey. The Mississippians, leading the advance, had seized a two-story stone house that overlooked the cathedral. From this vantage point, the Main Plaza could be seen over a block away to the southwest but was still out of the range of effective rifle fire. The Americans spotted another two-story stone house that overlooked the plaza, and this became the target of the next advance. But the streets that led to this building came under an intense fire from Mexican field artillery, and the combined force of Mississippians and Texans found it necessary to construct barricades for their protection while crossing the streets. Davis sent Sergeant Major Harlan for reinforcements, but minutes later a breathless Harlan returned with orders for Davis and Henderson (in command of the Texans) to withdraw their men from the city. Davis thought that the attackers would have been safer spending the night inside captured buildings close to the Plaza, but he obeyed General Taylor's orders, and the Mississippians retreated.

The retreating men were closely pursued by Mexican soldiers, who poured heavy fire into every street intersection from parallel streets. Lieutenant Howard was wounded by a musket ball while attempting to cross one of these heavily guarded intersections. The 3rd U.S. Infantry, which was supported by a piece of light artillery, forced back the Mexicans snipers and allowed the last American troops, the Mississippians and the Texans, to withdraw to the northeast suburbs.

On the western side of the city, Worth's forces had met with equal success, having fought to within a block of the Main Plaza. But Worth did not withdraw his troops from their advanced positions, and they remain posted throughout the night, and planned to continue their advance at daybreak. Major John Munroe, circling the city from the west, brought Worth the 10-inch mortar, which was advanced to the Plaza de Capilla, well within range of the Main Plaza. From this point, throughout the evening Munroe rained bombs on the Mexican troops that huddled together in the Main Plaza. Worth's artillerymen miraculously hoisted a 6-inch gun and two howitzers to the top of the tallest building in their area, and began to fire on the many targets within their range.

A feeling of hopelessness had begun to permeate the morale of the Mexicans. In early afternoon, General Pedro Ampudia, commander of the garrison, had requested a cease-fire to remove all civilians from the battle zones within the city, but Taylor, suspecting that the request was a ruse to interrupt the momentum of the American attack refused to agree. Now, as mortar shells fell among the Mexican soldiers huddled in the Main Plaza, hopelessness began to turn to panic.

At 9 P.M., General Ampudia wrote to General Taylor, offering to "evacuate the city and citadel, taking with me the personnel and material of war which is left."[49] Taylor responded promptly that "my duty compels me to decline acceding to it. A complete surrender of the town and garrison, the latter as prisoners of war, is now demanded."

The two sides, far apart in their demands, agreed to appoint commissioners to arbitrate a possible surrender. Taylor appointed Gen. James Pinckney Henderson of the Texas Volunteers, Gen. William Worth of the regular troops, and Col. Jefferson Davis of the Mississippi Rifles to represent the Americans. The Mexican commissioners were Gen. Tomas Requeña, second in command of the Mexican forces in the north, Gen. José Garcia Conde, and Don Manuel Maria Llano. A surrender treaty was finally agreed upon by parties of commissioners and readied for signature by Ampudia and Taylor.

The terms of surrender, considered by many to be overly generous, were approved by General Taylor on September 27. By September 28, 1846, the city of Monterrey was in the hands of the Americans.

FIVE

Victory in Monterrey—Censure in Washington

I forgot to say that Mexican balls were not cast to kill me; thank God, I have escaped unscratched.
—*Daniel R. Russell,*
writing home from Monterrey, September 25, 1846

Under the provisions for the capitulation of Monterrey, Mexican forces abandoned the Citadel on September 25, and lowered the Mexican flag with an eight-gun salute. American forces promptly entered the fort and raised the Stars and Stripes to the accompaniment of a twenty-eight-gun salute, one for each state in the Union. American volunteers resting in camp were unaware of the flag-raising ceremony, and the cannon's roar sent the weary men rushing to their guns, shouting, "They have begun again."[1] However, once Old Glory was seen flying over the Citadel, all the tense nerves went slack again.

The following day the first of three divisions of the Mexican Army marched out of Monterrey, leaving behind their sick and wounded, which the Americans had agreed to care for. The second division followed on the 27th and the third on the 28th. The retreating Mexicans looked to American observers more like a victorious army than a defeated one:

> I saw enough of the Mexican troops when they marched out, to satisfy me that they only lacked one daring leader to have made their escape or a successful defense. They went out sullenly, defiantly, and their attitude was such as to create a well-founded apprehension that a collision would occur between them and our troops who lined the roadside.[2]

Allowing the Mexican army to go free, retaining their small arms, was viewed by many of the American soldiers with mixed reactions. Capt. William P. Rogers wrote:

> This armistice and its terms I look upon as a great a piece of folly as could have been enacted, if we have to fight again and all seem to think we will. If we do Gen. Taylor and all his referees deserve the execretation [execration] of the whole American people for the Mexicans were in our power.[3]

John Kenly, a Maryland volunteer, made a shrewd judgment:

> The army was very much divided in opinion; those opposed to its terms as being too lenient increased in numbers with the number of days elapsing from the surrender of the town. . . . It is worthy to note that I met with no one who had been in the assaults of the first day on the eastern defenses that found fault with the terms. . . .[4]

The Mexican army moved to Saltillo for a short respite. From Saltillo, Antonio Lopez de Santa Anna, the commander in chief, ordered the Army of the North to San Luis Potosi, about 250 miles south of Saltillo. This was the base from which Santa Anna planned to organize a force that he hoped would drive the Americans from northern Mexico. The Mexican staff and line officers fresh from Monterrey visited the general there on October 18, and were very coolly received. Santa Anna lectured the officers on errors made during the late campaign for Monterrey, and ordered a court-martial to investigate the causes for the loss of that city, losses in ordnance, and an excessive casualty rate. Balbontin, an artillery officer at Monterrey, claimed that Mexican forces suffered no more than 200 casualties in the defense of Monterrey, but that figure was far too low.[5]

Victorious American volunteers encamped at Walnut Springs were eager to visit Monterrey, but Taylor had placed the city off limits, especially to volunteers. His experience at Matamoros made him distrust the unruly volunteer regiments, which had been known to rob and kill civilians. But gradually volunteers were allowed to visit the city in small unarmed parties, and they wrote home to describe the scenes of their victory. C. E. Smedes, a Mississippian from Vicksburg, was surprised that the Americans had won at all:

> And when I saw the place [Monterrey], every house of which is a perfect fort of itself, and *was* fortified; when I saw every street barricaded and ditched, . . . and that they had in addition to the private fortifications, some twenty or thirty forts and forty pieces of artillery, I cannot for the life of me see how we made such progress into the town as we did, without losing more men . . . we received from them thirty-four pieces of artillery and some forty barrels of powder, with any quantity of other ammunition and public stores.[6]

Lieut. Benjamin S. Roberts, an American observer who did not participate in the attack, visited Monterrey after the battle and wrote his observations of the defenses:

> The yards are all of stone masonry seven feet or more high, two or more thick, serving the best of purposes to cover sharpshooters. The streets were barricaded with walls of heavy stone and dirt embankments, five feet or more thick, high enough to cover infantry perfectly.[7]

The effects of the struggle in Monterrey had scarred that city. Lieutenant Roberts wrote:

> The houses are literally torn to pieces with the balls, cannister and grape from the Mexican batteries—the trees in the streets cut down with balls—the sides of the houses down the streets, commanded by the Mexican batteries, appear as though iron harrows had been dragged over them, so terribly were they raked in the showers of grape and cannister pounding down them.[8]

The official casualty report issued by General Taylor lists 487 Americans killed and wounded, although many feel that this figure was too low. Colonel Davis reported the casualties of the Mississippi Regiment: September 21, 7 killed, 47 wounded; September 22, 1 killed, 1 wounded; September 23, 1 killed, 4 wounded. Total Mississippi casualties: 9 killed and 52 wounded.

Attention was now centered on tending to the sick and wounded and burying the dead. Lieut. R. L. Moore of the Mississippi Regiment listed the following casualties,

> Mr. Fredrick Matthews was hit on the head with a grape shot, which fractured his skull and the wound was supposed to be mortal. Mr. J. P. Tennille had his head blown off by a cannon shot; Mr. D. D. Dubose was killed by a cannon shot . . . Lieut. M. Crump had two shots through his hat.[9]

Daniel Russell added to this list the following Mississippi casualties:

> We lost, mortally wounded, in the charge, Dr. G. W. Ramsey; A. Cobb was missing after the first day's fight, and was found dead yesterday. The Dr. received a four pounder through the left hip, and lived 30 hours.[10]

Among the wounded was Rufus Arthur, brother of the editor of the *Vicksburg Whig,* who was struck on the head by a spent musket ball. The only damage done was to "bruise my head a little, and bleed me rather freely." He rejoined the battle after Captain Crump had stopped the bleeding with his handkerchief.

Some of the dead lay exposed to the elements for three days, and many of the wounded died from lack of attention. The majority of the enlisted men and volunteers were buried in shallow graves close to where their bodies had fallen. The graves were so shallow that their bodies were later unearthed by wolves and packs of hungry dogs. However, at least two cemeteries were used to inter American soldiers, both located at the American camp at Walnut Springs, the first being a resting place for the officers of the 3rd Infantry and the second a resting place for enlisted men.[11]

The Mississippians were proud of their victory, and their letters home boasted of their accomplishments. Daniel Russell wrote:

> Next day, 23d, Col. Davis called out from the fort a portion of the regiment, my company among others, for a sally on the town. This was an interesting fight—every house a fort—every street fortified. . . . We crawled on roofs of houses, and with the true rifle curled the yellow scoundrels from the house-tops whenever they rose to shoot. . . . A more gallant set of men than we have, God never chose to send into battle.[12]

Captain McManus wrote to *The Southron* about the escapades of his company:

> The "State Fencibles" . . . were scattered on the tops of houses, and behind them, and in the open street, exchanging shots, and in every sort of exertion which such a fight would naturally give birth to, without a thought of giving ground until the order to "retire" was given. Wm. Low brought down a colored gentleman who had taken two fair fires at me; and he no doubt would have "got" me had not Low "stopped his game" by shooting him down.[13]

However, one of the most remarkable feats was performed by two men not belonging to the regiment, John Rhodes Smith of New Orleans and Ezra Price of Natchez.[14] These men were members of the 4th Louisiana volunteers, which was disbanded at Camargo. Hearing that Taylor had marched overland to attack Monterrey, the two struck out on foot to join the army. They walked from Camargo to Monterrey in six days, arriving at Walnut Springs on September 21. At the camp, each borrowed a rifle and marched off to fight with the 3d Infantry. Later during that same day they joined the Mississippi Regiment and finished up the day fighting in their ranks. Capt. George Crump, commanding the Vicksburg Volunteers, said that Mississippi regiment was "claiming them as one of us."[15] The citizens of Natchez, in honor of Price's valor, commissioned a rifle to be made and presented to him. The rifle was described as "handsomely mounted in silver, with a silver plate on the stock."[16]

Wounded American soldiers were moved to the palace of General Arista on the south side of Monterrey, to recover in the opulence of formal gardens and reflecting pools. From this location, Lt. Col. A. K. McClung reported to a friend in Columbus, Mississippi:

> About ten days ago I underwent a surgical operation, and had five pieces of bone extracted, one of them an inch and a quarter long

> and half an inch thick. One wound was through the middle of the hand, rendering an amputation of two fingers necessary, and stiffening the other two. I only retain the use of the thumb. Now these bones are out, the surgeons think I will improve rapidly. I have struggled up against these wounds wonderfully, and I now feel confident of a steady recovery.[17]

To honor his bravery, the citizens of Columbus, Mississippi, had a sword made for presentation to McClung. The scabbard and sword are described:

> The scabbard is embossed with appropriate designs, and on a gold plate is the inscription—"Presented to Lieut. Col. Alex'r K. McClung by the citizens of Lowndes county, Miss. for his gallantry at the battle of Monterey." On the sword are the words uttered by the gallant Colonel, when making his charge on the Mexican defenses—"Tombigbee Volunteers, follow me." The handle is covered with mother-of-pearl, richly inlaid with gold and precious stones, the guard is set with a large and beautiful topaz, and the guard chain is of massive gold. The whole is surmounted with a spread eagle, whose diamond eyes sparkle.[18]

William Henry Harrison Patterson, lieutenant in the Tombigbee Guards, was likewise honored for his bravery at Monterrey. The citizens of Charlottesville, Virginia, his birthplace, awarded Patterson a sword.[19] Private Samuel W. White of the Mississippi Regiment, wounded in the battle for Monterrey, was awarded a sword for his bravery there by his former classmates of the senior class of Yale University.[20]

Jefferson Davis received great praise from his troops for his actions at Monterrey. His insistence on endless drills and rigid discipline had been received with some criticism from his fellow Mississippians—criticism which had begun to appear in some of the newspapers of his home state before the attack on Monterrey. But Davis's handling of his men during this battle silenced his critics. Lieut. Daniel Russell wrote that his company had "been on the heels of Davis since the fight opened" and that "Davis is a gallant fellow." Rufus Arthur joined in the praise of Davis:

> Our field officers had a name when they were elected, but they have in this action ascended the ladder of fame. Col. Davis was in the front and head of the battles from the opening to the close,

cheering onward the men by his cool, pleasant, fearless and confident manner. He knew the men he had to command and felt confident, and they in return fought well, because they had confidence in the skill, discretion, and ability of their leader.[21]

The leadership qualities Jefferson Davis had demonstrated at Monterrey were to bring him national attention. Unfortunately he had also shown a rather petty side to his nature by becoming embroiled in a controversy.[22] Colonel W. B. Campbell of the 1st Tennessee Regiment challenged Davis's claim that the Mississippians were the first American regiment to enter the walls of Fort Tenería. One of Colonel Campbell's letters home claimed the honor for the Tennessee regiment. The letter, though written for private consumption, was published in a Tennessee newspaper and stirred up a regional controversy between the sister states. Balie Peyton, a fellow Tennesseean and aide to General Worth, substantiated the claim with another letter to the press. Davis was furious and stubbornly disputed this claim in speeches and public letters to the press. Colonel Campbell had only been attempting to make a good case for his regiment and had not intended any malice to the Mississippians, but his declarations hurt Davis's pride. Campbell had written in his diary on September 28, concerning the taking of the Tenería, "The Mississippians were on my right and rushed forward with my men; but the latter, being more directly in front of the fort [Tenería], and nearer to it, reached it sooner and stormed it."[23] General Quitman, a Mississippian, and brigade commander of the brigade containing both the Mississippi and Tennessee regiments, attempted to remain neutral in the contest but finally surrendered to the relentless pressure placed upon him by his fellow Mississippians and reluctantly entered the controversy on the side of the Mississippi Regiment. By February 19, 1847, Campbell's recollections had been hardened by the controversy, and he stubbornly wrote:

As soon as my regiment [Tennessee] charged they [Mississippians] did so. There was a simultaneous rush. Some of my men entered the fort first. Davis was on foot and in citizens dress. I received no orders from Quitman until after the fort was taken.[24]

This controversy was to rage on long after the Mexican War, with Davis's political enemies quick to accept the Tennessee claims and his friends adamant in his support of Mississippi.

While most of the Mississippi regiment battled in the streets of Monterrey, the men of Companies A and F, commanded by Captains John Sharp and William Delay had been ordered to stay behind in Cerralvo to guard the supplies left there. While in Cerralvo, these two companies came under the observation of one of the surgeons stationed there, S. Compton Smith. Smith would later write that the two companies were made up of mostly

> young men,—planters, and sons of planters,—and almost all men of education and responsibility. Many of the privates even, as well as the officers, were accompanied with servants, brought with them from home.[25]

The men stationed at Cerralvo were more than a little homesick and wished to taste again the famous Mississippi corndodger, rather than the flat Mexican tortilla. But dodgers were made of cornmeal, not the fine-ground flour used in tortillas, and for this a special grinding was needed. The head of commissary in Cerralvo, a recent West Point graduate, nursed a prejudice against all volunteers. He would issue neither cornmeal nor any of the many hand mills owned by the army to the Mississippi boys. Captain Sharp was informed, "The mills were intended for the use of the *regular troops* at Monterey, and he was not authorized to give them out to volunteers." When an angry Captain Sharp took his problem to Maj. S. Compton Smith, who outranked the officer of commissary, the major advised Sharp that his men could use the mills, but they must be returned when finished. Major Smith called upon the young commissary officer later that day and found him

> pacing up and down his narrow apartment, in a most furious but impotent rage. At the same time my ears were saluted with a loud roaring sound, that reminded me of the Falls of Niagara, which was issuing from the court; the sound was accompanied with the full chorus of a "corn song", such as I had often heard among the negroes of the southern plantations. I immediately perceived what was going on. With difficulty restraining an inclination to

> laughter, I inquired of the lieutenant the cause of his excitement. "Oh!" cried he, pointing to the court, "those blackguard volunteers!" The "blackguards", it seemed, were not content with the use of a few of the mills, but were determined, as they said, to give the lieutenant "a benefit" and had manned every mill they could muster, and were grinding and roaring away in the most approved plantation style.[26]

A grim incident occurred in Cerralvo on October 11, 1846, when the body of Pvt. A. M. Liles from Company F was found hanging from an orange tree. He had been strangled by a horsehair lariat, which was still firmly attached to his neck. This type of lariat was common among the vaqueros of northern Mexico, but the unique braiding in this particular lariat identified the owner as a certain Juan La Vaca. A reward was offered for his capture, and within a few days several of his countrymen brought him in to claim the bounty. La Vaca admitted the murder, caused by a dispute with Liles over a five-dollar gambling stake in a card game. The men of Company F passed sentence on La Vaca, and he was hanged on the same orange tree as Private Liles by the same horsehair lariat.[27]

The two left-behind companies of Mississippians rejoined their regiment in Monterrey on October 31, 1846. The Mississippians were still encamped at Walnut Springs, not far from the modest marquee of General Taylor, and from this vantage point they had ample opportunity to observe Old Rough and Ready.

General Taylor was quite a curiosity to the Mexicans, who could not understand either his language or his simple life-style. He failed to play the familiar role of "conquering general" that they had come to know only too well. He remained camped with the American volunteers outside the city, even at the urging of his aides, who wished him to establish headquarters in Monterrey, preferably in the lush environment of Arista's Palace. But Old Rough and Ready would not entertain the idea of such pomp and ostentation. Rowdy volunteers, especially Texas Rangers, had been committing depredations against the Mexican civilian populace and the area around Taylor's modest tent swarmed with Mexicans, who had established a market there for the sale of their produce to the Americans. The marketers were safe there under his eye, probably the only safe place around Monterrey at this time. The old general was never able to master much Spanish and used a translator to converse with the Mexicans. Taylor was sitting in his tent one morning when a Mexican was ushered into his presence. Through the services of a translator Taylor was told that the Mexican wished to lodge a complaint: Volunteers had been stealing his wood. The old gentleman, preoccupied with army problems and wanting to get rid of his pesky caller, pointed his finger toward the door of his tent and growled, "huevos [eggs], huevos!" The puzzled Mexican was hustled away, while one of Taylor's aides gently reminded the general that the word he wanted was "vamos."[28]

Mexican officers captured on September 21 were kept under guard near Taylor's tent during the night, and all eagerly awaited the dawn for a glimpse of the famous American general. He appeared early on the morning of September 22, "attired in blue-check frock coat, blue pantaloons, without stripes, white waistcoat, and a broad-brimmed straw hat." The Mexican officers, accustomed to seeing generals bedecked in yards of medals, plumes, and fancy gold frogging, were baffled by this garb. Finally they thought of an explanation: "The General was about to make some dangerous reconnaissance in person."[29]

The Polk Administration in Washington was the object of much of Taylor's concern during these idle days after the capture of Monterrey. The terms of the surrender treaty for Monterrey were scorned by politicians in Washington, especially articles 2, 3, and 6.

> ARTICLE 2. That the Mexican forces be allowed to retain the following arms, to wit, the commissioned officers their side arms, the Infantry their arms and accoutrements, the Cavalry their arms and accoutrements, the Artillery one field battery not to exceed six pieces with twenty one rounds of ammunition.
> ARTICLE 3. That the Mexican armed forces retire within seven days from this date, beyond the line formed by the Pass of the Rinconada, the City of Linares, and San Fernando de presas.
> ARTICLE 6. That the forces of the United States will not advance beyond the line specified in the 3d Article before the expiration of eight weeks or until the orders or instructions of the respective governments can be received.[30]

The treaty was sent by express to Washington on September 25, and received on October 11 by William Marcy, the Secretary of War. The reaction was swift; Polk wrote in his diary with righteous indignation:

> In agreeing to this armistice General Taylor violated his orders and I regret I cannot approve his course. He had the enemy in his power and should have taken them prisoners, depriving them of their arms, discharging them on their parole of honour, and preserving the advantage which he had obtained by pushing on without delay farther into the country. . . .[31]

At a meeting held the next day, Polk's acquiescent Cabinet unanimously agreed that Taylor had "committed a great error" and felt that the capture of the Mexican army at Monterrey would have ended the war. Polk and his Cabinet advisers agreed to order Taylor to terminate the armistice immediately and to renew a "vigorous" prosecution of the war. By October 22, such orders had been drawn up by the War Department and presented to Polk for his approval. Polk added some oral instructions to the bearer of this dispatch, Robert W. McLane, and McLane was sent on his mission.

Taylor received these orders on November 2 and reacted predictably with anger. Privately he expressed the opinion that these orders were maliciously intended to undermine his popularity with the American public—a hint that Taylor might already be considering a run for the presidency. Taylor the Whig and Polk the Democrat had been at odds since the early summer of 1846, and Taylor's suspicions were probably well grounded. Polk, a veteran politician, could sense the swell of positive public opinion generated by Taylor's victories in Mexico. Democratic efforts to downplay the general's role in the victory at Monterrey fell on deaf ears. The press continued to laud Old Rough and Ready and the roar of public approval echoed through the halls of Congress and the White House.

Were the generous terms of capitulation granted to the Mexicans an error in judgment, or were there extenuating circumstances? Zachary Taylor, shrewd and pragmatic, was much too clever to surrender a chance to capture the defenders of Monterrey if he had been able to do so. The very wording of articles 2, 3, and 6 in the capitulation agreement implied a weak American bargaining position. In truth, the strategic position of Taylor's forces was precarious.

On September 24, Taylor found himself with fewer than 5,000 effective soldiers, attempting to surround an army of about 10,000 Mexicans, housed in Monterrey in a very strong system of fortifications. The American army, bloodied in the attacks of September 21 on the eastern side of Monterrey, were fatigued and would not have been able to sustain the attack much longer without rest. The Mexicans had remained relatively intact, and their most powerful fort, the Citadel, remained virtually undamaged. Supplies and ammunition were critically low on the American side, while evidence suggested that the Mexican defenders had ample to withstand the siege for many more days. In fact, the term "siege" did not even apply in this case, for the city had never been completely invested. Only the road to Saltillo had been closed by the Americans; the road from Monterrey north to Marin remained open to movement by the Mexican Army. General Ampudia's army could have avoided capture simply by abandoning Monterrey and marching north out of town on this road. Worth's division was on the south side of the city and probably would not have been able to come to Taylor's aid to prevent such a breakout. Thus, it is doubtful whether Taylor had the strength to force a surrender of the Mexican army.

The army's supply of ammunition and food was quickly dwindling. Col. W. B. Campbell of the 1st Tennessee had noted in a letter that by September 21, "Our supply of ammunition was very limited; our provisions still more limited."[32] Taylor knew that he must either conquer Monterrey quickly or else disengage his forces and return to the Rio Grande. An organized retreat would have been impossible with the many untrained volunteers in his army. It is questionable if many of his weary soldiers had the strength for a forced march over more than 150 miles of rugged terrain. The many wounded had to be transported, and few wagons were available. The Mexican army, which abounded in superb horsemen, would have like nothing better than to take the offensive, attacking the rear of Taylor's retreating army while the front was held up on the narrow roads by the excellent Mexican cavalry. Retreat would have become rout.

In final analysis, it appeared that Polk's politically suspicious nature would not allow him to trust the military judgment of his field commander. As chief executive, he rarely delegated authority to others, and did much of his administration's work himself, down to the finest details. He literally worked himself to death during his single term in office, dying only a few months after the completion of his first term.

The grim reality of the American army's situation at Monterrey had not been communicated in the dispatches to Washington. But even if they had been, it is not clear in retrospect that they would have been believed.

SIX

The Expedition to Victoria

> The weather has been delightful and the country along the base of the mountains beautiful beyond description and abounding in all the tropical fruits. Delicious cold water from the mountains. Many of the streams full of trout and other excellent fish. Talk of marching against Tula. About 6,000 Mexicans there plus 2,000 light troops holding the passes. We could take no artillery except by carrying it some twenty miles by pack mules and men. If one or two light batteries could be taken along Taylor would be on his way there tomorrow. He has a strong desire to get hold of Valencia, who is said to be the best officer in the Mexican service.
>
> —*Lieut. Benjamin S. Roberts, letter, January 6, 1947*

General Taylor disregarded the orders from Washington received on November 12, 1846—orders hand carried by Maj. Robert W. McLane, directing General Taylor to assume a defensive posture and to proceed no farther south. Taylor marched the very next day with a force commanded by General Worth and captured the city of Saltillo, which was surrendered to the Americans without opposition.

Leaving Worth to garrison Saltillo,[1] Taylor returned to Monterrey to organize an expedition against Victoria, the capital of the state of Tamaulipas. The American force was divided into 1st and 2d Brigades. The 1st and 3rd U.S. Infantry and the Baltimore Battalion of volunteers was designated as the 1st Brigade, under Twiggs.[2] The 2d Brigade, under the command of Quitman, consisted of the volunteer regiments from Georgia, Tennessee, and Mississippi.

A major strategic objective of the expedition was to explore the spur of the Sierra Madres running east toward the Gulf Coast. Taylor and his staff were searching for alternate passes through this mountain chain large enough to allow for the passage of cannon and wagons. If the Mexicans could bypass the major pass at Monterrey, Santa Anna could move from his base at San Luis Potosi directly to the Rio Grande and cut Taylor's supply line, leaving the American army isolated in the Sierras. Tula Pass outside Victoria particularly needed to be scouted.

Taylor planned to rendezvous at Victoria with a force under the command of Gen. Robert Patterson, which was to march overland from Matamoros. Patterson's force was to continue on from Victoria to Tampico by land and garrison that city, which had recently been occupied without opposition by the United States Navy. The combined forces of Taylor and Patterson were thought necessary to take Victoria, and Taylor quite likely did not wish to repeat the lessons learned at Monterrey by attacking the city with too small a force. Heavy opposition was expected in that area since the Mexicans were commanded there by the firebrand Gen. Gabriel Valencia.[3]

Along the line of march, American soldiers met Mexicans who greeted them with the salutation "Fandango poco tiempo," meaning "the ball" was soon to open—fighting would begin soon. Balbontin notes that Valencia's forces numbered more than 2,000 veteran troops comprising some of the finest regiments in Mexico. The long lines of the American advance were closely scouted by the Mexican cavalry, and appeared to the Mexicans to be "prolonged and disorderly." Campfires were seen in the Sierras in the evenings by American soldiers on the march, no doubt those of these scouts. Even civilians expressed a willingness to fight the American invaders.

Taylor's forces in northern Mexico, never large in number, were now spread thinly among a few small garrisons several days' march from one another. By late December, they were positioned so that it would require more than ten days' time to concentrate into a size capable of resisting a major Mexican attack. Santa Anna's army in San Luis Potosi was now estimated by observers to exceed 20,000 troops, and the Mexican government burned for a Mexican military victory, no matter how small, to bolster the country's sagging morale. Santa Anna had correctly surmised from his many sources of information—Mexican spies efficiently reported every American move—that the time was quickly approaching for military action against Taylor.

Taylor's forces left Monterrey on December 14, 1846, and proceeded by easy marches over the mountainous terrain to Montemorelos. The Sierras that rim the landscape throughout this region give the state its name: Tamaulipas, which means high mountains in the Indian language of Nahuatl. At Montemorelos the expedition was joined by the 2d U.S. Infantry and the 2d Tennessee Regiment, which had marched from Camargo to join the expedition. Quitman's Brigade camped outside Montemorelos on December 17, near an irrigation ditch named Garrapatas. The men of the brigade quickly added another word to their Spanish vocabulary: "garrapatas," meaning ticks. "Ticks cover it [the camp]," reported Quitman, "crawling about on the grass . . . to look out for something to bite."[4]

That evening while the Americans were gathered about campfires outside Montemorelos, admiring the grandeur of an early sunset in the mountains, a horseman galloped into Taylor's camp. He carried an emergency express from the American forces at Saltillo. General Worth had received word that Santa Anna was advancing from San Luis Potosi with a large army to attack the garrison at Saltillo. Taylor was now on the horns of a dilemma. If he returned to Saltillo, he risked the safety of General Patterson's forces with which he had planned to link up. If he failed to reinforce Worth at Saltillo, he risked the loss of Worth's forces and possibly even Monterrey. Taylor quickly made a compromise decision. While the 2d Brigade was pressing on to Victoria, he himself would return to Monterrey with the 1st Brigade, thence to proceed to Saltillo. But in Monterrey he learned that the Mexican advance guard had gotten less than halfway to Saltillo (Matehuala) when it was ordered to turn back. Taylor angrily denounced Worth for a "false alarm," and backtracked toward Victoria. Other such false alarms, jokingly called "stampedes" by the men in the ranks, continued to occur throughout the winter and served as a sobering reminder of the serious threat posed by the Mexicans in San Luis Potosi.

Taylor had barely reached Montemorelos on December 25, 1846, when he received another dispatch rider from Monterrey—this time relaying a message from Gen. Winfield Scott. Scott's plan for the invasion of Central Mexico through Vera Cruz had been approved by President Polk, and Scott was trying to locate the troops for his expedition. Scott told Taylor that he was planning to be in Camargo on December 23, and he requested a meeting there to discuss strategy. Considering the distance between Montemorelos and Camargo, it was impossible for Taylor to meet this deadline. Besides, his concerns and thoughts were now concentrated on the expedition en route to Victoria. Therefore Taylor ignored this request and resumed his march.

Meanwhile, Quitman's 2d Brigade continued on to Victoria. Davis was on leave of absence, so the 1st Mississippi was temporarily under the command of Maj. Alexander Bradford. To set a good example for his company, Captain Rogers often abandoned his horse and marched on foot at the head of his column, limping along with a slightly pained smile. He confessed to his diary on December 22, "The latter two days I walked every step of the way and oh! how I suffered but I will not complain."[5] This was an old problem for Rogers. On October 8, during the march to Monterrey, he had confided to his wife, "I thought I could habituate myself to fatigue but do not think that I can ever learn to walk far at a time. . . ."[6]

Beyond Montemorelos vast fields of sugarcane lined the roads on both sides, and every man on the march was seen to be chewing a stick of the sweet cane. The brigade passed through Linares and pronounced the town to be a handsome place filled with respectable-looking citizens. The ladies of Linares were not afraid of the formidable looking Yankee Volunteers and lined the streets to greet them; probably the first Americans they had ever seen. Many of the citizens kept green parrots as pets, which perched on their hands. A hotel in the middle of Linares sported the presumptive title

"Tienda de Abundancia."[7] East of Linares, the country changed from cultivated fields of cotton, corn, and sugarcane to a lush forest of ebony trees, broken by sparkling mountain streams of clear water. These forested hillsides were home to vast flocks of green parrots, deer, turkey, wild boar, and birds described as "like a pheasant," probably chachalacas.

The long dusty marches began to tire the men, and the column became strung out along the road. When a Mexican happened by on horseback, one of the foot-weary Mississippians attempted to ride double. Stopping the horseman, the dusty young man handed his rifle to the Mexican to hold while he climbed aboard and, once seated, he found the riding bumpy. The Mexican horseman "soon dexterously twitched" the Mississippian from the hurricane deck of his pony and galloped away in possession of the Mississippian's rifle.[8]

Christmas Eve was celebrated by the men of the army with the manufacture of "eggnog." Foragers into the countryside returned with eggs and bottles of mescal (a potent distilled beverage produced from the fermented juice of the lechiguilla, a succulent) that were added to a camp kettle filled with boiling water and sugar.[9] On Christmas Day, the soldiers marched through the small town of Hidalgo, a dilapidated village with a strong Moorish appearance; the church in the center of town looked to the Americans like a mosque.

General Valencia had kept the uneven advance of the Americans under close observation, and had repeatedly pleaded with Santa Anna for orders to attack. No such orders came, but some minor engagements did occur. While scouting Santa Rosa Canyon near Linares, a party of engineers and dragoons was cut off by the Mexicans, losing the baggage train and eleven men. Word of this attack sent alarm through Quitman's Brigade; arms were loaded, bayonets fixed, and stragglers hastily closed up the line of march. Most American soldiers by now had heard or even seen what the Mexican rancheros could do to soldiers that fell behind, and "you might have covered the whole division with a blanket, so closely did they keep their ranks."[10] On the night of December 27, the army camped at an abandoned sugar mill, and before dawn the pickets on the Victoria road were attacked. The small Mexican force quickly retreated, but the firing created a minor panic among the soldiers. The Mississippians were no exception.

> This news caused the utmost confusion—soldiers running hither and thither hunting their officers—officers hunting their men—nobody knew from what point the attack was expected, and everybody under the impression that the Mexican cavalry were just ready to make a spirited assault. In the midst of this confusion the major [Bradford] mounted his bobtailed horse, and after a great deal of exertion brought his men into line of battle, which was in itself a matter of surprise, as he was more madly excited than "any four men" under his command. Observing that there was still much confusion and apprehension, resulting from the peculiar circumstances which surrounded the boys at that critical moment, the major drew himself up to his full height, and called out in a loud voice—"Keep cool, boys! keep cool! Look at me! (putting spurs to his horse and galloping off at full speed,) I'm as cool as h—ll!"[11]

No units of cavalry accompanied Quitman's Brigade, so on December 28, a makeshift troop was organized by Quitman to scout the hostile countryside in advance of the approaching infantry.[12] Under the command of Lieut. William Patterson of the 1st Mississippi, whom Quitman deemed "an active and enterprising officer," the newly designated troopers immediately departed to explore the route.

Santa Anna ordered a distraught and angry General Valencia not to provoke a battle with the Americans in Victoria, since this region of Mexico was isolated by the mountains from San Luis Potosi, the Mexican base of supply. Mexican cavalry, obeying orders, galloped out of Victoria to the mountains around Tula Pass only a short time before the Americans entered on December 29, 1846.

American entrance into Victoria was faithfully reported by Rufus K. Arthur, a Mississippi Rifleman, in a letter home to Vicksburg:

> On the morning of the 29th December we started in fine order to enter [Victoria] peacefully or forcefully. Our company was the front of the advance guard on that day, and we all indulged the pleasant anticipations of a passage with the Mexicans, but a deputation, consisting of the State and city authorities, met us about

three miles from the city, and gave General Quitman a hearty welcome. . . . They informed General Quitman that they were authorized to surrender the city with all the public property, . . . We then marched on into the city, through the principal street, and formed in the Grand Plaza with great ceremony—it was the most imposing scene I ever witnessed. The surrender was then formally made, and the American flag was then hoisted on the State House.[13]

Samuel French, a young lieutenant in Capt. George H. Thomas's artillery battery, did not remember the surrender ceremony at Victoria as being quite so formal.

The alcalde left his office, crossed the plaza, and after a short address presented the keys of the city to General Quitman. The Mexican standard was hauled down, and as the United States flag was thrown to the breeze the band began to play, when all at once, in emulation, three or four jackasses begin to bray, and bray, and drowned all the proceedings, amidst roars of laughter that could not be restrained, especially among the volunteers.[14]

The army camped one mile from the town leaving five companies to garrison Victoria. From the 1st Mississippi, the Vicksburg Southrons and the Raymond Fencibles were chosen, the Southrons quartered in the State House of Tamaulipas. On January 4, 1847, Generals Taylor and Patterson arrived in Victoria with the remainder of the forces, bringing aggregate troop strength to better than 5,000 American soldiers. Col. Jefferson Davis and Capt. George Crump also arrived with this party of soldiers, returning from a sixty-day leave of absence to Mississippi.

Correspondent Rufus K. Arthur reported to the citizens of Vicksburg the novel settings that the Mississippians had encountered in Victoria:

We are now pleasantly situated—keeping out the enemy, preserving order in the city, *sleeping in houses,* eating oranges, bananas, . . . in short enjoying all the luxuries of a tropical life . . . the thermometer stood at 96 degrees on the 30th December; figs are growing, the trees green and in bloom and the men bathing in the mountain stream every day.[15]

Many of the new volunteers brought from Matamoros by General Patterson had never met General Taylor. The Illinois volunteers were visited by the old general on January 4, accompanied by an aide attired in a "clean and handsome" uniform and astride a magnificent thoroughbred dragoon horse. Old Rough and Ready himself rode a gentle mule and wore a dusty old black frock coat from under which protruded his sword. He greeted the men by doffing his big Mexican straw hat but the men mobbed the aide with outstretched hands, mistaking him for Taylor. One of the new volunteers was heard to comment, "Why do they call him old Taylor?" Once the mistaken identification had been rectified, the volunteers swarmed over the old man, and he tried to shake each of the many hands extended to him in respect and admiration. Still skeptical, one of the Illinois men was heard to wonder if *that* (the mule) was the animal the general was on when he charged the Mexicans.[16]

On January 3, 1847 Gen. Winfield Scott arrived in Camargo on the steamboat *Corvette,* to be greeted by military bands and the roar of cannons.[17] When Scott found that Taylor, unable to attend the meeting, was now far away in Victoria, he did not tarry. Dashing off direct orders to General Butler, with a copy to Taylor, Scott reembarked at 3:00 P.M. that same afternoon to return downriver to Brazos Island. The severity of these orders made it clear why Scott had wanted to meet with Taylor in person: He had hoped to soften the hard blow.

Scott, with the permission of the president, would divert more than 9,000 troops—4,500 regulars and 4,500 volunteers—from Taylor's already undermanned army for use in the planned invasion of central Mexico. Taylor was to be left with fewer than 7,000 men—no regulars except the 2d Dragoons under Col. Charles May, and a battery of light field artillery, and only 700 volunteer troops with actual battle experience. This 7,000-man figure included all troops on garrison duty at the many posts from the mouth of the Rio Grande to Saltillo.

The orders were received by Butler and acknowledged, and the copy for Taylor was forwarded to Victoria by a small party of dragoons, under the command of Lieut. John A. Richey. The party passed through Villa Gran on the evening of January 13, 1847, and passed on the outskirts of the village while Richey returned to town for supplies, alone. In Villa Gran, Richey was lassoed from his horse by unknown parties and brutally murdered.[18] The dispatch case was removed from his body, and the important orders therein forwarded immediately to Santa Anna at San Luis Potosi.[19] The American army in northern Mexico was now in grave danger.

When Taylor finally received a second copy of Scott's orders, he was greatly disturbed. The men reported that the demeanor of the old general changed—not only irritable and moody at the loss of his troops, but so preoccupied that he once put mustard into his coffee rather than sugar.[20]

From that portion of his command stationed in Victoria, General Taylor decided to send the majority to Tampico with General Patterson and retained only Thomas's artillery battery, two squadrons of dragoons under Colonel May, and the Mississippi Regiment. The men of the Rifles were proud of this honor and their apparent elevation over their rivals, the 1st Tennessee.

In late January, Taylor left Victoria without a garrison, and put his now much reduced army on the road back to Monterrey. En route he stopped in Villa Gran to settle a little unfinished business. With the artillery battery and the dragoons stationed in the main plaza, Taylor summoned the alcalde of that village to an informal court of inquiry on the murder of Lieutenant Richey.[21] Taylor demanded that the murderers be given up. The alcalde, pale and trembling, pleaded ignorance, stating that he could not produce them. Taylor threatened to hang him if he did not cooperate. But a lengthy examination of witnesses was equally useless. Finally a frustrated Taylor closed the hearing by informing the alcalde that he was levying a contribution on the village of $50,000, to be paid in three weeks if the murderers had not been identified by that time.

Old Taylor was in very bad mood by the time this hearing was over, and his disposition was not improved by discovering that an artillery piece blocked the road outside Villa Gran, holding up the baggage train. He galloped up to the traffic block with a scowl on his face, and a hushed silence fell on the idle teamsters gathered about. Dismounting, Taylor approached the driver of the team and began to pull his ear. He ordered the artillery off the road, and to remain off the road until all wagons had passed. As soon as Taylor galloped off again, Lieutenant French, fresh from West Point, reported that he had "assumed command" of the situation and ordered the artillery piece back on the road.

The expedition returned to Monterrey by January 24, 1847, to their old campgrounds at Walnut Springs, but remained there only a short while. Taylor disobeyed Scott's specific orders to abandon Saltillo and instead decided to push his little army eighteen miles south of Saltillo to Agua Nueva, on the main road to San Luis Potosi.

Taylor reasoned that Santa Anna must have learned, from the Richey documents, the official timetable for the Vera Cruz invasion and would soon concentrate his forces to defend that city. However, if Santa Anna should decide to push north and attack Taylor instead, the best place to intercept the Mexicans was not Monterrey, where the American army could be trapped and where supply lines could be easily cut. Since there were not enough troops remaining along the Rio Grande to relieve the siege, it would be a simple matter to starve out the defenders. Moreover, retreats and defensive holding operations did not suit the general's temperament. "Let them come; damned if they don't go back a good deal faster than they came," muttered a belligerent Taylor to a correspondent of the *New York Tribune*.[22]

The most opportune strategy, reasoned Taylor, was to confront the Mexican army before it reached Saltillo. The 250 miles of road between San Luis Potosi and Saltillo passed mostly through a desert region, which, lacking adequate food and water, would have to be crossed by forced marches on limited rations. The Mexican army would be its most vulnerable at the end of such a march and must not be allowed to rest and obtain provisions in Saltillo.

Santa Anna, still in San Luis Potosi, would not be allowed to remain inactive much longer. The press in Mexico City criticized him almost daily for his reluctance to take offensive action. The Mexican people desperately needed a victory over the Americans to bolster their sagging morale. Santa Anna envisioned a daring plan. He would move his army north and overpower the American forces at Saltillo and then return in glory to lead his army against Scott—an army whose ranks were certain to be filled with men stirred by the feelings of patriotism that a Mexican victory would create. Santa Anna felt that Taylor's depleted army could be overwhelmed by his own 16,000 men—12,000 infantry and 4,000 cavalry.

Santa Anna was a daring strategist, but his grasp of logistics fell short. He had never been known as a great provider for his armies, but now matters were even more desperate than usual. The Mexican government was virtually bankrupt. There was no money for tents or ambulances or medical supplies.[23] The Mexican Army of the North had not been paid for a long time, and most of its soldiers had no money of their own to provide even the most basic necessities. The army was expected to rely mainly on the "resources of the country" through which it was passing for subsistence, and this time it was about to pass through the high desert country. But these details were evidently not important to Santa Anna and his staff.

The first Mexican soldiers left San Luis Potosi on January 27, 1847, other troops on January 28 and 29. Santa Anna and his staff and the rear guard departed by February 2 for Saltillo. The weather turned harshly colder; within a week, icy rain was falling on the troops. By February 13, soldiers began to die from exposure to the elements and lack of provisions. By February 19, they began to desert the ranks, and at nightfall the camp was organized in the shape of a pentagon, the perimeter policed by cavalry with orders to shoot anyone trying to desert. By February 20, the Mexican Army had reached as far north as Encarnación, forty-eight miles from Saltillo, and was reviewed there by General Santa Anna. The Mexican army now consisted of 10,000 infantry, 4,000 cavalry, and sixteen cannon, according to a Mexican officer with the army.

On February 8, 1846, Colonel Davis wrote his wife from Agua Nueva:

> We are here on the table-lands of Mexico, at the foot of the Sierra Madre. We came expecting a host and battle, have found solitude and externally peace. The daily alarms of this frontier have ceased, the enemy I believe has retired to San Luis de Potosi, and we are waiting reinforcements, while General Scott is taking all who can be seized and incorporates them in his division of the army. We have a beautiful and healthy position, and are waiting only action or such excitement as reconciles man to repose.[24]

Davis's solitude was about to be broken by a small cloud of dust that was just now visible on the southern horizon, the dust of thousands of marching feet.

SEVEN

The Battle of Buena Vista

> Our forces on the Rio Grande, and especially General Taylor's advanced position, were in a very critical position. If General Taylor's army be in that position it has grown out of his own imprudence in advancing without orders beyond Monterey and too far into the interior. General Scott seems to have assumed the command with the single idea in his head of taking Vera Cruz, and with this view has probably reduced General Taylor's forces to too small a number.
> —*President James Knox Polk, diary, entry for March 22, 1847,*
> *prior to receiving news of the victory at Buena Vista*

Geography heavily influenced the Battle of Buena Vista, so it is important to understand the topography of the valley in which the battle was fought, February 22–23, 1847.

About three miles south of Saltillo, the road from San Luis Potosi passed through a mountain defile called La Angostura (the Narrows). North of this pass a mile or so lay the hacienda of Buena Vista—aptly named, since the mountain setting was a spectacular one. To the west of Angostura, the land fell away from the road in a series of stony gullies and ravines, some of them 20 feet or more deep, creating a landscape impassable to artillery and cavalry both. To the east rose rugged bluffs, carved up by more ravines into steep-sided canyons topped with plateaus—like a hand with many fingers—and joining to form a continuous plateau at the foot of a towering range. The largest of these "fingers" was Middle Plateau, flanked by North and South Plateaus to either side of it. Gen. John Wool, scouting the area in December 1846, had recommended Angostura to Taylor as an excellent defensive position.[1]

Taylor had already pushed through Angostura Pass and taken up a position fifteen miles south at Agua Nueva. By early February, the countryside abounded with rumors about Santa Anna's advance, and the situation was tense. On January 23, an American scouting party, sent forth earlier from Saltillo, had been surprised by elements of Santa Anna's cavalry screen. Gen. José Vicente Miñon and his men encircled the blissfully sleeping camp of volunteers at Encarnación and captured it without firing a shot.[2] Two days later, another scouting party, dispatched from Saltillo to locate the first patrol, was also captured by General Miñon.

On February 20, Col. Charles May led a reconnaissance party of three hundred troopers from the 1st Dragoons southeast of Agua Nueva to the rancho of Hedionda. In that vicinity, Trooper Samuel Chamberlain topped the rise of a slight hill and reported seeing, "To the South, away in the distance, vast clouds of dust rolled up for miles reminding me of my first sight of Taylor's Army." A large army was heading north. May and his troopers soon made contact with an advanced unit of Mexican cavalry, and fearing that capture was imminent, raced back to camp, dashing into Agua Nueva before dawn on February 21. Colonel May reported the massive advance of Mexican infantry and indicated that the Mexican Army might be attempting to flank Agua Nueva by passing to the east, a movement that would cut off Taylor's army from Saltillo.[3]

This last inference was quite correct. The previous evening, General Santa Anna had ordered General Miñon and his cavalry brigade of 1,200 men to proceed to Saltillo in a flanking movement, by way of an unguarded alternate route. This narrow mountainous trail, too rugged for artillery but accessible to light cavalry, crossed the mountains at a small pass east of Hedionda and crossed back through the high pass named Palomas Adentura, due east of Saltillo. Miñon had been assigned to attack Taylor's rear, disrupting communications between Saltillo and Monterrey and harassing the defenses of Saltillo.

This unsettling news was confirmed soon after dawn, with the arrival of Ben McCulloch, a Texas Ranger.[4] McCulloch, disguising himself as a ranchero, had slipped into the Mexican camp at Encarnación and completed an accurate inventory of the enemy's strength.

These two reconnaissance reports painted a grim picture for the American army. Santa Anna was advancing with an army of better than 10,000 infantry, accompanied by an excess of 4,000 excellent cavalry and sixteen pieces of artillery. In the open plain around Agua Nueva, American forces were extremely vulnerable to this much larger army, open to being flanked by the cavalry and encircled. Once trapped, the Americans—operating from a small defensive enclosure on level ground and without any natural cover—could then be systematically destroyed by the Mexican artillery. Taylor's army needed to retreat to a better defensive position, a defensive site that ideally

- blocked the advance of the Mexican Army on Saltillo, where it hoped to obtain provisions,
- neutralized the advantage that a larger force had in flanking a smaller one,
- had an irregular topography that offered cover for American defenders from Mexican artillery,
- had a rugged terrain over which it was virtually impossible to ride a horse, ending the advantage of cavalry.

Fortunately just such a location was not far away: Angostura Pass.

But the plan to retreat from Agua Nueva to the pass faced opposition from General Taylor. Taylor felt that a retreat in the face of an advancing Mexican army would demoralize the largely volunteer American army and offer encouragement to the Mexicans. A heated meeting ensued between Taylor and his staff, and Taylor reluctantly gave way to the power of Wool's logic. In the early afternoon of February 21 the American army retreated northward into Angostura Pass, and hoped that it would not become their Thermopylae.

General Taylor and his staff, accompanied by the Mississippi Regiment and May's Dragoons, marched to Saltillo to prepare the defenses of that city. The bulk of the army, under the immediate command of General Wool, prepared defensive positions, and the Arkansas Mounted Regiment was left at Agua Nueva to load army supplies and baggage for shipment to Saltillo. But the Arkansas volunteers, apparently unaware of their perilous situation, balked at their assignment.

When the supplies did not arrive, May's Dragoons were ordered back to Agua Nueva to find that the Arkansas Regiment had refused to perform the "demeaning task" of loading wagons. The Dragoons arrived in Agua Nueva at midnight to find the "Rackensackers" playing cards in small groups or sleeping while a long line of empty wagons waited to be loaded. The grumbling Dragoons commenced to load the wagons themselves and were making some progress when the sound of shots were heard from the San Luis Potosi road. Chamberlain reported the resulting bedlam:

> Cries of "Run boys, run! The Mexicans are on us!" were heard and great confusion ensued. The Arkansas Cavalry became panic stricken, sprang to their saddles and fled, nearly stampeding our horses. Captain Steen gave orders to fire the place; blazing logs were thrown into the chapel and all the houses, bacon and pork thrown on, the large barley stack fired, and soon the whole place blazed up grandly . . . . the hill back of the place fairly glittered with the sheen of the Mexican lance points.[5]

Santa Anna, with the vanguard of the Mexican infantry, arrived in Agua Nueva on the morning of February 22, 1847, to find only smouldering ruins. From this scene of disorder, the general concluded that his march had surprised the American garrison at Agua Nueva and that the entire American army was retreating in a state of panic.[6] Barely allowing his men the time needed to refill their canteens, the elated Santa Anna pushed his weary troops forward toward Saltillo.

The personnel of Taylor's army, present on February 22, 1847, were as follows:

Battle of Buena Vista

UNIT	NUMBER	COMMANDER/KEY SUBORDINATES[7]
1st Illinois Infantry	580	John J. Hardin
2nd Illinois Infantry	573	William H. Bissell
2nd Kentucky Infantry	571	William R. McKee Henry Clay, Jr.
2d Indiana		William A. Bowles
3d Indiana		James H. Lane
Indiana Aggregate	1,253	
1st Mississippi Infantry	368	Jefferson Davis
1st Arkansas Cavalry	479	Archibald Yell
1st Kentucky Cavalry	305	Humphrey Marshall
1st U. S. Dragoons	133	Enoch Steen
2nd U. S. Dragoons	76	Charles May
Texas Ranger Company	61	P. Edward Conner
McCulloch's Spy Company	27	Ben McCulloch
Battery, 4th U. S. Art.	117	John M. Washington
Battery, 3rd U. S. Art.	150	Braxton Bragg
Battery, 3rd U. S. Art.	150	Thomas W. Sherman
General Staff	41	Zachary Taylor John Wool
TOTAL	4,884	

Of this number, 364 were reported on sick leave, leaving 4,520 effective troops.

The morning of February 22, 1847, dawned brightly over the sierras of northern Mexico. A crisp breeze ruffled and snapped the battle flags of the American army poised for action south of Saltillo. A general feeling of anticipation was felt throughout the army. Bands played "Hail Columbia," and the password of the day was "Honor of Washington," since it was the birthday of our first President.[8] While Taylor prepared the defenses of Saltillo, Wool had the troops in Angostura Pass busily constructing a few simple defensive structures; time did not allow for more elaborate preparations.

Santa Anna arrived at Angostura Pass in midmorning accompanied only by his staff and an escort of cavalry. He was unpleasantly surprised by the natural strength of the American positions and quickly set his staff to work to reconnoiter. In the meantime, to occupy the Americans until his infantry arrived, Santa Anna dispatched a note to Taylor demanding his immediate surrender. Taylor curtly refused. While these notes were being exchanged, Santa Anna's engineering officers were scouting the pass and returned with sobering news.

American forces had been positioned by General Wool in the following order: The road to Saltillo was blocked at its narrowest point by three guns of Washington's battery (Capt. John Washington was a distant relative of America's first president), supported by the 1st Illinois and the 3d Indiana, posted on the bluffs to the east of the road. The west side of the road, as we have seen, was so deeply carved up by steep arroyos as to be impassable. These units constituted the American right wing.

The center of the American defenses was placed on Middle Plateau and was manned (west to east) by the 2d Kentucky, 2d Illinois, and the 2d Indiana; the latter was placed farthest south in the most advanced position.

The left wing of American defenses, placed on the high plateau at the foot of the mountains, consisted of the Arkansas and Kentucky cavalry and the U. S. Dragoons. This site was about the only location on the battlefield having level enough terrain for the extensive use of mounted troops.[9]

The Mississippi Regiment was placed on the North Plateau behind the American defenders occupying the Middle Plateau. Two companies of the Rifles were left behind as a guard for the headquarters camp near Saltillo and the supply wagons. The Mississippians could muster only 368 effective soldiers for the upcoming battle, so for men in the battle line, fire power would be critical. Colonel Davis issued rifles to his junior officers and flag bearers to compensate for the shortage in manpower. The regimental flag was carried into battle, but inside the pack of the flag bearer, not on a staff.

Henry R. Kenna, of Captain Sharp's company, recorded the arrival of the 1st Mississippi at its assigned post on the North Plateau:

> Our regiment arrived on the ground about 2 o'clock, and took our position on the side of a hill, out of sight of the Mexicans. We were not long here when Gen. Wool and staff rode up and saluted Col. Davis. He said he was glad to see our regiment there, &c. We

> presented arms, and he rode bare-headed along the line to our left and returned again to the centre. We were brought to a "shoulder and order arms," successively. Col. Davis then addressed us in the following words: "Fellow-soldiers, Gen. Wool would remind you that this is the birth day of Washington, and he expects you to perform deeds worthy of the occasion. The General now wants to hear three Mississippi cheers." After we had given three huzzas, a fine looking old gentleman belonging to the General's staff, resembling Major Dunn rode out and said, "Three cheers for Mississippi," which the staff gave in pretty good style.[10]

Artillery support for the infantry was as follows: three guns from Washington's battery were placed with the 2d Indiana, two guns from Bragg's battery with the 2d Illinois, and three guns from Sherman's battery with the 2d Kentucky.

Without waiting for his full complement of men, Santa Anna sent light infantry under Gen. Pedro Ampudia to test the far left wing of the American defenses. Colonel Marshall's Kentucky cavalrymen responded to the advancing Mexican troops by dismounting and climbing the mountainside in an attempt to establish an advantageous position. The Mexicans executed similar tactics, scrambling up the rocky slopes. The two parties were separated by a deep ravine that extended far up the flank of the mountain. The signal for the Mexicans to commence firing was given at 3:27 P.M., according to Mississippi rifleman, James C. Browning, with the discharge of a cannon by a Mexican gunner.[11] Marshall's and Ampudia's men exchanged fire across the ravine as each side climbed farther up the mountain, seeking a better vantage point. Men from both armies watched this lone struggle develop throughout the afternoon. Santa Anna could not launch a full-scale attack, until the major part of his infantry, still on the road from Agua Nueva, arrived at La Angostura.

Taylor sensed that a major battle would not develop that day in Angostura Pass, so he returned to his headquarters south of Saltillo to improve the defenses of the city. He was accompanied by May's Dragoons and the Mississippi Regiment. The rear of Taylor's army, his supplies and wagons, and the city of Saltillo, now appeared to be in the greatest immediate peril. Early in the afternoon, Miñon's cavalry brigade had driven in the pickets on the road leading to Saltillo from the east.[12] His cavalry, reinforced with about 500 rancheros from the surrounding countryside, were now visible to the residents of Saltillo. Taylor's line of retreat to Monterrey was now cut off.

The defenses of Saltillo were far from adequate. A fort on the hill overlooking Saltillo was manned with two 24-pound howitzers under the command of Lieutenant Webster, and nearby were stationed two companies of the Mississippi Regiment. In Saltillo a cannon was mounted to cover the four streets leading from the plaza, and the streets were blocked by overturned wagons. The musket barrels of American defenders protruded from the tops of the main buildings.

In clear view of Saltillo, Miñon's forces were seen maneuvering in the plain outside the city, and the sound of gunfire was heard from the direction of Angostura Pass. Capt. Albert Pike, stationed in Saltillo on that day, reported, "The heavy volleys of the Mexicans, fired with huge charges of powder, were distinctly heard by us, and mistaken for cannon."[13] After dark the firing ceased, and the city, spared attack, posted pickets and sentries for a watchful night.

Back at Angostura Pass, American soldiers dined on hardtack and raw bacon, while the Mexicans for the most part fasted. Thousands of small campfires twinkled in the night from hillsides south of the American positions. Mexican lancers on picket duty were to be faintly heard singing in fine voice the popular ballads "Love Not" and "Adios" as they performed their lonely duties.[14] On the evening breeze floating from the south were faintly heard the sound of vivas, as the Mexican soldiers responded to an impassioned harangue delivered to the troops by General Santa Anna.

In his memoirs, James Carleton, a member of Taylor's army, paraphrased the general's heartfelt eloquence:

> The United States of the North . . . had provoked this war under the cover of other objects to be gained, but really for their own aggrandizement, and the acquisition of territory clearly the property of the United States of the South [Mexico]. . . . He called upon them to look upon their country. What met their sight? Its possessions wrested away; its dignity insulted; its fair fields ravaged; its citizens slaughtered; its hearths and homes made deso-

late. . . . He reminded them that they had crossed deserts, had suffered hunger, and thirst, and fatigue, without a murmur. Long and weary had been their march. . . . This address was received with loud cries of "Viva Santana!" "Viva la Republica!" "Libertad o Muerte!"—distinctly heard in our lines.[15]

Early morning on February 23, 1847, temperatures were quite chilly, and teeth chattered uncontrollably in the ranks of the soldiers of both sides. Santa Anna ordered the buglers to sound reveille, one corps at a time, hoping to impress the Americans with the vast size of his army. As the sun cleared the eastern sierras, the American army was greeted with a sight that deeply impressed all observers. In the words of Samuel Chamberlain:

> I doubt if the "Sun of Austerlitz" shown on a more brilliant spectacle than the Mexican army displayed before us—twenty thousand men clad in new uniforms, belts as white as snow, brasses and arms burnished until they glittered like gold and silver. Their Cavalry was magnificent—some six thousand cavaliers richly caparisoned in uniforms of blue faced with red, with waving plumes and glittering weapons, advanced towards us as if they would ride down our little band and finish the battle at one blow. They formed in one long line with their massed bands in front, and then a procession of ecclesiastical dignitaries with all the gorgeous paraphernalia of the Catholic Church advanced along the lines, preceded by the bands playing a solemn anthem. . . . The infantry knelt down, the Cavalry lowered their lances and uncovered, and their colors drooped as the benedictions were bestowed. This ceremony offered a striking contrast to conditions in our lines; there was not a Chaplain in our army![16]

At headquarters, the 1st Mississippi was ordered to accompany General Taylor back to Angostura Pass in anticipation of a battle, leaving two of its companies to man the fort south of Saltillo. No company wished to be left out of the action. Capt. William P. Rogers had avoided that duty on February 22: "Col. Davis as is his wont ordered me and Colonel [Captain] Cooper to remain with our companies at camp. I refused to do so and was then permitted to lead my company to the field." However, on this morning Captain Rogers was not able to have his way:

> He [Colonel Davis] came to me early and told me that I was the only captain in the Regiment who had not been on detached service and that he hoped inasmuch as we were surrounded by Mexicans that I would not again refuse to take a separate command and defend the post of headquarters . . . the post he assigned me he said was a post of honor and that he desired that I might have the glory of leading an independent command to action. The enemy was then approaching and I thought as did all others that we would be charged in two hours. I could not again refuse and accordingly took command of the foot with two comps. of Mississippi and one detachment of artillery.[17]

Before Taylor and his Mississippi escort left headquarters, a roar of cannon and discharging musketry was heard to the south, and the "ball had opened."

Santa Anna realized that his troops would not be able to force the Americans from their strong positions with a frontal assault; he would have to turn their left flank. An excellent route existed for such a flanking movement, level enough for both infantry and cavalry—along the plateau at the foot of the mountains. The infantry divisions of Manuel Lombardini and Francisco Pacheco were chosen to lead the attack and were massed in the ravine south of Middle Plateau with orders to climb the north side of the ravine and throw themselves without warning on the American defenders.

This ravine was deep, and the movements of the massed Mexican divisions could not be seen by American observers on Middle Plateau. The point of the Mexican attack was aimed at the most forward position along the American line, that of the 2d Indiana. To support this infantry attack, the Mexicans had positioned a battery of artillery close to the base of the eastern mountains.

In an attempt to divert attention from his primary objective, Santa Anna ordered an attack on Washington's artillery position at Angostura Pass.[18] Gen. Santiago Blanco's Division, composed of the Regiment of Engineers, the 12th regiment, the Fijo de Mexico, the Battalion of Puebla, and the famous Guarda Costa de Tampico was to advance northward along the road and overrun American artillery emplacements.

Because of the deep gulleys on one side of the road and the steep bluffs on the other, Blanco's troops were able to advance only along the narrow roadway. American artillery was zeroed in for the road, and Blanco's troops were literally torn to shreds by the exploding shells and canister. Every discharge of Washington's guns wreaked havoc among the closely packed ranks of attacking Mexican infantry, and the column quickly fled the roadway for shelter in the gulleys. The diversion, however, had achieved its purpose. While all American eyes were focused on Blanco's attack, the forces of Pacheco and Lombardini had been formed for attack on the Middle Plateau without opposition.

On the Middle Plateau, the 2d Indiana suddenly found itself confronted by three regiments of Mexican infantry: the veteran Corps of Guanajuato and a body of Mexican cavalry estimated to total at least 4,000 men. B. F. Scribner, a young private in the 2d Indiana, recorded the painful scene:

> It was an awful moment to face the thousands of veterans in solid column, with their gaudy uniforms and showy banners . . . before our line was formed they had fired two rounds. . . . About this time the battery on our left opened upon us a deadly fire of grape, which raked our flank with terrible effect; still we stood front to front, and poured our fire on the infantry. . . . Apollos Stevens was the first of our Grays to fall. He received a grape shot in the head, and fell back almost into my arms. O, how shall I describe the horror of my feelings? . . . We had fired about twenty-one rounds when I hear someone say, "They are all retreating!" and turning, I saw the [Indiana] right wing had gone, and the left starting . . . the retreat was general, and the enemy fast advancing upon us, led on by a large force of lancers.[19]

Pacheco's veteran infantry, with the help of the Mexican artillery of Capt. Ignacio Ballastra had routed the 2d Indiana.[20] The Indianians could not be re-formed and raced from the Middle Plateau in a panic.[21] Lieut. John Paul Jones O'Brien, who commanded the three-gun artillery battery supporting the Indiana troops, was left without protection from the oncoming Mexican infantry. Loading his guns with double canister, he inflicted a heavy price on the advancing Mexicans, but could not sustain his battery without infantry support in this forward position. O'Brien retreated with two of the guns, but was forced to leave the third behind for the Mexicans. The horses and men serving this piece had been killed.

To the left of the 2d Indiana's vacated position, Pacheco's advancing forces flanked the 2d Illinois. The Illinoians fired a few volleys at the Mexican infantry and then began to execute a disorganized retreat northward along the Middle Plateau. These green troops had been shaken by the stampede of the Indiana regiment and were on the verge of panic as their officers, Col. William Bissell and Lieut. Col. Don Morrison, struggled to rally them. Two senior officers appeared, Capt. George Lincoln, General Wool's adjutant general, and Maj. Roger Dix, the army paymaster. Dix seized the national colors from the Illinois regimental colorbearer, and waved the flag aloft from his huge bay horse, a most prominent target for Mexican gunners.[22] The Illinois regiment had abandoned its assigned post, exposing the artillery battery of Lieut. George H. Thomas to capture by Pacheco's infantry. Lincoln exhorted the Illinoisans, "Come on, my brave Illinoisans, and save this battery."[23] A moment later, he was struck by musket balls in the waist and head, and slumped to the ground dead. But the 2d Illinois rallied and remained on the battlefield throughout the day.

With the defeat of Blanco on the Saltillo road and the crisis that was now developing on the Middle Plateau, American troops and artillery were frantically pulled from the inactive right wing to reinforce the middle. Four companies of Hardin's 1st Illinois were sent, and the artillery of Bragg and Sherman ringed the plateau to send a hail of metal into the advancing Mexicans. Santa Anna, escorting the infantry of Pacheco, was himself injured during this attack. His horse was struck on the head by American grapeshot, and the general suffered a severe fall, which injured the stump of his amputated leg (lost in a battle with French forces in 1838). His Excellency retired from the field with a painful but not dangerous wound, and Pacheco's infantry was driven back into the ravine by the concentrated artillery fire. Next it was the turn of Lombardini, to the right of Pacheco. His infantry division joined up with the light infantry division of Ampudia and some units of Mexican lancers, and advanced upon four companies of the Arkansas Mounted Regiment. These cavalrymen turned in panic and fled their posts. Capt. Albert Pike saw this stampede and reported:

> The battery on our left [Ballastra] so plagued the Arkansas cavalry, that Col. [Archibald] Yell ordered it to retreat a little way, in

> order to avoid the cannon range, intending then to await a charge of the lancers supporting the battery. But the men, untaught to maneuver, and totally undisciplined, understood the word *retreat,* to be an order to make, each man, the best of his way to the rear; and turned and ran off in great confusion. Col. Yell . . . Lieut. Col. [Gaston] Mears, McVicar, . . . and others succeeded in rallying a portion of them, and the approaching lancers retired on their showing a firm front.[24]

General Lombardini was wounded and had left the battlefield; his infantry division was placed under the command of Gen. Francisco Perez.[25]

The Mexican divisions of Perez and Pacheco had succeeded in driving a wedge in the American defensive line. The Kentucky cavalry of Col. Humphrey Marshall, posted near the eastern mountain range, was now isolated from the main American force. Capt. Pike reported the reaction of the Kentucky volunteers:

> The skirmishers fled from the mountains in utter confusion, and a great many of them ran to Saltillo, including one Captain of the Arkansas regiment. It is said that the order was understood to be *retreat to Saltillo.* I think that is probable. The others fled to the rancho [Buena Vista] and were no more seen in the field.[26]

Santa Anna had accomplished his first objective: to turn the American left flank. The Mexican infantry was now moving westward on the North Plateau. Their objective was to reach the Saltillo road north of the position held by Washington's artillery. The Angostura road battery could then be easily overwhelmed from the rear and the road to Saltillo opened for the advance of the Mexican army.

It was now 9:00 A.M., and General Taylor, accompanied by the Mississippi Regiment and May's Dragoons, reached the ridge that overlooked the battlefield. A scene of pandemonium was unfolding below and around them. Indiana troops raced past the Mississippians to seek refuge in Saltillo. "Indiana troops filled the ravine [North Ravine], . . . and were in every other direction flying from the field, throwing away their arms, and some even crying like children for terror." No form of pleading was able to stop the panic-stricken troops. "Rally on the Mississippians" was the unanswered cry.[27] Down in the ravines and along the North Plateau Mexican lancers were seen riding down the fleeing refugees. Some of the retreating American troops halted and turned to defend themselves; some fell to their knees and begged for mercy, but none were spared. Off in the distance to the east, a cloud of dust marked the hasty retreat of several companies of the Arkansas Mounted Cavalry, followed closely by Mexican lancers. To the southeast of the Mississippi Regiment, a body of Mexican soldiers estimated at between 4,000 and 5,000 men was advancing toward the ridge.

This was to be a watershed moment in American history. The actions of Jefferson Davis and the Mississippi Rifles in the next few minutes were to decide the outcome of this battle, who was to be the next President of the United States, and the ownership of vast territories in the southwestern United States.

Davis later wrote, "But in view of my own responsibility, it may be permitted me to say in relation to our first attack on the enemy, that I considered the necessity absolute and immediate. No one could have failed to perceive the hazard."[28] General Wool, who was with the Mississippians, had been attempting to rally the retreating Indianians in a line of defense, but to no avail. Davis approached Wool and asked him if he would send forces to sustain the Mississippians in an attack upon the rapidly advancing Mexicans. Wool promised support and went in person to summon reinforcements. Davis then ordered his regiment to advance, alone and unsupported, against the oncoming Mexican infantry.

Fewer than 370 Mississippians were left, but they were prepared to advance alone on 4,000 Mexican troops. The men of the Mississippi Regiment had placed the utmost confidence in Jefferson Davis. "The men cheerfully, ardently entered into the conflict . . . the Regiment never faltered, nor moved except as ordered."[29]

The Mississippians were rapidly formed into order of battle, and the line advanced toward the Mexicans in double-quick time. Now within rifle range, Davis ordered the regiment to "fire advancing." The red-shirted Mississippians scrambled across a steep gully, estimated to be 10 feet deep, dodging a hot fire poured on them by the Mexicans, and dragged themselves out. The regiment was reformed on the other side of the gully and continued its advance in good order—at a high price. The majority of the casualties suffered by the Mississippians at Buena Vista were to occur during this attack. But now Mexican soldiers were seen falling from their ranks, victims of the steady firing of red-shirted marksmen. The Mexican advance along the North Plateau was halted, and their forward elements were driven back on the reserves. The 1st Mississippi had saved the American army from being encircled.

Meanwhile, a party of Mexican cavalry had ridden onto the North Plateau behind the Mississippians, and the regiment now began to receive fire from the rear as well as the front. Still fighting alone on the North Plateau, the regiment was ordered by Davis to about-face and confront the Mexican cavalry. The Mexicans quickly mounted their horses and escaped back into the ravine. Davis, riding ahead of his regiment, spotted them cautiously attempting to descend the steep banks and summoned his men. "The nearest of our men ran quickly to my call, attacked this body, and dispersed it with some loss. I think their commander was among the killed."

General Wool had made good on his promise to bring reinforcements, and the Mississippians were now joined by the 3d Indiana, commanded by Col. James H. Lane, and one piece of artillery under the command of Lieut. Charles Kilburn, which opened fire as soon as it was unlimbered. The Mexican advance slowed to a standstill. Davis and the Mississippians had bought the time needed to summon reinforcements.

From the Middle Plateau, the batteries of Sherman and Bragg were turned to face the North Plateau, and their shells also exploded among Mexican forces. The combined force of Mississippi and Indiana regiments then advanced to drive the retreating Mexicans from the plateau. Mexican soldiers were seen scrambling desperately to escape the deadly effects of the artillery, and both infantry and cavalry retreated into a small canyon in the eastern mountains and paused there to await further orders.

In the meantime, the American left flank—the Kentucky Cavalry and a portion of the Arkansas, positioned close to the foot of the eastern mountains—came under attack from a unit of Mexican lancers. Without orders, Colonels Marshall and Yell withdrew their horsemen and retreated northward into the open plain. They had intended to make a stand just east of the Hacienda Buena Vista, but by leaving their assigned positions, the volunteers had opened a gap in the American defenses. The army wagon train parked near the hacienda was exposed to attack from the oncoming lancers. General Wool, fearing that the volunteer cavalry could not contain the Mexicans, dispatched May's Dragoons to defend the wagon train. Samuel Chamberlain, a trooper in May's command, reported:

> We were half a mile from the waggons, the enemy much nearer, and advancing at a gallop, straight for the volunteers who sat quietly on their horses. The Colonels, Yell, and "Falstaff" Marshall, were having a lively little dispute as to which one was the senior in rank, and this when fifteen hundred of the fiercest horsemen in the world were coming down on them at full speed![30]

The resulting clash of arms was reported by Capt. Albert Pike:

> They waited until they [Mexicans] came within forty yards, when each man raised his carbine and fired—and as some say, our men charged—as other say, the Mexicans dashed among them. The fire did but little harm. The utmost confusion ensued . . . Col. Yell's command was routed. He himself, facing the foe and trying to rally his men, was killed with many wounds—so disfigured that hardly one could recognize him.[31]

After the initial shock of contact, most of the Arkansans and Kentuckians fled the field, racing to the cover afforded by the walls of the hacienda. Colonel Yell was killed, while trying to rally his troops, by a lance thrust through his mouth. The body of Capt. Andrew R. Porter of the Arkansas Cavalry was found beside him. The Arkansas color-bearer was killed in the charge, and the regimental flag was captured by the Mexicans. Lancers pursued the fleeing Americans to the walls of Hacienda Buena Vista. But at this location a heavy fire from the occupants inside and on the roofs of the buildings succeeded in driving them off. This contingent of defenders at the hacienda was made up of teamsters from the wagon train and soldiers who had abandoned their posts on the battlefield during one or another of the various panics. But at the hacienda they had rallied.

The Mexican lancers, having retreated, were regrouping when they were struck from the flank by May's Dragoons. The Mexican horsemen were driven by the Dragoons, and retreated from the plain east of the hacienda into the mountains east of Saltillo. Mexican cavalry, riding the smaller mustangs, were often no match for the Dragoons mounted on big American Thoroughbreds. These big horses were held in awe by the Mexicans. Trooper Chamberlain reported that Soldan, his American Thoroughbred mount, would literally "ride over" Mexican horsemen during a charge, and while there was often no blood on his sabre, he would find "plenty on his spurs."[32]

The fighting spirit of many of the Arkansas and Kentucky troops had been broken, and as Albert Pike reported:

> By degrees some rallied and joined us—but the mass both of Arkansas and Kentucky troops dispersed, and many fled to Saltillo, in such numbers that Lieut. Donaldson of Capt. Webster's artillery, told me, he thought the whole army was in full retreat. He requested the officer commanding the Mississippi companies near town, to place his men across the road, and stop the fugitives. He did so, and stopped about fifty; but the most broke through and entered the town.
>
> The runaways carried fearful reports to Saltillo. Several times that the left wing was defeated and was retreating—once that the whole army was in full retreat—alarming those left to defend the town. Some seemed mad with terror, and went crying and blaspheming around the streets, creating most extraordinary confusion, nor could [they] be formed, even when in safety.[33]

Not everyone in Saltillo was frightened by the rumors. Wash (George Washington) Trahern relayed an incident with a fugitive soldier that occurred in Saltillo at the height of the panic. Sarah Bourginnis, known to Taylor's soldiers as the Great Western, had followed the army all the way from Corpus Christi to Saltillo. She functioned as nurse, laundress, cook, and barkeep, and at that time ran a restaurant in Saltillo. As her nickname suggested, she was of ample dimensions, measuring 6 feet 2 inches in height; Trahern swore that she could "whip most anybody in a rough and tumble fight." On February 23, at the height of the battle, an Indiana deserter came dashing into her restaurant out of breath and reported to all within hearing distance:

> General Taylor is whipped and the army was cut to pieces, and the Mexicans under full headway for Saltillo. She just drew off and hit him between the eyes and knocked him sprawling; says, "You damned son of a bitch, there ain't Mexicans enough in Mexico to whip old Taylor." She says, "You just spread that report and I'll beat you to death."[34]

By now Santa Anna had lost most of his earlier gains. In an effort to turn the tide of battle again, he sent Gen. Anastasio Torrejón's brigade of cavalry to link up with the forces of Ampudia, forming a cavalry force of about 2,000 men, and to move onto the North Plateau; they were ordered to force a passage through American defenses onto the Saltillo road. Ahead of them the lancers could see the *Camisas coloradas* with their Whitney rifles. What they could not see was the 3d Indiana, which had taken refuge in the ravine from Mexican artillery.[35]

Davis hastily requested an artillery piece from Capt. Thomas Sherman and summoned the 3d Indiana Regiment from the ravine to renew the fight.

The classic defense for infantry against cavalry attack had always been the hollow square, pronged with bayonets, but there was no time to organize such a formation with unschooled volunteer troops in the face of an advancing enemy. Besides, Whitney rifles were not equipped with bayonets. Davis quickly assembled the combined force of Mississippians and Indianians into a novel defensive formation that would later attract worldwide attention from students of military science. He formed the troops into a V, with the Indiana troops lining the south edge of the ravine, and the Mississippi regimen forming the side that extended from the edge of the ravine into the North Plateau. The two sides met at an angle of about 120 degrees, with the open end pointed toward the Mexican cavalry. Davis reasoned that the converging lines would produce a zone of increasing firepower. Cavalry charging into the mouth of the V would be destroyed.

Davis moved to the left end of the Mississippi line and there placed an artillery piece that had been hastily delivered by Sherman. The fate of the battle was again in the hands of Davis and his Mississippians.

> The enemy was now seen to be a body of richly caparisoned lancer, came forward rapidly and in beautiful order—the files and ranks so closed, as to look like a solid mass of men and horses. Perfect silence, and the greatest steadiness prevailed in both lines of our troops, as they stood at shouldered arms waiting an attack. Confident of success, and anxious to obtain the full advantage of a cross fire at a short distance, I repeatedly called to the men not to shoot.
>
> As the enemy approached, his speed regularly diminished, until when within 80 or 100 yards, he had drawn up to a walk, and seemed about to halt. A few files fired without orders, and both lines then instantly poured in a volley so destructive, that the mass yielded to the blow, and the survivors fled. Captain Sherman having come up with a field piece from his battery, followed their retreat with a very effective fire, until they had fled beyond the range of his gun.[36]

The artillery of Sherman and Bragg, located on the Middle Plateau, were both turned upon the retreating Mexican troops to produce a perfect rain of shot and shell. The Mexicans took refuge in a small recess in the eastern mountains, a topographical feature known in the American West as a box canyon. Its steep walls and mouth faced onto the North Plateau, in direct line of fire for artillery. The small canyon was choked with a huddled mass of horses, riders, and infantry, and artillery projectiles were bound to strike some target. A lull in fighting had occurred on the Middle Plateau and Bragg's battery was ordered to move from there to the North Plateau to join the artillery already there in "unlimbering" on the Mexicans trapped in the canyon. The battery of O'Brien remained to guard the Middle Plateau which was then quiet.

The canyon and its environs became a slaughter pen. At about 1 P.M., a party of Mexican officers ran up a white flag, and American artillery ceased firing.

The Mexican officers, escorted into General Taylor's presence, asked, "In the name of Santa Anna, what did the American general want?" The best sense Taylor could make of this strange message was that Santa Anna wanted a parley. He dispatched General Wool under a white flag to the Mexican camp—only to find that the Mexican gunners refused to honor the white flag and cease fire.

When Wool returned, it was discovered that the Mexicans in the box canyon had taken advantage of the situation to escape. The white flag had been a mere ruse to free the trapped Mexican soldiers.

A lull in the fighting occurred in the early afternoon, and a review of the field indicated that Santa Anna's forces were now in about the same position as when the battle had commenced that morning. Early Mexican successes had been reversed by hard fighting and the accurate and incessant bombardment of American field artillery. Days were short in February in the high sierras of Mexico; the first shadows were beginning to be seen making their way across Angostura Pass. If Mexican forces intended to win the day, then they were impelled to start another operation immediately. Santa Anna organized his exhausted infantry into one more attack force, under the command of Gen. Francisco Perez.[37] Among the units in this force were the 11th Regiment and the Battalion of León. This force was to make a last attempt to drive the Americans off the Middle Plateau.

General Taylor, a man never known to relish the defense in a battle, interpreted the afternoon lull in fighting as a sign of weakness and indecision on the part of the Mexican forces. He planned to seize the initiative and launch a probe against the Mexicans on the South Plateau. The last, and in many ways the most desperate, struggle of the day was about to begin.

General Perez, repeating a tactic used earlier in the day, advanced his troops eastward in the South Ravine, out of sight of the Americans and safe from their deadly artillery. General Taylor, at the same time, sent six companies of the 2d Illinois, led by Col. John J. Hardin, to attack the center of the Mexican line on the South Plateau. The two attacking forces quickly met. The left wing of the advancing Mexicans stumbled into Hardin's Illinois battalion, then in the process of crossing the South Ravine. Gen. Perez ordered his force to pivot on its left flank and attack. Greatly outnumbered and taken in flank, the Illinoisans faced rapid annihilation, but Cols. William H. Bissell and William R. McKee, seeing the perilous situation, advanced their forces to Hardin's aid. Lieutenant O'Brien turned his two remaining 6-pounders on the Mexicans in the South Ravine with good effect, but the advancing Mexican infantry could not be stopped. They struck Hardin, Bissell, and McKee in flank, and drove them. The Mexican force was too large to be contained by the disorganized and outnumbered American forces, who were told "Retreat or you are lost."

The only route open to the trapped Americans was westward in the South Ravine, which opened upon the Saltillo road in view of Washington's battery. Americans scrambled down the rocky gulch, closely followed by Mexican soldiers with bayonets, while from above Mexicans lined the rim of the South Ravine and fired down into the retreating mass. When a line of Mexican lancers sealed off the mouth of the South Ravine, the fleeing Americans were trapped. Hardin was killed by a lancer while gamely fighting for his life; McKee died at the head of his troops, and Henry Clay Jr., son of the famous American senator, suffered a broken thigh bone from a Mexican musket ball. Clay's comrades in arms attempted to carry him out to safety, but young Clay would not permit the progress of their retreat to be slowed. He handed his expended pistol to his fellows, asking that it be returned to his father, and drew his saber, prepared to fight to the death. His body was later found in the South Ravine stripped of clothing and horribly mutilated.[38]

From his position on the Saltillo road at Angostura Pass, Washington saw the lancers formed at the head of the South Ravine to block the passage of retreating Americans. He opened fire, pouring spherical case shot on the Mexican horsemen. This barrage of flying metal drove the lancers for cover and opened the mouth of the South Ravine. American survivors burst onto the Saltillo road and raced for the protection of Washington's battery. The artillery battery lobbed shells over their heads, scattering death among the oncoming lancers. Pursuit of the retreating Americans was effectively halted.

The Middle Plateau was now almost empty of American infantry. The right wing of Perez's infantry had scrambled up the South Ravine and organized in a column to advance westward along the Middle Plateau to the Saltillo road. Only two guns of O'Brien, posted on the Middle Plateau, remained to dispute the Mexican advance. They were without infantry support, but he and his men courageously remained at their posts, firing double loads of canister into the advancing Mexican infantry, and succeeded in slow-ing them long enough for American reinforcements to reach him. O'Brien's positions were overrun, and he lost two artillery pieces to the Mexicans.

Bragg and his guns, now on the North Plateau, moved rapidly to counter this new menace. His drivers lashed their tired horses to a gallop on the torturous and winding trek to the Middle Plateau. Sherman's men limbered up, and their artillery followed Bragg in a cloud of dust. The 3d Indiana was summoned on the double, and Davis reported that one of Zachary Taylor's aides, "called from the other side of the ravine . . . that General Taylor wanted support."[39] The Mississippians, at their post on the North Plateau, recognized the gravity of the situation and took the direct route through the North Ravine to the Middle Plateau, reaching it just in the nick of time. Capt. Reuben Downing of Company G reported:

> After resting from the fatigues of the day, we were ordered to the front, near the center of our line to assist our friends who were gallantly struggling against terrible odds. When advancing to their relief we discovered a large body of Mexicans, charging in fine style down the hill on the artillery. We opened fire upon them at the distance of two hundred yards, which arrested their progress, We gave many hearty cheers & charged them—the enemy broke & fled over the point of the hill, we pursuing—we perceived a Mexican Battery to our left next the mountains which commanded this hill, I ordered my company & those of the Riflemen, who followed, to pass with me rapidly over the point of the hill, to the next ravine where I supposed the enemy were . . . & were ordered to retire, which was done, not however until we had succeeded in killing & despersing this force of the enemy.[40]

The artillery position reported by Captain Downing was Bragg's battery, now on the Middle Plateau without infantry support and about to be overrun by Mexican infantry. Davis reported:

> We saw the infantry [Mexican] advancing in three lines. . . . We pressed on, climbing the rocky slope of the plain on which this combat occurred, reaching it's brow so as to take the enemy in flank and reverse, when he was about one hundred yards from the battery. Our first fire—raking each of his lines, and opened close upon his flank—was emminently destructive. His right gave way, and he fled in confusion.[41]

The combined forces of American infantry and the guns of Bragg, Sherman, and Thomas finally succeeded in driving the Mexicans from the Middle Plateau.

The day's fighting had ended on this last note as the sun descended behind the western sierras, and a cold chill in the air began to be felt. Sporadic firing was still heard to reverberate from the mountains, but most of the combatants were either spent from their exertions or dead. Exhausted American troops dropped in their tracks. But Taylor still held Angostura Pass—just barely.

EIGHT

A Review of the Battle of Buena Vista

In a battle so fierce and protracted as this, where there were so many exhibitions of coolness and bravery, it is a difficult and delicate task to particularize. But justice compels me to mention Colonel Davis and his regiment of Mississippians, who so nobly and so bravely came to the rescue at the proper time to save the fortunes of the day.

—*Brig. Gen. Joseph Lane,*
Commander, Indiana Volunteers

. . . For the details of the military operations &c on this line I refer you to Genl Taylor's despatches. They are generously full so far as good conduct went, but rather silent on the subject of volunteers running &c &c. A few facts on this subject may interest you. The great Baltimore Battalion which boasted so much of taking Monterey fled in a body very early in the action and never got into the fight. From five companies but nine men remained on the field at night. With the exception of the Miss. regt. under Col. Davis, a graduate [West Point] you may say *ditto* of almost all who were here.

Capt. Braxton Bragg, a private letter
to William T. Sherman, March 1, 1848.

General Taylor returned to his headquarters outside Saltillo on the evening of February 23, 1847, accompanied by the exhausted Mississippi Regiment. They had lost thirty-nine slain and fifty-six wounded—proportionately higher casualties than any other regiment in Taylor's army. Still, they were ordered on to Saltillo to garrison the city, as Miñon's cavalry continued to threaten an attack.

Miñon had made a feeble attempt on the city in the afternoon, and Captain Rogers, in command of the two companies of the Mississippi Regiment left behind to guard the city, reported:

> Gen. Menyon [Miñon] charged up upon my command to in about 400 yds but I operated on him a rapid and heavy fire of round shot and bombs, which together with a squad of cavalry which had run from the foe and which had rallied at the rifle noise soon drove him off. Of these there were about 2000 or 2500 and we killed about 50 or 60.[1]

Rogers was posted in a redoubt near the southern approach to the city, charged with defending Taylor's headquarters and the wagon park, which consisted of more than 200 vehicles. The redoubt was armed with two 24-pound howitzers, and to the right of the redoubt a 6-pounder, one of Bragg's field pieces, under the command of Lieut. William Shover. Shover had pursued Miñon's fleeing cavalry with his field piece, accompanied by "a promiscuous crowd of mounted and foot volunteers, teamsters, and citizens."[2] The Mexicans were driven more than three miles from Saltillo before pursuit was abandoned.

The scene at Hacienda Buena Vista on the evening of February 23 was one of extreme confusion. American deserters from the battlefield crowded around the buildings, interfering with the work that needed to be done. Lieut. Samuel French, who had been shot in the thigh by a Mexican musket ball during the battle, had been moved to the hacienda for treatment. He reported the scene there:

> There must have been seven or eight hundred able bodied men at the buildings who had left the ranks. When the firing ended Gen. Taylor came. . . . I said to the General I hoped he would gain a complete victory on the morrow, and his reply was: "Yes, yes, if too many of my men do not give me the slip to-night." I think he made this reply because he was mortified and pained to find so many men at the hacienda who had deserted the field, many of

> them by carrying off the wounded and not returning to their companies.[3]

As the battle had raged during the day, Mexican lancers had been observed murdering any American wounded found lying on the battlefield. For this reason, commanders of the American units had allowed their soldiers to carry wounded comrades from the field to a safe haven. Thus shirkers could easily abandon their posts on the battlefield simply by not returning. By afternoon, soldiers were desperately needed to man the depleted American lines. Trooper Samuel Chamberlain observed that:

> Every wounded man found himself surrounded by a host of new friends, who felt the greatest solicitude for his safety. I saw one volunteer, shot through the arm, with no less than eight of these benevolent chaps assisting him off the field. One of them was even carrying his hat! General Wool sent us to drive these good Samaritans back to their duty, which we done with no gentle hand.[4]

General Taylor's quip about his men giving him the slip probably masked a genuine worry: could the American army, whose ranks were filled by volunteer soldiers, withstand another pounding like today's? The army's casualties had been heavy, but desertion had caused a greater loss in soldiers. It was estimated that 1,500 to 1,800 Americans had deserted their posts during the day's fighting.[5] From the rim overlooking Angostura Pass, one could see the twinkling lights of Mexican campfires dotting the south end of the valley. A large force of the enemy remained to take up the battle tomorrow. Throughout the cold and rainy evening, Taylor's staff and others advised him to retreat, but he stubbornly refused to abandon Angostura Pass.

However, he needed the heavy artillery and additional forces stationed now at Rinconada,[6] about twenty miles north of Saltillo, on the Monterrey road. This force consisted, according to Albert Pike, of about 600 cavalry under Gen. Thomas Marshall, and Capt. Benjamin Prentiss's battery of 18- and 24-pounders. But the road from Saltillo were blocked by Miñon's cavalry, plus a large force of irregular cavalry known as rancheros. Captain Pike's company of Arkansas Cavalry, supporting a train of ninety wagons, had been turned back two days earlier.[7] Early in the evening, Taylor had sent a corporal and ten men with dispatches to Rinconada, but Mexican patrols along the road had stopped them. The old general must have remembered the services rendered by Ben McCulloch and the men of his spy company, for he summoned two of them, known by reputation to be the best horsemen in the army. Wash (George Washington) Trahern, accompanied by Morris (Maurice) Simons were in for the ride of their young lives. Wash Trahern:

> I walked into the marquee. The old General was a rough old fellow, the wickedest man I ever saw in my life, but a kind man at heart. . . . He says, "I sent for you, and have got an extra and very dangerous ride for you if you will attempt it." He says, "I want you to go down to Rinconada tonight and carry a dispatch to General Tom Marshall to bring up the heavy artillery." . . . He says, "Do you think you can get through?" Says I, "General, I will try."[8]

Wash and Morris left Saltillo and abandoned the road to proceed to Rinconada by an overload route. Guarding the road that night were more than a thousand mounted Mexican rancheros, recruited from Monclova, Buenaventura, and Parras, under the command of Col. Miguel Blanco. After being chased and narrowly avoiding capture, the two American messengers reached Rinconada with the dispatches. General Marshall quickly formed an armed convoy and set out for Saltillo, arriving there by dawn with the heavy artillery.

Col. Jefferson Davis had been wounded early in the day; a musket ball had entered his right foot near the ankle, shattered his spur, and imbedded brass shards from the spur in the wound. Davis had refused to leave the field for medical attention, and the wound was temporarily wrapped while he remained on horseback.

Davis spent a painful and sleepless evening, while his friends washed the wound to prevent infection. In his state of pain, Davis could not sit a horse or walk, but refused to relinquish command of the regiment. Before daybreak, he had commandeered a wagon and team to drive him to the battlefield at the head of his regiment.

The Mississippi Rifles had spent a gloomy night in contemplation of a resumption of hostilities the next day. But with the coming of dawn, they had a pleasant surprise: the Mexican army had all but vanished.

Santa Anna had abandoned his positions on the South Plateau during the night and was retreating to Agua Nueva. Only the rear guard had remained throughout the night, keeping campfires lighted to deceive the Americans. A relieved and rejoicing American army swelled with pride at their apparent victory, then began to swarm over the battlefield, looking for the wounded and dead. William H. Scott of the Mississippi Regiment reported finding the body of his comrade, Dick Eggleston:

> But for his straw hat and a few other articles of clothing which the ruffians had left on him, I should have failed to recognize the body of young Eggleston, he was shot, stabbed, and otherwise abused—This was indeed the fate of all whom I saw—Lieut. Moore, and a man named Couch, of our company, were the only persons whose bodies I easily recognized. . . . I rode over the whole field; parties were engaged burying the dead, but there were still hundreds of bodies lying stiff and cold, with no covering save the scanty remnant of clothing which the robbers of the dead found too valueless to take from them. I saw the human body pierced in every place. . . . Some seemed to die execrating their enemies, and cursing them with their last breath—others had the most placid and resigned expression; some appeared to have died defending their lives bravely to the last, while others evidently used their last words in supplicating for mercy. Here lay youth and mature age calmly reposing in untimely death.[9]

Rufus K. Arthur, brother of the editor of *The Daily Whig* in Vicksburg, described what he saw:

> We have to mourn the loss of that true and gallant soldier Lieut. R. L. Moore. He was wounded in the leg while advancing at the head of his company in the first desperate charge upon the enemy . . . being wounded he sought protection in a ravine; but he there met a more brutal and horrible death . . . they pierced his body in various places, and stripped him of his clothes, money, &c. leaving him a striking monument to the barbarity and cruelty of the mode of Mexican warfare. . . . In our company we lost four of our friends and comrades, Wm. Couch, D. H. Eggleston, James Johnson, and John Preston. The list of the dead will also disclose the fate of poor Frank M. Robinson, who was as noted in the Regiment for goodness of heart as he was for brilliancy of intellect and gallantry of conduct—also, Henry G. Trotter, (son of

> Judge Trotter) and many others, highly esteemed by their comrades and beloved by friends at home. Most of those in the list of killed were only wounded by the enemy's fire and subsequently murdered by the lanceros. The comrades of the fallen men wreaked terrible vengeance upon the inhuman monsters.[10]

Henry R. Kenna of the Mississippi Regiment reported that, "Captain Sharp was severely wounded in both legs, and had the handle shot off his Bowie knife, and a pistol out of his belt; he would not retire either, but mounted a dead Lancer's pony which Adj't. Griffith caught for him and stayed with us till late in the afternoon."[11] Captain Albert Pike of the Arkansas Cavalry reported seeing a wounded Mississippian named Malone limping from the field with a wound in the thigh. In passing, Malone "heard Capt. Linnard trying to turn back five or six of the Indianians—but in vain—burst into tears, and limped back to the field again."[12]

Colonel Hardin's body was discovered, and Maj. H. W. Benham reported that, "He was killed by one or two lance wounds . . . and his sword scabbard was belted to his body when found, the Mexicans had not had time to take that [along] with the sword. A dead lancer and a horse lay near him, and a lance with a fresh cut on the staff was brought in with him, and was sent to his wife, as I am told."[13]

The body of the oldest man in the army, 2d Lieut. William Price, was found in one of the ravines pierced with multiple lance wounds. The seventy-two-year-old man, who had organized a company of the 2d Illinois, had put up a game fight for his life. It was reported that the Mexicans had thought the white-haired elderly gentleman to be General Wool.[14]

Manuel Balbontin, a Mexican officer present at the Battle of Buena Vista, writing in later years about the battle, was silent about Mexican atrocities. He did however seem to sense how the Mexican practice of killing American wounded would look to later generations, and offered this incident by way of an explanation:

> The commander of a squadron of a regiment of hussars, D. Juan Luyando, was about to lance a rifleman, who, getting down on his knees, implored mercy. Luyando let him alone and passed on. The rifleman raised himself immediately, and firing upon him, to whom he owed his life, shot him from his horse, piercing him

through and through with a ball. The murder of the commandant was in an instant revenged by his soldiers.[15]

The final official American casualty list reported 272 killed, 388 wounded, and six missing. An official Mexican casualty list was not produced, but Manuel Balbontin says that the Mexicans suffered 591 killed, 1,049 wounded, and 1,854 missing—most of the missing being deserters from Santa Anna's retreat.

William P. Rogers visited the battlefield on February 24, and reported:

> I passed over the Mexican slain. There they lay in heeps, the dead and the dying. The wounded have by their sides small sacks of parched meal. They have evidently been poorly fed and clothed as was indicated by their emaciated forms. Some would eagerly beg for "Agua and Pan" while others would exclaim "Ciete me Senor" [sense unknown] as I passed. Others also we would see who had passed unhurt through the fight, but who from exhaustion and emaciation were scarcely able to speak. Our soldiers were kind to them, giving water and bread and speaking kindly to them.[16]

Mexican dead and wounded littered the road from Angostura Pass to Encarnación, and large complements had been left behind in Agua Nueva and Encarnación to fend for themselves without medical supplies or food. Taylor sent both commodities to the wounded at those sites and dispatched wagons to pick up the Mexican wounded from the battlefield. "After the battle, our men brought their wounded [Mexican soldiers] down from the mountains on their back, and treated them with great humanity," reported Albert Pike.

The Cathedral of Santiago was used as a hospital for the soldiers of both armies. Many Americans wounded on February 23 had been conveyed to the cathedral by a wagon train organized for that purpose by Enoch C. Marsh, a native of Illinois connected with the army in a civilian capacity.[17] A Mississippian reported, in a letter home, that,

> Saltillo is one vast hospital. Besides our own wounded, (four to five hundred in number), Gen. Taylor has collected all the

> wounded Mexicans who were left by their army and put them in hospital. It is most disgusting to visit one of those places. All of them, (the Mexicans) are badly wounded, for those who were slightly sounded went off. They are dying every hour in the day, but they die better than we could under similar circumstances, for their priests are always at hand to set the sails of their last voyage in a proper manner. It is a first rate kind of religion, and is the only good thing I have seen in Mexico, except oranges and grapes, and they are all gone.[18]

The American dead of Buena Vista were buried at two sites, adjacent to the hospitals in which they were treated. The first site was near the Hacienda Buena Vista, now on the grounds of the Antonio Narro Agricultural College, located in the southern suburbs of Saltillo. The second site was within a few blocks of the magnificent Santiago Cathedral, located in downtown Saltillo[19] (On neither site are there markers to commemorate the dead, and the battlefield itself is remembered only by a rather plain marker found on the east side of the road through Angostura Pass.)

Some American bodies, buried in temporary graves, were later disinterred and shipped back to their native states: William R. McKee and Henry Clay Jr., returned to Kentucky; Archibald Yell buried at Little Rock, Arkansas;[20] the body of George Lincoln shipped to his father, Levi Lincoln, former governor of the state of Massachusetts;[21] the bodies of several Mississippians to their home counties, probably returning the regiment as it was mustered out of service in June, 1847. The *Vicksburg Whig,* in an article discussing Lieutenant Moore, state, "Such steps shall be taken as may be necessary to have his body brought to this place to be interred in the burial ground of this corps."[22] *The Southron,* of Jackson, reported on June 25, 1847, the funeral of Joseph C. Reveille and William W. Phillips, killed at Buena Vista.

It was difficult to understand Santa Anna's rather precipitous retreat from Angostura Pass on the night of February 23. Balbontin reported that the close of day found the Mexican soldiers, "happy and content for having overcome thus far the obstinate resistance of the Americans." By nightfall, the order to retreat was issued, causing, "general and profound disgust" among the Mexican soldiers. The feeling was—and they were probably right—that another day's battle would bring victory over the Americans.

Perhaps Santa Anna felt that this victory could only be gained by the destruction of his army—an army that had to kept intact to counter the imminent invasion of central Mexico by Winfield Scott. His critics in Mexico City had demanded action from him, and he had given it to them. Now, at least, he could report to the Mexican Congress how well the Mexican soldiers had performed their duties on the battlefield and how gallantly they had stood up to the horrors of American artillery.[23]

But even with all this rationalization, the grim fact remained that a third day of battle would quite likely have resulted in an American defeat. In such a case, Santa Anna could have pushed on easily to the Rio Grande and perhaps even to the Nueces, erasing all American gains of the war. Quite likely Scott would have had to abandon his assault on Vera Cruz, and with opposition to the war now springing up at home, popular opinion might have hardened against further aggressive policies toward Mexico. A victory at Buena Vista would have united all the various Mexican political parties and splinter interests under Santa Anna's banner, and monies and men would have been recruited for a larger, more resolute army of citizen-patriots. It could literally have been the event that brought on the birth of a new nation. But Santa Anna, mercurial and unprincipled, often lacked resolution. Unwilling to venture any more than had already been risked, he opted for the half measure.

Santa Anna's coach left the weary Mexican army behind, plodding in disarray, disease, and disgust toward San Luis Potosi, and hurried on to Mexico City. The general brought with him the regimental flags of the Arkansas and Kentucky Cavalry and cannon taken from John Paul Jones O'Brien on the Middle Plateau as proof of a "signal Mexican victory."[24] Word of a victory caused the citizens at San Luis Potosi, through which he had passed, to celebrate and cheer the name of Santa Anna. A few days later when the ragged and starving remnants of the army began to arrive in that city, the cheering died away.

Gen. Vicente Miñon, commanding a brigade of Mexican cavalry

at Buena Vista, wrote a rebuke of Santa Anna's actions at Buena Vista:

> The nation will know, one day, . . . That it had brave soldiers, worthy to rival, in ardor and enthusiasm, the best of any army whatever; that it had entrepid officers, who led them gallantly to the combat,—but it had no general who knew how to make use of these excellent materials. . . . The battle of La Angostura was nothing but an unconnected succession of sublime individual deeds—partial attacks of the several corps that entered the action. . . . General Santa Anna cannot conceive how it happens that a victory may be gained over an enemy by wise and well-calculated manoeuvres. . . . I disapproved of his retiring from the field of Angostura . . . the army which had left San Luis might have remained at that point, and completed the great work, which it had undertaken, of destroying the enemy. . . . It is false that there was not food and water. There was everything,—I myself supplied General Santa Anna. I had not less than 700 beeves confined within an enclosure, all of which I shared with him as opportunity offered. His retirement was unjustifiable. . . .[25]

Many American military experts agree with this analysis—that Santa Anna's piecemeal attacks enabled Taylor to shift reinforcements here and there as needed whereas a general assault all along the line would have overwhelmed him.

The American public received news of Buena Vista slowly; all American communication from Monterrey to Camargo had been halted by the guerrilla activities of Mexican rancheros. Most newspaper correspondents, concluding that there would be no more fighting to report in northern Mexico, had left Saltillo prior to the battle to accompany Scott's soldiers on the invasion of Vera Cruz.

However, when the news was received, it was reported as another victory for American arms, and lavish credit for the victory was heaped upon Zachary Taylor. Newspaper editors in small towns as well as large cities continued to build upon the legend of Old Rough and Ready, which they had created themselves. Taylor easily became the most popular man in America, and his candidacy for President seemed a foregone conclusion.

But among official circles in Washington, the news of Buena

Vista was received with a flurry of finger pointing. Polk blamed Taylor and Scott, both Whigs, for provoking an apparently unnecessary battle. Taylor was blamed for disobeying orders not to move his troops south of Monterrey, and Scott was blamed for depleting Taylor's army for the troops needed to invade Vera Cruz.[26] The charge against Taylor was weak on tactical grounds, because a defensive battle fought at Monterrey by the American army was bound to fail; Santa Anna could easily have invested Monterrey with a small army and starved Taylor into submission. To succeed, Taylor knew he must stop the Mexican army before it reached Saltillo and was resupplied, and he simply used the discretion normally allowed a field commander in choosing a battle site. The American public took Taylor's side and blamed Polk for allowing Scott to strip Taylor of troops.

On the other hand, Taylor blamed Scott and Polk for removing his regular soldiers and leaving him in a position where he was sure to fail. The press of that time backed up Taylor's opinions, and soon the American public was also convinced of a deep dark plot by the Polk Administration against Taylor.

Taylor's chief assets to the army at Buena Vista had been his leadership qualities and the personal example he offered his men. There had been no more prominent target on the field of Buena Vista than Taylor astride Whitey, his knock-kneed horse. When the day was going badly for the army at Angostura Pass, many a frightened volunteer was reassured by the sight of the old general calmly sharing their perils.

The battle of Buena Vista had shown the superiority of the new highly mobile 6-pounder field artillery. This field artillery and the tactics necessary for deployment of it were brought to this country from France by Capt. Samuel Ringgold.[27] Ringgold had been sent to France in 1842 by the army to study French artillery, and was strongly influenced by what he had observed. He was instrumental in developing an elite corp of artillery staffed by dashing young officers. Capt. Braxton Bragg, one of this new breed of artillerists, wrote that Buena Vista was "an awful fight and nine-tenths of the killed & wounded of the enemy were by artillery. I fired 250 shot to the gun."[28] Taking into consideration the short length of this winter's day, that figure averages to about one shot every three

Jefferson and Varina Howell Davis. *Courtesy of National Portrait Gallery, Smithsonian Institution, Washington, D.C.*

The canton of the flag of the First Mississippi Regiment showing missing stars removed by Varina Howell Davis. *Courtesy of the State Historical Museum/Mississippi Department of Archives and History*

Model 1841 percussion rifle, the Mississippi rifle. The bayonet in the lower right is not used with the rifle. *Courtesy of Fuller Gun Collection, Chickamauga-Chattanooga Military Park*

Model 1822 flintlock musket, the standard issue weapon for the American soldier of the Mexican War. *Courtesy of Fuller Gun Collection, Chickamauga-Chattanooga Military Park*

Andrew Keith McClung. *Courtesy of State Historical Museum/Mississippi Department of Archives and History*

View of the Main Plaza at Camargo, Mexico, 1846. *Woodcut taken from John Frost,* Pictorial History of Mexico and the Mexican War *(Philadelphia: Thomas, Copperwait and Co., 1848)*

Camargo, Mexico, garrisoned by American Troops as seen from across the Rio San Juan. *Woodcut taken from John Frost,* Pictorial History of Mexico and the Mexican War *(Philadelphia: Thomas, Copperwait and Co., 1848)*

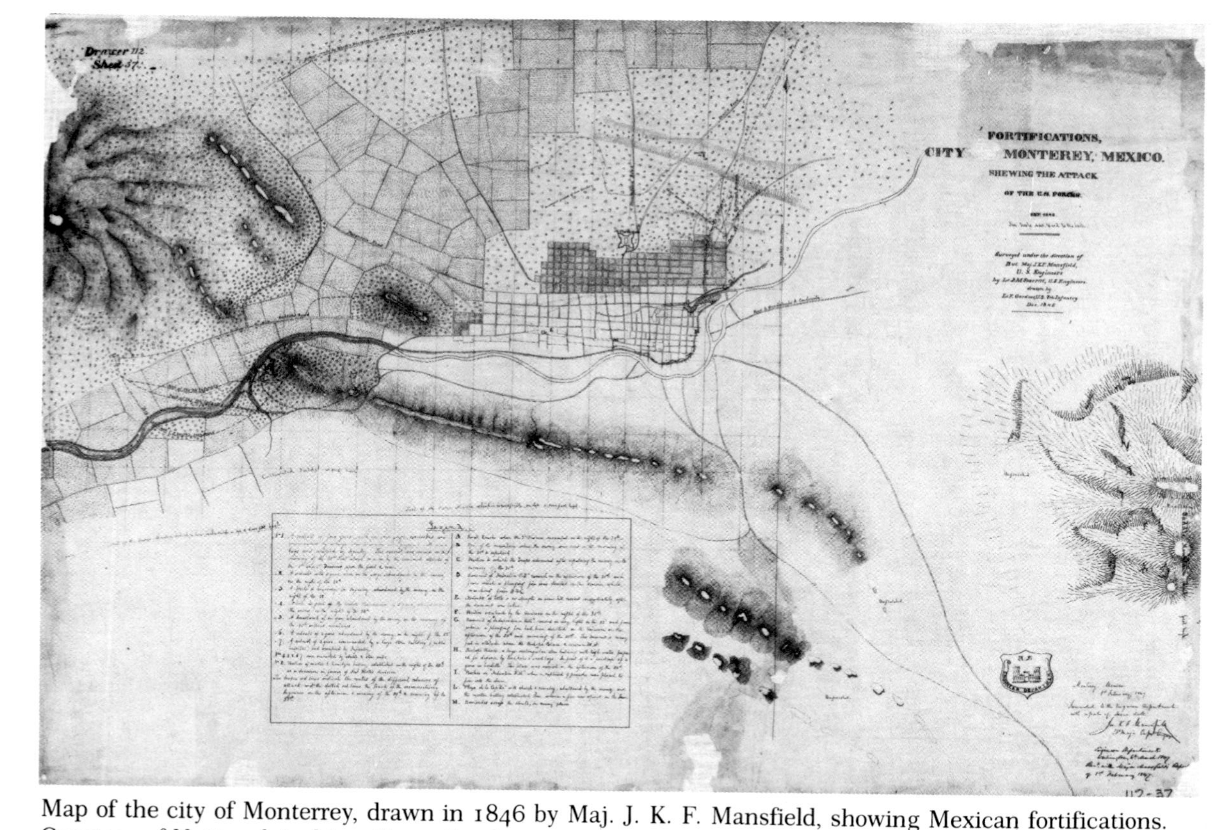

Map of the city of Monterrey, drawn in 1846 by Maj. J. K. F. Mansfield, showing Mexican fortifications.
Courtesy of National Archives Trust Fund

Death of Henry Clay, Jr., at the battle of Buena Vista, Currier lithograph

The Virginia Regiment in formation on the streets of Saltillo, Mexico, 1847.
Courtesy of Beinecke Rare Book and Manuscript Library, Yale University

General John Ellis Wool (center) and staff, Saltillo, Mexico, 1847. *Courtesy of Beinecke Rare Book and Manuscript Library, Yale University*

Santiago Cathedral, Saltillo, Mexico, 1847. *Courtesy of Beinecke Rare Book and Manuscript Library, Yale University*

minutes per gun throughout the day, mighty tall shooting even for a soldier of Braxton Bragg's caliber!

If American artillery had been the high point of the day, surely the lowpoint was to be found among certain volunteer regiments. The American press tended to gloss over the great number of men who had deserted the battlefield. One conspicuous example of such a unit, although by no means the only one, was the Arkansas Mounted Regiment. This cavalry unit, according to Samuel Chamberlain, was composed of excellent material, "quite famous in their own locality as fighting men," but possessing an independence of character and self-confidence "fatal to their efficiency as soldiers." The Arkansans created discipline problems for the army from its earliest entry into Mexico. Josiah Gregg, who accompanied Wool's army into Mexico as a translator, reported that their officers often acted toward General Wool in an insubordinate manner.[29] Taking their cue from the officers, the men of the regiment likewise insulted Wool and his staff.[30] General Wool put his finger on the problem facing this regiment when he wrote, prior to the battle, "Col. Yell's regiment is composed of very good materials but without any instruction. They do not appear to be under the control of their officers."[31] Col. Archibald Yell, commander of the regiment, was a former congressman and governor from Arkansas and a brave and gallant man, but not a soldier. He knew nothing about military training and had not mastered even the most elementary drill formations. Consequently, his men received no regimental drill. Maj. Solon Borland replied, when informed of the poor condition of the Arkansas regiment by the inspector general, "We come here to fight sir! not clean old iron and groom horses sir! and doggoned if we do it sir!"[32] Borland, a politician-officer, considered every soldier in the regiment a potential voter, and feared that Arkansans would later express displeasure at the ballot box if ordered to perform menial military duties. The men of the regiment were allowed to rob and steal from helpless Mexican civilians, even commit rape and murder, while their officers turned a blind eye. This regiment, in fact, compiled its fighting record mostly against the women, children, and old men of Mexico. Its officers equated war with fighting and reasoned that since they were good brawlers, they must also be good warriors. The soldiers and officers of the regular army, they reasoned, could teach them nothing that they did not already know. Buena Vista was a sad lesson. Capt. Albert Pike was one of the few members of the regiment courageous enough to send an honest letter home about the battle. Appearing in the *Arkansas State Gazette,* April 24, 1847, this letter documented a history of poor discipline:

> It is a sad thing that brave men, for they were brave, should be so destroyed, for want of discipline. In the first place, the companies of our Regiment engaged there, had been hardly drilled at all, except what little the company officers had done. The Colonel and Lieutenant Colonel had never drilled them since they left San Antonio. Their order once broken could not be restored; and a retreat was bound to be a rout. In the next place, it was a great error to receive the enemy's charge—and indeed to use the carbine at all. After firing they had no time to draw the sabre, and the impetus of the Mexican charge demolished them at once. Had they charged sabre in hand, and possessed that mobility and facility of changing front which only discipline could give, they could not have been routed as they were. Poor Yell! He atoned for his error with his life: but other brave men died with him, who were not in fault. . . . It will not answer to take undisciplined troops, and especially undisciplined cavalry into the field. It is murderous. Men must not only be drilled but disciplined. They must not only like, but respect their officers for their superior knowledge. . . .[33]

The Arkansas Regiment was certainly not the only lawless element of the American military in northern Mexico. The volunteer and regular soldiers who committed crimes against the civil population were protected from punishment by a loophole in the military law. The military laws of the time did not anticipate an American force fighting in a foreign country. Military laws assumed that American soldiers were to be operating within the United States and were therefore covered by civilian statutes and could be tried by a civilian court. Military tribunals were only to be used to try offenses involving the Articles of War. The War Department had asked Congress as early as December 1845 for the power to extend the jurisdiction of courts-martial to offenses committed by American soldiers against civilians in foreign countries, but Congress, ever sensitive to political overtones, had failed to produce any legislation. Taylor, although shocked and angered by the criminal acts committed against the Mexican populace, was virtually powerless to punish these violations; his only recourse was to dismiss the guilty parties from the service and have them sent home in disgrace.[34]

If the Arkansas Regiment represented the worst aspects of the volunteer army in Mexico, the Mississippi Regiment offered one of the best. Col. Jefferson Davis was absent from Vicksburg when the election of officers occurred. It was a mark of the good sense of the Mississippi volunteers that they chose someone with his military experience as their colonel. During the first days in Mexico, the diaries of the men of the regiment and the letters sent home were filled with complaints about having to march in the hot sun, and the incessant routine of drill. A disgruntled Mississippian wrote in this letter of August 13, 1846:

> He is the only Colonel of a volunteer regiment who has kept a guard during the day at or near this point exposed to the overpowering heat of the hottest sun imaginable; in fact, a thousand instances of his severity, even in the short period we have been under his command, rush to my mind. . . .[35]

Even Davis's brother, Joseph, writing on October 7, 1846, cautioned him that "Some complaints have been uttered against you for the severity of training. . . ."[36] Davis was quickly tested while in Mexico by the spirited young men of the regiment, who slipped into a Mexican cornfield and stole an abundant supply of roasting ears. Davis paid the complaining Mexican for the damages incurred, and ordered the men assembled. Davis sensibly did not attempt to identify the culprits of the cornfield raid, but simply announced that in the future any man caught stealing from or abusing the civilian population would be sent home in disgrace.[37] This policy of discipline must have made an impression on the men, because the names of Mississippi men were conspicuously absent from the proceedings of the military tribunals of Taylor's army. In fact, the 1st Mississippi had a good name with other regiments. From the camp at Monterrey on November 24, 1846, Rufus Arthur wrote home about their good conduct.

> Within the past week there has been several broils between the volunteers and the Mexicans in Monterey and the neighborhood, which have resulted in the death (or murder) of several volunteers and Mexicans. . . . As yet no Mississippian has tarnished the character of the Regiment, and I feel assured they will not. In an open and honorable warfare with the Mexicans, the Mississippians have proven themselves brave and chivalric, and I know that none of them will play the assassin, and imbrue their hands in blood of the humble and crouching citizens whom they have conquered. Numerous instances of their noble, generous, and humane conduct, to the citizens, and particularly to the females on the 23rd of September in Monterey, might be cited to their lasting credit. Even money, in some instances, was offered by the alarmed Mexicans (private citizens) for their lives, but all our noble boys refused to receive it, and most gallantly protected those who were found unarmed. . . . Not withstanding the reputation our Regiment had for "wild spirits," it thus affords me pleasure to say they have demeaned themselves so gallantly and so well that they have won the highest rank in the volunteer service for good order and good soldiers.[38]

Jefferson Davis the politician had risked his popularity with his men and the voters of Mississippi to do what had to be done to prepare his troops for battle. But moral courage alone was not enough to prepare his regiment for service; military experience was also required. The Battle of Monterrey offered his troops an opportunity to see the good that Davis's training had wrought. In a letter sent on October 13, 1846, by Joseph Howell to his sister Varina, her husband was discussed as a military man:

> If the time of our regiment expires, and our Colonel, Jeff Davis, even then thinks we could be useful, there is not a man in his regiment who would not sacrifice his life to obey him, so much has his gallant conduct raised him in their estimation. The degree of power his coolness, courage, and discretion have acquired for him in the army generally would hardly be believed at home. Everything difficult of decision is left to him, and I verily believe that if he should tell his men to jump into a cannon's mouth they would think it all right, and would all say, "Colonel Jeff," as they call him, "knows best, so hurrah, boys, let's go ahead." He is

> always in front of his men, and ready to be the first to expose himself; and moreover, he has taken them into so many tight places, and got them out safely, that they begin to think if they follow him they will be sure to succeed. . . . I wish never to be commanded by a truer soldier than Colonel Davis.[39]

This letter, while admittedly partisan, was a true representative of the feeling found in the letters and public comments by the members of the regiment.

The regiments that failed at Buena Vista all suffered from the same glaring defect: lack of leadership. Why would a man with no military experience permit his name to be placed in nomination as an officer for a volunteer regiment? Surely blind ambition would serve as a quick answer to that question, but a deeper look into the circumstances is required. Men reared in the American tradition of the volunteer militia had come to feel that military training was unnecessary. Volunteer militia, hastily organized in the tradition of the "minuteman," could function well against Indians and could even on occasion stand behind cotton-bale breastworks and trade volleys effectively with professional troops, but facing a professional army in the field was a different matter.

Up to the time of the Mexican War, Americans had never had to engage in a war of conquest, and fight battles in a foreign country. West Point was created in 1802, and from its inception had faced criticism from politicians and the general public. The Military Committee of the House of Representatives, meeting in 1837, referred to West Point graduates as, "novelists and magazine writers, effete, arrogant dabblers in art, French, and drawing."[40] This unfortunate attitude toward military training was a cause of the failure of many volunteer militia regiments to respond to the requirements of a war of conquest such as the Mexican War. One of the most important lessons learned by the Battle of Buena Vista, and indeed the entire Mexican War, was the value of professional military training.

The Battle of Buena Vista has been studied extensively, but the best summary analysis is probably the one proposed by Col. William Campbell, commander of the 1st Tennessee regiment, who had served under Taylor at the Battle of Monterrey. Transferred to Scott's army, he was stationed near Vera Cruz when he heard on March 20, 1847, of the American victory at Buena Vista. He wrote in his diary, "Old Zack is the most lucky man alive. He is brave, kind, and good, and clever, but especially he is lucky."[41]

NINE

Final Muster

> The "bravest of the brave," the heroes of Buena Vista and Monterey, the invincible riflemen of the Mississippi, the volunteer veterans of a most eventful campaign, arrived on Saturday in our city, and were received by our people with joy and enthusiastic admiration. Well have they deserved all the praise and public demonstrations of approval and respect which a generous people could bestow.
>
> —*The New Orleans Delta, June 10, 1847*

In compliance with orders issued by Santa Anna, Mexican Gen. José Urrea and a division of light cavalry entered Tula Pass by mid February 1847. This steep and narrow pass through the Sierra Madre, located southwest of Victoria, was too narrow to admit either cannon or wagons. General Urrea had been ordered to disrupt the supply lines for Taylor's army between Camargo and Monterrey and to encourage the many rancheros of this region to employ a more aggressive policy of resistance. Urrea's actions were timed to support Santa Anna's planned attack on Taylor's army. If the American army was driven from Saltillo to the garrison at Monterrey, General Urrea's command would be in a position to put the Americans in grave jeopardy.

In anticipation of Urrea's arrival, the activities of Mexican guerrillas under the command of Gen. Antonio Canales were stepped up. By February 24, 1847, Canales and Urrea had teamed up to attack an American supply train of wagons at Marin, about twenty miles north of Monterrey.[1] The train consisted of 110 wagons and 358 pack mules containing subsistence and forage for the army and merchant's goods for commerce. Resistance from the small armed escort was quickly silenced, and the unarmed teamsters and mule drivers were captured, brutally tortured, and put to death by their Mexican captors. Among those killed was the English consul at Saltillo, a Mr. Burns. Most goods were spirited away by the Mexicans, and those goods not used were put to the torch along with the wagons.

On the next day, five companies of the 2nd Ohio under the command of Colonel G. W. Morgan were attacked near Marin while on their way to Monterrey. But Morgan was alert and repulsed the attack in fine style.

Around March 6, another wagon train proceeding to Monterrey was attacked, just north of Cerralvo. Using Cerralvo as a base, the Mexican forces advanced on a wagon train of about two hundred wagons being escorted by two companies of Kentucky and two companies of Ohio volunteers. In addition, the American escort, under the command of Maj. Luther Giddings, had two cannon, one placed in front and the other back of the train. The wagon train, over a mile in length, was advancing single file over the narrow mountain roads when the mounted Mexicans swept past the lead wagon and attacked the middle of the train. Several of the mule teams panicked and stampeded, their wagons bumping and jolting over the rough countryside. These wagons were set afire by the rancheros before Giddings was able to come to their rescue. One of the burning wagons, filled with gunpowder, ignited in a brilliant fireball, killing seven of the attacking rancheros. Before another massacre could occur, Giddings attacked the Mexicans with his small detachment and forced them back to Cerralvo. From Cerralvo the rancheros abandoned their attack and retreated farther north to the little village of Puntiagudo.

The combined forces of Urrea and Canales were gaining strength daily as more and more Mexican civilians enlisted. General Canales boasted that, in the month of February alone, his forces had killed 161 Americans.[2]

Dispatches sent to Taylor in Saltillo from Monterrey described the attacks on supply lines and urgently requested reinforcements. On March 8, General Taylor himself set out for Monterrey with a relief force. The Mississippi Regiment was among those sent, and Captain Rogers wrote of the experience:

> Gen. Taylor has provided a train of camp wagons to transport our Reg. So I can ride my cabillo [caballo]. This delights me for I have walked and walked until my whole heart sickens at the prospect of a tramp. 15 or 20 miles a day with no comfort at night is not inviting. By the way however I am a pretty fair pedestrian and would make a good lecturer on walking if from sad experience we are supposed to learn.[3]

The relief party arrived in Monterrey on March 10, and Rogers noted, "Our regiment is received with great eclat. . . . We are all Lions here".

From camp at Monterrey, Taylor reacted angrily to the attacks on his supply lines. He was convinced that the guerrillas had been aided and abetted by the civilians of the region. He placed a levy of $96,000 on the people of the State of Nuevo Leon to pay for the burned wagons and supplies and dispatched mounted Texas volunteers to collect the debt.[4]

Thus began one of darkest periods of the Mexican War in northern Mexico. Of this period, Samuel Chamberlain was later to write:

> General Taylor not only collected the money assessed by force of arms, but he let loose on the country packs of human bloodhounds called Texas Rangers. Between the Rangers and the guerillars the unfortunate inhabitants of the states of Nuevo Leon and Tamaulipas had a hard time of it during the summer of 1847, plundered by both sides, their lives often taken, and their wives and daughters outraged and carried off. The names of "Old Reid," Captain Bayley [sic], Harry Love, Ben McCulloch and, more terrible than all, "Mustang" Gray will always remain fresh in the memory of the Mexicans, as the fearful atrocities committed by them now form part of the Nursery Legends of the country.[5]

From Mexico City, Gen. Mariano Salas proclaimed to his countrymen, "I have obtained permission to raise a guerrilla corps, with which to attack and destroy the invaders in every manner imaginable. . . . *War without pity unto death!* will be the motto of the guerrilla warfare without *Vengeance*."[6] Canales, not to be outdone, announced that every American, armed or unarmed, and every Mexican living peacefully was to be shot. The peaceful rural population was bewildered by the violent turn of events, suffering attacks in turn from both Americans and Mexicans. A hacienda that did not wish to furnish supplies for the guerrillas was burned for being unpatriotic. But if it did furnish supplies, Americans would burn the hacienda for being a guerrilla camp. There were no civilians in northern Mexico now, and many of the people fled their homes to hide in the mountains.[7]

The mounted Texas volunteers and a group of civilian teamsters murdered twenty-four civilians from a village near Marin to exact vengeance for the Marin wagon-train massacre. The village of Puntiagudo, about twenty miles south of Camargo, was declared a haven for guerrillas by Col. Samuel Curtiss of the Ohio volunteers and burned in early March 1847. By June 1847, General Taylor relented on his levy, commenting that "the Texas horse had scarcely made one expedition without committing murder, and asked that no more be sent to him."[8] General Wool was disgusted by the actions of the Texans, and ordered that Texas volunteers not be sent on distant expeditions except under "extraordinary circumstances"; but the genie had already been let out of the bottle.

By the summer of 1847, Major Giddings of the 1st Ohio reported that the trip from Monterrey to Camargo was "over a road numerously dotted with the skeletons of men and animals past roofless and ruined ranchos and many a dark and smoldering heap of ashes."[9]

Compton Smith reported the scene of destruction:

> Leaving Mier, we next encamp at Punta Aguda. This place, when we first visited it, contained a population of some fifteen hundred rancheros, who furnished us with a plentiful supply of fresh provisions, and were very friendly disposed toward us. A few months after, on the passage of Colonel Curtiss, of the 3rd Ohioans, this pretty village was laid to ashes, in retaliation for some depredations which had been committed upon some of our

> trains, while on the road; and of which, there is no doubt, these people were entirely innocent. The march of that regiment, all the way to Monterey, was marked with devastated fields, and the smoking ruins of villages and ranchos, where the advancing columns of our army had met with shelter and friendly receptions. Such are the horrors of war: the innocent and friendly peasantry are oftenest made to suffer its penalties. These unwarranted acts of cruelty were severely censured by General Taylor, who immediately issued orders, forbidding a repetition of them. The next usual encamping ground, on the upward march, after leaving Punta Aguda, is the spot where stood, when we first rested here, the little ranchita of Chicharrones. Not an adobe remained upon another of its walls, after the passage of our modern Attila.[10]

The Mississippians were now placed on escort duty for the wagon trains that traveled the narrow road between Camargo and Monterrey. They rode the empty wagons from Monterrey to Camargo and marched beside the full wagons on the return trip. The first train to be escorted reached Camargo by April 2.

This hot dusty duty had the men of the regiment on edge; William P. Rogers' diary entry for April 5 recorded this terse note: "Insulted to day by a Dutchman knocked him down and stamped on him." The train departed Camargo on April 8, with the Mississippians afoot. Unaccustomed to the arduous rigors of lengthy marches, the line of troops began to straggle, and Rogers reported, "A soldier lagged behind and was killed his body dreadfully mangled. We have two Mexican prisoners for it and if proof is strong they will be shot." By the next day,

> The prisoners were shot this evening. One of them was game to the last, the other lagged like a dog. Poor fellows I was sorry for them, but the proof was too strong to let them pass and being called on for an opinion I gave it for shooting them.[11]

The wagon train reached Monterey without further incident, and the escort was given some free time before the return trip to Camargo. In Monterrey, on the night of April 21, two Mississippians engaged in a loud drunken brawl with one of May's Dragoons and a man from the Quartermaster's Department. A military patrol, under the command of Col. A. M. Mitchell, arrested the dragoon and the man from the Quartermaster's Department but returned to find the two Mississippians still violating the peace. The Mississippians exchanged some unpleasant words with the men on patrol, and a scuffle ensued. During this scuffle, a musket discharged, striking Lieut. Wm. H. H. Patterson, of the Mississippi Regiment, in the thigh. He was removed to the hospital where the wounded leg was amputated. The regiment was outraged, and Rogers reported that, "2nd Lieut. Wade desired me to bear a challenge to the officer who ordered Patterson shot. I done so but the fellow declined fighting."[12]

Another train of empty wagons left Monterrey on April 27, and Rogers's company was sent again on escort duty, probably to get them out of Monterrey before revenge could be exacted for the wounding of Lieutenant Patterson. On April 28, south of Cerralvo, near the little village of Papagayos, Rogers reported, "Today our butcher rode ahead of the train with 2 or 3 others and was shot in the thigh—his leg was taken off he killed one of the Mexicans that shot him." The man wounded was Maurice Kavanaugh Simons, the young man who had ridden with Wash Trahern to bring up the artillery from Rinconada for Taylor's forces. Simons was left in Papagayos in critical condition, and the good people of that little village nursed him back to health in the next few months.[13] Rogers' company escorted the train to Cerralvo and remained there to garrison that small city.

The Mississippi Regiment was one of those volunteer regiments mustered in for one year's service from June 1846 to June 1847, and time had just about run its course. The Mississippians stood muster for the last time in Monterrey on May 17, 1847. A parade of the garrison troops was held in their honor, followed by an address to the Mississippians from their commander, Zachary Taylor. Young William Estes, from Brandon, Mississippi, remembered the solemn occasion:

> We had never seen the old hero in uniform, but on this occasion he came out in our front in the regulation blue "from trip to toe." He made a short speech to us and during its delivery attempted to "pull down his vest frequently." The purport of the speech was "that he hoped we would all reach home in safety, and that our career in private life would prove as happy as our military career had been bright and glorious."[14]

As a parting gesture of his gratitude to Davis for all that he had done, Taylor remarked to Davis, "My daughter was a better judge of men than I."[15] The ceremony was concluded as Davis brought the regiment to attention in a manner described by a North Carolina volunteer in attendance:

> In dress parade on the same ground in the same place they did the evening before the battle of Monterey . . . each standing in the tracks he then stood in near as could be. It was a solemn sight. There were great gaps and not a man to fill it up—here were three—then one farther along two The Regiment looked like an old comb with most of the teeth broken out.[16]

This ceremony caught the imagination of a young man in the audience, Theodore O'Hara of the Kentucky Cavalry. From his experiences and observations as a soldier in Mexico he wrote the famous poem, "Bivouac of the Dead." Here is the original version of the stanza written to honor the Mississippians:

> On Fame's eternal camping ground
> Their silent tents are spread,
> And glory guards with solemn round
> The bivouac of the dead.
> No more on dress parade will meet
> That brave and gallant few. . . .[17]

The regiment that left for Mexico with 926 recruits was now returning home with 376 weary veterans.

The regiment moved through Cerralvo, collected the two companies there on garrison duty, and arrived at Camargo on May 22. The Rio Grande was very low, and steamboats had been unable to move up the river any farther than the city of Reynosa. The regiment did not tarry in Camargo, but marched overland to Reynosa. From there, eight companies were sent down to the mouth of the river on the steamboat *Rough and Ready,*[18] and the two remaining companies followed later, passing Matamoros on May 27 aboard the steamer *Whiteville*. Colonel Davis wished to make passage to New Orleans for the regiment on a steamship, but had to settle for the schooner *P. B. Savory* and the brig *Forest*, which departed from camp at the mouth of the Rio Grande on May 30, and reached New

Orleans by June 5. The other two companies left the mouth of the river a few days later and reached New Orleans by June 11.

The legislature of the State of Mississippi presented each member of the regiment a new blue uniform, which was received by the men of the regiment prior to their departure from the mouth of the Rio Grande.

The city of New Orleans turned out in a "vast crowd" to greet the returning Mississippi Regiment, and a celebration for the veterans was held on June 10. A parade wound its way along Camp Street to Lafayette Square. The highlight of the ceremony was a speech delivered by Davis who stood, supporting his wounded leg on a chair.[19] Young William Estes recalled the occasion thus:

> The whole city was thrown open to us, and we were banqueted and re-banqueted. But the people insisted on each occasion that we should appear in our army uniforms and carry our rifles.[20]

Colonel Davis and four companies of the regiment continued their journey on June 12, and boarded the two steamers *Natchez* and *St. Mary* for Natchez. These steamboats were hailed from every landing along the way by the sounds of cheering voices and firearms discharged in honor of their passage. Steamboats passing in the other direction hooted salutes from their whistles to honor the Mississippians. The distinguished passengers were greeted at Natchez by a large and enthusiastic crowd in a ceremony punctuated by another round of speeches. At this stop Davis and his wife Varina were reunited, and the procession proceeded to the steamboat landing, "in a barouche, nearly hidden with flowers."[21]

Their next stop was home base for the regiment, Vicksburg, Mississippi. The homecoming was probably one of the greatest celebrations ever put together in this city.[22] The arrival of the party was heralded by a five-gun salute from artillery on the Court House square and a procession from the landing to the square, in this order:

1. The Committees of Reception and Arrangement.
2. Vicksburg Volunteers.
3. Hills-City Guards.
4. Mayor and Council.
5. Clergy, and surviving soldiers of former wars.

6. First Mississippi Rifles.
7. Southrons.
8. Vicksburg Blues and Cadets.
9. Volunteer companies from abroad.
10. Orator of the day.
11. Chief Justice and Associate Judges of the High Court, Chancellor, and other Judges of the State.
12. Invited Guests.
13. Masonic Lodges, and I.O.O.F. Fellows, according to their order of precedence.
14. Sons of Temperance.
15. Mechanic's Mutual Benefit Association.
16. Citizens on foot.
17. Citizens on horseback [for obvious reasons].
18. Ladies in carriages.
19. Warren Cavalry.[23]

After the oratory, the parade continued to Camp Independence, the site at which the regiment was first organized, for a barbecue. After a fine meal was served, "sufficient to feed several thousand people," social liquids were distributed and a round of toasts became the highlight of the day. Thirteen regular toasts were given, which were responded to by the men of the regiment with an additional ten. Where were the Sons of Temperance when this was going on?

On that note, the bleary-eyed men of the regiment proceeded to their homes, and one of the most gallant regiments to serve in the Mexican War was disbanded sine die.

Governor Albert Gallatin Brown, in a communication to Davis, felt that "there should be no divorce between the gallant soldier & his Gun," and expressed the desire that the men of the regiment should retain their fine Whitney rifles after being mustered out of the service of their state.[24] On March 1848, the State Legislature passed a resolution to that effect.

The Whitney rifle was indeed a fine firearm and its merit was commented on by Colonel Davis in a letter to Col. George Talcott of the Army Ordnance Department:

> The fine rifles which you issued to the Regt. I had the honor to command in Mexico are worthy of the highest commendation, I

> doubt whether as many pieces are ever issued from any other ordnance Dept. so perfect in their construction and condition, In accuracy of fire they are equal to the finest sporting rifles, their range I think exceeds that of the [old pattern] Musket, and they less often miss fire or want repair than any small arms I have seen used in service.[25]

This paragraph was reprinted widely in advertisements issued by the Whitney Arms Company of New Haven, Connecticut, to praise the merits of a "new model Percussion Rifle" in 1850, and a "New Model Mississippi and Minnie Rifle" in 1860.[26] Later in the same month, in a letter addressed to William L. Marcy, Secretary of War, Davis wrote to endorse Eli Whitney's arms:

> Sir, at the request of Mr. Eli Whitney constructor of the rifles issued to the 1st Rgt. of Missi. Vols. I have the honor to address you and to bear testimony to their high value . . . and recommend the constructor to the most favorable consideration of your Department.[27]

It is of interest to conclude this history with a brief discussion of the life of one of the most flamboyant characters in the regiment: Alexander Keith McClung. Immediately after his military career climaxed on this June day of 1847, he began his campaign for the office of congressman of the Second District of Mississippi. As the Whig candidate for this position, he faced a stiff challenge from his Democratic rival, Winfield Scott Featherston. On the speaking junkets arranged for candidates he confided to friends that the crutches on which he leaned were "in themselves sufficient token of his claims upon the popular vote." However, the public thought otherwise, electing Featherston to the position.[28] This defeat was taken bitterly by McClung. By 1849, he had received a political appointment from his old commander Zachary Taylor, now President: chargé d'affaires to Bolivia. But his temper continued to control his actions, and he fought several duels in Bolivia. In one, he killed the British military attaché, whom McClung referred to as "one overbearing Englishman." He received cards from other English officers who wished to avenge the death of their comrade, but before these could be obliged, Her Majesty's government requested that the State Department recall McClung. McClung was returned to the United States, and he settled again in Mississippi. John A. Quitman, who in 1850 had been one of a group of men plotting to invade Cuba with the aid of the Cuban revolutionary known as Lopez, wrote McClung to join his expedition, destined to "decide the great question of American or European dominance of this Continent." McClung refused the invitation from Quitman, deciding rather to enter the congressional elections of 1851 in Mississippi as a Whig candidate for congress.[29] He ran as an ardent Unionist, and was again defeated. His nature, which earlier had exhibited violent tendencies, now darkened with melancholia, and he became a man to be feared by his fellow citizens.

Reuben Davis narrated a chilling encounter with McClung during this latter period of McClung's life:

> I was in Jackson . . . and while walking with Governor Alcorn and Governor Clark, invited them to go with me to a certain restaurant. . . . Colonel McClung was in the eating-room . . . he had driven everyone out of the house. He had been drinking heavily for some days, and had reached a state of actual insanity . . . we saw McClung seated at the head of one of the tables. . . . He had a large duelling pistol on either side of a bottle of wine that stood before him, and a bowie-knife was disposed between them. His face was deeply flushed, and his bloodshot eyes gleamed angrily. . . .
>
> McClung did not like Clark, and he hated Alcorn. . . . I whispered to Alcorn not to exasperate McClung by seeming to ignore his presence, but to ask him to take a glass of wine. He did so, and McClung after glaring at him for a moment, replied with a fierce emphasis, "Not with you, sir; I drink my own wine." . . .
>
> I don't suppose three men ever despatched food with more celerity than we did . . . or with less appreciation of its flavor. McClung had now begun to tell a story of how he had that day been attacked by three assassins in that very room, and got up to show just how he drove them off. Brandishing his bowie-knife, he rushed down between the two tables, just grazing Clark's back as he passed him with a furious lunge. When he sat down again, he began to flourish his pistols, regardless of the fact that they were hair trigger, liable to go off at a touch. As soon as it seemed prudent, our party rose to leave . . . McClung jumped up with a pistol in each hand, and ordered us to stop. . . . Wheeling

around, he pointed both pistols at Alcorn and said, "Do you believe I told the truth?" Alcorn immediately replied, as blandly as possible, "Why colonel, do you suppose any gentleman ever questions what you assert?" McClung scowled at him and turned upon Clark, who made the same reply. We were then permitted to depart. . . .[30]

In a last desperate attempt to take control of his life, McClung applied to the Administration of Pres. Franklin Pierce for a military commission; he asked to be appointed colonel of a new regiment of "voltiguers" cavalry, being formed for use against the Indians on the frontier. Jefferson Davis was Secretary of War in the Pierce Administration, and must have decided the final fate of this application, which was denied. It must have been clear to Davis that McClung had deteriorated so badly over the years that he no longer was able to command men.

Now dangerously unstable, Alex McClung was avoided even by his friends. His finances were depleted, and he had to resort to borrowing money to get by. He finally took the only escape open to a gentleman of his time: suicide. On March 25, 1855, while staying in the Eagle Hotel in Jackson, Mississippi, he placed a small derringer to his head and ended his turbulent life. By his body was found the poem "Invocation to Death,"[31] which he had composed for the occasion. McClung was buried in the Vicksburg Cemetary in the Coleman family lot beneath a small marker.

The only battle flag of the 1st Mississippi still known to exist resides in the Mississippi Department of Archives and History.[32] The flag was donated to the Department by Mrs. Sarita Tamplet of Brenham, Texas, daughter of George W. Campbell, the regimental flag bearer. This flag was made by the ladies of Columbus, Mississippi, and presented to the Tombigbee Volunteers by the daughter of Maj. Thomas Blewett. The design consists of thirteen red and white silk stripes with a blue canton on which was displayed twenty-eight silver stars, one star for each state in the union at that time. The present physical condition of this flag is poor, all of the stars having been cut out by Varina Howell Davis during the years immediately following the War Between the States. At that time Jefferson Davis was perceived by critics to be almost solely responsible for the Confederacy's defeat, and several of his old friends had denounced him publicly. To some of those who had remained true to their friendship, Mrs. Davis presented a star taken from the flag. Whether any of these stars yet exist is not known, but their ownership must have represented a very special badge of honor.

APPENDIX A

Personnel of the Mississippi Rifles

The list of personnel in this appendix was transcribed from three rolls of microfilm (National Archives Microfilm Series, M-863, Records of the Adjutant General's Office, Compiled Service Records, Mexican War). The microfilm was generously lent to the author by The Papers of Jefferson Davis, of Rice University.

Before using this roster, the reader should observe several caveats. The microfilm records were holographic copies of copies of original holographic records, often transcribed with phonetic spellings. One should expect, for example, to see names like "Schaefer" spelled "Shaifer" or some other phonetic variation. The temptation to change such spellings was resisted; the roster in this appendix lists names exactly as they were recorded for the compiled service record. One should also be aware that this roster might not be complete; the list simply contains those names that appeared on the compiled service record—no more, no less. A more informed reader might want to pencil in correct spellings and add names to this list that have been inadvertently omitted.

Beside each soldier's name, short comments will usually appear. These summaries have been taken from the compiled records, and have been included as points of interest and to amplify on the data appearing in the narrative. For example, when one reads that illness took a heavy toll on the Mississippians when they were camped at the mouth of the Rio Grande River, one needs only to enumerate from this list to verify the truth of that statement. For economy of effort, a soldier's rank is not included if he remained a private throughout his tour of duty. All other ranks are included. The comments are sometimes amusing, but are mostly grim reminders of the many sacrifices made by the volunteers from Mississippi to serve their country.

Company A: The Yazoo Guards

John Akin	
D. F. Bailey	discharged for disabilities at the mouth of Rio Grande, Aug 19, 1846.
Winston Banks	
Daniel H. Batton	promoted Corp., Feb, 1847.
James H. Bell	Corp., discharged for disabilities at the mouth of Rio Grande, Aug 25, 1846.
Noah Bisbee	left in hospital, Monterey, Dec 10, 1846.
Ferdinand Bostick	Sgt., elected 1st Lieut., Sept 7, 1846, absent without leave since Oct 1, 1846, dropped from rolls, Feb 10, 1847.
Edward Bowman	promoted to Sgt., discharged for disabilities, Cerralvo, Oct 29, 1846.
John Bradley	
George Brook	wounded, Battle of Buena Vista, Feb 23, died of wounds, Mar 2, 1847.
Alonzo Brown	
Philip J. Burris	1st Lieut., resigned July 22, 1846.
Samuel S. Caldwell	musician.
A. C. Capshaw	discharged for disability, mouth of the Rio Grande, Aug 22, 1846.
William W. Capshaw	died at Matamoros, Oct 2, 1846.
Samuel K. Carter	
Henry D. Clark	wounded, Battle of Buena Vista, Feb 23, lost rifle and equipment on battlefield.

Francis Colton	discharged for disability, mouth of the Rio Grande, Aug 8, 1846.
Amos B. Corwin	elected 1st Lieut., Feb 15, 1847.
Andrew J. Cowart	died, Matamoros, Sept 15, 1846.
John Dillon	discharged for disability, Cerralvo, Oct 29, 1846.
Elijah Dixon	discharged for disability, Matamoros, Sept 28, 1846.
Thomas J. Ellis	died, mouth of the Rio Grande, Aug 17, 1846.
Robert Fisher	promoted to Sgt., Mar 10, 1847.
Elijah Floyd	
Henry Floyd	discharged for disability, mouth of the Rio Grande, Aug 19, 1846.
Daniel Forbes	died, Matamoros, Sept, 1846.
Edwin Fox	discharged for disability, Cerralvo, Oct 29, 1846.
Solomon Gardner	discharged for disability, Monterey, Dec 4, 1846.
Richard S. Gerrald	deserted, Vicksburg, July 7, 1846.
William G. Gerrald	discharged for disability, mouth of the Rio Grande, Aug 28, 1846.
Charles R. Gordon	discharged for disability, Matamoros, Sept 19, 1846.
Richard Green	discharged for disability, Monterey, Dec 4, 1846.
R. Henderson Griffin	discharged for disability, Cerralvo, Oct 19, 1846.
Thomas R. Griffin	promoted Corp., Sept 18, 1846.
Caleb Grimes	died, Cerralvo, Oct 6, 1846.
Meredith Hart	discharged for disability, Monterey, Dec 5, 1846.
Andrew J. Herrod	
Thomas Higginbotham	promoted Sgt., Mar 10, 1847.
Albert P. Hill	promoted to 1st Sgt., Sept 8, discharged for disability, Monterey, Jan 10, 1847.

D. W. Hollingsworth	musician, promoted Sgt. Jan 15, 1847.
Daniel Hughes	drummed out of the service July 22, 1846, by sentence of court martial, New Orleans.
William Ingraham	appointed Sgt., Feb 1847, killed, Battle of Buena Vista, Feb 23.
Albert Johnston	teamster, Dec 9, 1846.
John Johnson	
Henry R. Kenna	
John W. Kirk	discharged for disability, mouth of the Rio Grande, Aug 8, 1846.
Samuel D. Lavender	discharged for disability, mouth of the Rio Grande, Aug 8, 1846.
Charles A. Leake	discharged for disability, mouth of the Rio Grande, Aug 19, 1846.
Henry S. Little	
Madison M. Mason	discharged for disability, Monterey, Dec 4, 1846.
Charles I. Miller	promoted Cpl., Sept 18, 1846.
James M. Miller	discharged for disability, mouth of the Rio Grande, Aug 22, 1846.
William J. Miller	Cpl., died, Matamoros, Oct 1, 1846.
Middleton R. Mobley	
William Moore	discharged for disability, Matamoros, Oct 1, 1846.
Joseph W. Morris	wounded in left wrist, Battle of Buena Vista, Feb 23.
Joseph W. Morton	discharged for disability, Matamoros, Oct 1, 1846.
James O'Bryant	
Cornelius O'Sullivan	killed, Battle of Buena Vista, Feb 23.
Samuel C. Parker	discharged for disability, mouth of the Rio Grande, Aug 8, 1846.
Peter A. Paul	discharged for disability, Matamoros, Sept 28, 1846.
William H. Peaster	died, mouth of the Rio Grande, Aug 10, 1846.

Joseph H. Penny	
Moses S. Phillips	Cpl., elected 2nd. Lieut., date unknown.
W. A. Prestridge	discharged for disability, Matamoros, Sept 28, 1846.
Emory Prewett	discharged for disability, Matamoros, Oct 1, 1846.
Jesse Read	discharged for disability, New Orleans, July 23, 1846.
Licurgos D. Reed	died, Monterey, Nov 13, 1846.
James Richards	discharged for disability, mouth of the Rio Grande, Aug 19, 1846.
Benjamin F. Ridley	discharged for disability, mouth of the Rio Grande, Aug 27, 1846.
Calvin Schnebely	died, Matamoros, Sept 13, 1846.
John M. Sharp	Capt., severely wounded, Battle of Buena Vista, Feb 23.
Robert L. Shook	wounded, Battle of Buena Vista, Feb 23.
Thomas P. Slade	2nd Lieut.
John Standin	discharged for disability, Monterey, Dec 4, 1846.
David Stephens	died, Matamoros, Sept 25, 1846.
Wm. H. Stubblefield	wounded, Battle of Buena Vista, Feb 23.
S. Stubblefield	wounded, Battle of Buena Vista, Feb 23.
Robert Swisher	discharged for disability, Monterey, Nov 29, 1846.
James W. Thomas	discharged for disability, Matamoros, Dec 5, 1846.
John R. Ware	
Christopher Wedekin	Due Government one brass mounted rifle.
Harry West	died, Cerralvo, Nov 2, 1846.
Samuel W. White	severely wounded, Battle of Monterey, Sept 21, 1846, elected 2nd Lieut., Feb 3.
James W. Whitman	discharged for disability, Matamoros, Sept 25, 1846.
Ulysses Whitman	died, Camargo, Sept 7, 1846.

George Williams	discharged for disability, mouth of the Rio Grande, Aug 22, 1846.
Robert F. Williams	Sgt., discharged for disability, mouth of Rio Grande, Aug 19, 1846.
John Wooldridge	died, Cerralvo, Sept 28, 1846.

Company B: The Wilkinson Guards

James B. Baird	detailed for duty at Cerralvo, left sick on the march.
Benjamin Bass	
Francis Best	Cpl. promoted to Sgt., Dec 18, 1846.
William J. Bryan	
Albert G. Cage Jr.	transferred to Col. John Hays Regt. Mounted Rifles, Sept 3, 1846, Camargo.
Benjamin M. Cage	promoted Cpl., Dec 18, 1846.
William L. Cage	discharged for disabilities, Monterey, Oct 13, 1846.
James Calhoun	2nd Lieut.
Ido Carriger	
James D. Caulfield	discharged, Sept 14, 1846, employed as Asst. Surgeon Sept 15.
Reuben W. Chance	wounded in forehead, Monterey, Sept 23, died of wounds, Sept 25, 1846.
Richard F. Clampett	discharged for disability, mouth of the Rio Grande, Aug 10, 1846.
Thomas G. Conner	
Douglas H. Cooper	Capt., acting Major, Oct 20, 1846.
William A. Cotton	
Noland Dixon	discharged for disability, mouth of the Rio Grande, Aug 24, 1846.
James W. Donnelly	wounded, Battle of Buena Vista, Feb 23.
Charles Erambert	Cpl., promoted to Sgt., Dec 13, 1846.
Claiborne Farish	Sgt.
Joseph S. Fuqua	discharged for disability, mouth of the Rio Grande, Aug 2, 1846.

J. G. Gayden	
Thomas H. Hampton	
David B. Harris	
Samuel R. Harrison	2nd Lieut.
John Q. Herbert	discharged for disability, Monterey, Nov 22, 1846.
James Hill	
James L. Hodge	discharged for disability, Monterey, Oct 14, 1846.
William I. Hodge	promoted Cpl., Dec 13, 1846.
John L. Holt	private secretary to Gen. Quitman.
John T. Holt	Cpl.
William G. Hope	discharged for disability, Camargo, Sept 6, 1846.
Irenius Hutchinson	
James H. Jackson	wounded, Battle of Monterey, Sept 21, died in hospital, Oct 2, 1846.
George H. Jones	wounded slightly in the back of the neck at Monterey.
Seaborn Jones	killed, Battle of Buena Vista, Feb 23.
James J. Kearsey	
A. Lanehart	discharged for disability, Monterey, Dec 1, 1846.
A. C. Lanehart	discharged for disability, mouth of the Rio Grande, Aug 19, 1846.
William A. Lawrence	
Thomas H. Law	drummer, discharged for disability, Monterey, Oct 3, 1846.
James Lennex	
Hugh N. Linsey	discharged for disability, Monterey, Oct 13, 1846.
Robert H. Lowry	discharged for disability, Monterey, Oct 13, 1846.
James Martin	
Eugene Massell	Sgt., discharged, Dec 7, 1846, reenlisted, Jan 29, 1847.
J. F. N. McClure	discharged for disability, mouth of the Rio Grande, Aug 10, 1846.

Robert McConnell	Sgt.
Daniel R. McGahee	
James M. Miller	wounded, Battle of Buena Vista, Feb 23.
Robert Miller	Cpl., died at Victoria, Jan 8, 1847.
William H. Miller	severely wounded in left knee, Battle of Monterey, Sept 21, discharged, Jan 28, 1847.
Hiram Morgan	
Mayberry S. Morris	discharged for disability, Camargo, Sept 6, 1846.
David Murray	
Barney Murtough	
Robert H. Neeland	discharged for disability, Monterey, Feb 12, 1847.
Alexander Newman	discharged for disability, Matamoros, Sept 24, 1846.
Solomon Newman	wounded, Battle of Buena Vista, Feb 23.
James Nicholson	discharged for disability, Matamoros, Oct 26, 1846.
Henry F. O'Neal	discharged for disability, Monterey, Feb 16, 1847.
Carnot Posey	1st Lieut., slightly wounded, Battle of Buena Vista Feb 23.
William R. Rhea	
George P. Richardson	discharged for disability, Matamoros, Oct 18, 1846.
Saul I. Richardson	
James Riddle	
George Rivercomb	promoted Cpl., Feb 14, 1847.
John Robinson	
William S. Rotrammel	discharged for disability, Camargo, Sept 6, 1846.
Samuel Small	died, Saltillo, March 16, 1847.
George A. Smith	
Hampton Smith	discharged for disability, mouth of the Rio Grande, Aug 10, 1846.
James L. Smith	
Peter Smith	discharged, Monterey, Nov 2, 1846.

Frederick Schneider	taken prisoner by the enemy, Buena Vista, returned in exchange, March 3, 1847.
Walter Spurlock	
Weldon W. Strauss	discharged for disability, mouth of the Rio Grande, Aug 10, 1846.
James D. Steward	discharged for disability, mouth of the Rio Grande, Aug 24, 1846.
Wesley Steward	discharged for disability, Matamoros, Sept 24, 1846.
C. J. Strangher	discharged for disability, Monterey, Oct 13, 1846.
Clarke H. Tigner	discharged for disability, Monterey, Feb 2, 1847.
Thomas H. Tilley	killed, Battle of Buena Vista, Feb 23.
B. Lewis Turberville	killed, Battle of Buena Vista, Feb 23.
William D. Way	discharged for disability, Matamoros, Oct 18, 1846.
Douglas West	Sgt., discharged for disability, Monterey, Dec 7, 1846.
J. Monroe Westrope	
Theodore White	discharged for disability, Monterey, Oct 13, 1846.
Kinyon R. Whittington	discharged for disability, Monterey, Nov 2, 1846.
William I. Wilkinson	killed, Battle of Buena Vista, Feb 23.
William Woosley	
Charles Wolger	discharged for disability, Matamoros, Oct 23, 1846.

Company C: The Vicksburg Southrons

R. H. Abbott	discharged for disabilities at mouth of Rio Grande, Aug 19, 1846.
Henry L. Armour	discharged for disabilities at the mouth of Rio Grande, Aug 20, 1846.
Rufus K. Arthur	elected from sergeant to 2nd Lieut.,

	July 1, 1846, wounded Monterey, Sept 21, 1846.
Robert B. Banks	discharged, Saltillo, March 1, 1847, to be employed as surgeon at hospital.
Charles Barnes	sick in Cerralvo, Sept 15, discharged at Monterey, Nov 20, 1846.
John M. Barnes	wounded, Feb 23, 1847.
Theodore Batts	discharged for disabilities at Matamoros, Sept 21, 1846.
Charles T. Bradford	
Ira O. Bradford	discharged for sickness, Matamoros, Oct 8, 1846.
William H. Bright	discharged for disabilities, Monterey, Oct 9, 1846.
George W. Brown	discharged for disabilities, Matamoros, Sept 28, 1846.
Adam Brownlee	discharged for disabilities, Matamoros, Sept 28, 1846.
Francis Clark	
William H. Clements	
J. N. Collier	promoted to Cpl., Jan, 1847, slight wound in back, [Battle of Buena Vista?].
Samuel Collins	discharged for disability, Matamoros, Sept 28, 1846.
James W. Conn	severely wounded, Battle of Buena Vista, Feb 23.
Benjamin Conner	
Henry F. Cook	1st Lieut., slightly wounded, Monterey, Sept 21, 1846.
William Couch	killed, Battle of Buena Vista, Feb 23.
John Craft	
Edward Currie	
John M. Daughtry	
Robert H. Davis	discharged for disability, Monterey, Oct 9, 1846.
John S. Denson	musician, enlisted July 20, 1846, New Orleans.

A. L. Dixon	discharged for disability, Matamoros, Sept 28, 1846.
Philip B. Dixon	discharged for disability, mouth of the Rio Grande, Aug 7, 1846.
Stephen Dodds	appointed drum major, Aug 8, 1846.
John Dugan	absent without leave after May 20, 1847.
George H. Dunn	
Dick H. Eggleston	killed, Battle of Buena Vista, Feb 23.
Charles H. Ellis	
William H. Fleming	wounded, Battle of Monterey, Sept 21, discharged, Nov 2, 1846.
Henry F. Ford	
Benjamin Forkes	discharged for disability, Matamoros, Sept 28, 1846.
James Forkes	discharged for disability, Matamoros, Sept 28, 1846.
William J. Frier	discharged, May 15, 1847 to reenlist in 2nd Miss. Rifles.
Edward Gaffney	
Josiah H. Godwin	discharged for disability, Monterey, Oct 25, 1846.
George H. Gray	
Richard Griffith	2nd Lieut, Adjutant, appointed July 24.
J. M. Guy	deserted, Vicksburg, July 10, 1846.
James Gwinn	musician, discharged, mouth of the Rio Grande, unworthy for the service.
Seymour Halsey	transferred, appointed surgeon by the President, July 7, 1846.
William E. Harris	died of diarrhea, Cerralvo, Oct 4, 1846.
Andrew Hartley	discharged for disability, Matamoros, Oct 29, 1846.
William R. Hamby	discharged for disability, mouth of the Rio Grande, Aug 19, 1846.
William V. Hickie	Cpl., promoted to Sgt., July 1, 1846.
Samuel Hindman	discharged for disability, Matamoros, Sept 28, 1846.
Joseph D. Howell	discharged for disability, Monterey, Dec 5, 1846.

James Irvine	
John Jeter	
James Johnson	killed, Battle of Buena Vista, Feb 23.
P. W. Johnson	severely wounded, Monterey, Sept 21, discharged, Monterey, Oct 23, 1846.
Wesley Maples	discharged for disability, Matamoros, Sept 28, 1846.
John B. Markham	Cpl., wounded severely, Monterey, Sept 21, discharged, Monterey, Oct 20, 1846.
Russell M. Martin	
Daniel A. McKay	discharged for disability, Camargo, Sept 6, 1846.
Robert McKay	discharged for disability, mouth of the Rio Grande, Aug 22, 1846.
J. A. McLaughlin	Cpl., wounded, Battle of Buena Vista, Feb 23, promoted Sgt., April 9, 1847.
George E. Metcalf	
Joseph Miller	
Howard Morris	promoted Cpl., July 1, 1846, severely wounded, Battle of Buena Vista, Feb 23.
William M. Nutter	
James D. Peck	discharged for disability, Matamoros, Sept 28, 1846.
John Preston	killed, Battle of Buena Vista, Feb 23.
Henry L. Puckett	Sgt.
Andrew L. Richards	discharged for disability, Matamoros, Sept 28, 1846.
Robert E. Richardson	
C. H. Russell	discharged for disability, Monterey, Oct 20, 1846.
William Henry Scott	Sgt., slightly wounded, Battle of Buena Vista, Feb 23.
Benjamin M. Sims	
David Sims	discharged for disability, Matamoros, Nov 3, 1846.
William R. Skelton	

J. N. Stephenson	
Levi H. Stevens	wounded slightly, Battle of Buena Vista, Feb 23.
Henry Stout	
John Stout	discharged for disability, Matamoros, Sept 28, 1846.
William G. Street	
F. J. Streibeck	
Samuel C. Sust	wounded, Battle of Buena Vista, Feb 23.
Green B. Taylor	
Washington Thames	discharged for disability, Matamoros, Sept 28, 1846.
Henry B. Thompson	wounded, Battle of Monterey, Sept 21, discharged, Oct 20, 1846.
Thomas W. Tilden	discharged for disability, Monterey, March 11, 1847.
Louis Tillman	discharged for disability, Matamoros, Oct 29, 1846.
Lewis M. Turner	killed, Battle of Monterey, Sept 21, while advancing on the third fort.
Edward L. Vantress	
N. G. Watts	Sgt. acting Sgt. Maj., June 10 to Dec 20, 1846.
Samuel Wharton	
George D. Williamson	discharged for disability, Monterey, Oct 23, 1846.
John Willis	Capt.
John C. Winn	discharged for disability, Monterey, Dec 5, 1846.
James N. Wood	discharged for disability, Matamoros, Sept 28, 1846.
J. O. Woodruff	discharged for disability, Monterey, Oct 3, 1846.

Company D: Carroll County Guards

F. Marion Adaire	
J. Granger Adaire	promoted sergeant Jan 1847.

Pinckney G. Adkinson	
Richard Applegate	left sick at Monterey, Jan 30, 1847.
Egbert F. Beall	promoted from Cpl. to Serg., Feb, 1847.
Harrison B. Beard	
John C. Benthall	discharged Sept 18, 1846, at Matamoros, wounded in line of duty, Matamoros.
James W. Blake	promoted Cpl. Sept 14, 1846, discharged for disabilities, Apl 29, 1847.
Thomas Brown	sent back to Camargo sick, Sept 8, 1846.
John Buckholts	discharged for disabilities, Matamoros, Sept 12, 1846.
James Burrell	discharged for disability in line of duty incurred near Monterey, Dec 12, 1846.
David Capshaw	
Young Carr	discharged for disability, Matamoros, Sept 18, 1846.
Robert Clark	discharged for disability incurred in the line of duty, Monterey, Dec 4, 1846.
Alpheus Cobb	found on Sept 23, dead on battlefield of 21 inst. shot in head, chest, and thigh.
Daniel P. Cocke	promoted to Cpl., Aug 6, 1846.
John Cokely	promoted to Cpl., Dec 10, 1846.
Samuel Colbourn	discharged for disability, mouth of the Rio Grande, Aug 23, 1846.
Henry Creamer	
Thomas B. Davidson	
David R. Doyle	discharged for disability, Monterey, Oct 12, 1846.
J. Durden	Cpl., discharged for disability, mouth of the Rio Grande, Aug 10, 1846.
W. T. S. Durham	discharged for disability, Monterey, Oct 12, 1846.

John G. Elliott	
John Erwin	
Andrew Ewing	
R. Fields	discharged for disability, Matamoros, Sept 11, 1846.
Joel Forbes	discharged for disability, Matamoros, Sept 18, 1846.
Charles A. Forster	musician, transferred to Alabama Vols., Sept 6, 1846.
J. D. M. Gage	discharged for disability, Monterey, Oct 12, 1846.
James Z. George	discharged on petition, Monterey, Oct 12, 1846.
William P. Gray	dishonorably discharged, March 29, 1847.
William Gunter	discharged for disability, Monterey, Dec 12, 1846.
Harmon G. Hall	discharged for disability, Matamoros, Sept 12, 1846.
Marion Hanks	discharged for disability, Matamoros, Sept 12, 1846.
T. Hanks	discharged for disability, Matamoros, Sept 18, 1846.
John R. Harper	discharged for disability, Matamoros, Sept 18, 1846.
Wells C. Harrell	promoted 1st Sgt., Aug 8, 1846.
J. B. Heath	discharged for disability, Monterey, Oct 12, 1846.
Benjamin Hodge	elected 2nd Lieut., resigned Aug 19, 1846.
Warren Hoffman	wounded, Battle of Monterey, discharged for disability, Oct 18, 1846.
E. W. Hollingsworth	elected 2nd Lieut., Jan 5, 1847.
Bainbridge D. Howard	Capt.
Lewis T. Howard	2nd Lieut., wounded, Battle of Monterey, Sept 23, resigned Dec 30, 1846.

Alford Hudson	discharged for disability, Monterey, Oct 23, 1846.
David W. Jefferson	
James Johnson	died, Matamoros, Sept 11, 1846.
William H. Jones	
Owen W. Jones	absent without leave since June 12, 1847.
Thomas J. Kyle	Cpl., elected 2nd Lieut. Sept 6, resigned Dec 30, 1846, Monterey.
Robert A. Lewis	promoted Sgt., Sept 14, 1846.
William Lott	discharged for disability, mouth of the Rio Grande, Aug 9, 1846.
David E. Love	Sgt.
Richard Martin	discharged for disability, mouth of the Rio Grande, Aug 9, 1846.
William D. Martin	discharged, Aug 10, 1846.
Neil McAllister	
John McCauly	discharged for disability, mouth of the Rio Grande, Aug 9, 1846.
Andrew J. McClenden	discharged for disability, Matamoros, date unknown.
James A. McCoy	discharged for disability, Matamoros, Sept 18, 1846.
Lewis Mootry	
Samuel S. Monday	discharged for disability, mouth of the Rio Grande, Aug 9, 1846.
Ceasar L. Nixon	died, Cerralvo, Oct 9, 1846.
Benjamin F. Newman	hospital steward.
Hiram G. Norman	discharged for disability, mouth of the Rio Grande, Aug 9, 1846.
William Orr	
Frank F. Pleasants	promoted Cpl., Aug 23, discharged for disability, Matamoros, Sept 17, 1846.
Andrew Powell	discharged for disability, mouth of the Rio Grande, Aug 21, 1846.
George W. Ramsey	killed from a wound in the belly, Battle of Monterey, received Sept 21, died Sept 23, 1846.

James M. Ramsey	Sgt., discharged, Monterey, Dec 12, 1846.
Hugh A. Reynolds	promoted Cpl., April 29, 1847.
John Q. Reynolds	died, Matamoros, Nov 6, 1846.
Sherod Reynolds	discharged for disability, Cerralvo, Oct 31, 1846.
Benjamin B. Rhodes	discharged for disability, mouth of the Rio Grande, Aug 8, 1846.
Daniel R. Russell	1st Lieut., elected Capt., Aug 23, 1846
L. H. Russell	discharged for disability, Monterey, Feb 1, 1847.
John Shooke	discharged for disability, Matamoros, Sept 25, 1846.
James Somerville	
Jessie Strickland	fifer, discharged for disability, Monterey, Dec 12, 1846.
Benjamin F. Taylor	promoted Cpl., Apl 29, 1847.
Memory Taylor	discharged for disability, mouth of the Rio Grande, Aug 9, 1846.
Leonidas Trousdale	promoted Cpl., Jan 5, 1847.
G. W. Vance	
John D. Vance	
Daniel Waganon	killed in an affray, Feb 27, 1847.
Marcus C. Wellons	Sgt., discharged for disability, mouth of the Rio Grande, Aug 23, 1846.
David Wilgus	discharged for disability, Matamoros, Sept 25, 1846.
Richard Williams	
John N. B. Williamson	
George Wills	wounded, Battle of Monterey, Sept 21, discharged, Monterey, Oct 22, 1846.
F. Parker Wood	discharged for disability, mouth of Rio Grande, Aug 10, 1846.
Robert P. Wynns	promoted Cpl., Sept 14, 1846.
Albert Young	discharged for disability, Monterey, Dec 12, 1846.
Samuel A. Young	Sgt., discharged for disability, mouth of the Rio Grande, Aug 9, 1846.

Appendix A

Company E: Jackson Fencibles

John H. Bowman	promoted to Sgt., March 1, 1847.
Charles M. Bradford	elected 2nd Lieut., July 1, 1846.
Henry H. Bryan	
A. P. Burnham	wounded, Monterey, Sept 21, died of wounds, Sept 25, 1846.
William A. Butler	discharged for disability, Vicksburg, July 10, 1846.
John Campbell	discharged for disability, New Orleans, July 22, 1846.
Richard Clariday	wounded, Battle of Buena Vista, Feb 23.
Edward W. Cohea	
John Coleman	discharged for disability, Monterey, Oct 12, 1846.
Daniel Conner	
Solomon M. Coulter	
Patrick Deigman	discharged for disability, New Orleans, July 23, 1846.
James Donald	
B. H. Edwards	discharged for disability, Matamoros, Sept 12, 1846.
William E. Estes	Cpl., promoted to Sgt., March 1847.
George H. Farrar	discharged for disability, mouth of the Rio Grande, Aug 24, 1846.
Fred. Fauntleroy	discharged Dec 1, 1846.
George P. Findley	discharged for disability, Matamoros, Sept 24, 1846.
Crawford Fletcher	1st Lieut.
Marsellus A. Foute	Cpl., discharged for disability, Monterey, Oct 12, 1846.
Robert Fox	wounded, Battle of Buena Vista, Feb 23.
David Frazier	
Jacob Freidrick	discharged for disability, Monterey, Oct 12, 1846.
Hugh Gourley	discharged for disability, mouth of the Rio Grande, Aug 9, 1846.

Milton F. Gourley	discharged for disability, mouth of the Rio Grande, Aug 19, 1846.
James S. Griffin	
John Harrison	
William B. Hasty	
James Higdon	
Henry Hipple	
Calvin Hobbs	musician, fifer.
John M. Hooker	discharged for disability, Matamoros, Sept 24, 1846.
Archibald M. Hughes	Sgt.
James H. Hughes	2nd Lieut.
James W. Hunter	
Robert A. Joyce	killed, Battle of Buena Vista, Feb 23.
Henry V. Keep	discharged, Monterey, Oct 12, 1846, under age.
John Kennedy	wounded, Battle of Buena Vista, Feb 23.
William Kenny	
James H. Kilvey	
George W. Laird	promoted Cpl., March 1, 1847.
Isham C. Laird	wounded, Battle of Buena Vista, Feb 23.
Jeremiah E. Lairy	
Samuel Lane	promoted to Cpl., March 1, 1846.
Joseph H. Langford	Sgt., killed, Battle of Buena Vista, Feb 23.
William R. Langford	Cpl., discharged for disability, mouth of the Rio Grande, Aug 15, 1846.
William Lowe	discharged for disability, Monterey, Nov 13, 1846.
James Lowry	
James B. Lyerly	discharged for disability, Monterey, Nov 2, 1846.
William H. Marrs	discharged for disability, Matamoros, Sept 24, 1846.
Samuel Marsh	
William S. Martin	transferred to Tenn. Vols., Oct 19, 1846.
John L. McManus	Capt.

Evander McNair	Cpl. promoted Sgt., date unknown.
Z. McNully	discharged for disability, mouth of the Rio Grande, Aug 8, 1846.
Silas Meachem	killed, Battle of Monterey, Sept 21, 1846.
James Moore	discharged for disability, mouth of the Rio Grande, Aug 15, 1846.
Jessey W. Moss	
J. M. Myrick	
M. G. Myrick	
Andrew B. Patterson	Sgt.
I. Camp Perkins	
William W. Philips	Sgt., killed, Battle of Buena Vista, Feb 23.
George Phillips	
Hugh W. Pierce	wounded, Battle of Monterey, Sept 21, discharged, Monterey, Oct 10, 1846.
Henry Pomroy	
Archibald G. Price	promoted Cpl., March 1, 1847.
Anthony B. Puckett	promoted Cpl., March 1, 1847.
James Rawlings	died, Carralvo, Oct 1, 1846.
Joseph C. Revill	killed, Battle of Buena Vista, Feb 23.
John Ritch	
Edward W. Roberts	discharged for disability, mouth of the Rio Grande, Aug 15, 1846.
D. H. Robinson	discharged for disability, mouth of the Rio Grande, Aug 19, 1846.
James M. Robinson	Cpl., killed, Battle of Buena Vista, Feb 23.
A. Govan Rowe	discharged for disability, Monterey, Dec 12, 1846.
E. J. Runnels	discharged for disability, mouth of the Rio Grande, Aug 18, 1846.
William Schad	wounded in right thigh, Battle of Monterey, Sept 21, discharged, Monterey, Jan 27, right leg amputated.
Samuel Scruggs	died, Monterey, Oct 18, 1846.

William Sellers	killed, Battle of Buena Vista, Feb 23.
Calvin A. Shelton	
James M. Shelton	died, Matamoros, Sept 23, 1846.
Lewis Siples	
Marshall M. Smith	discharged for disability, Monterey, Nov 2, 1846.
Thaddeus T. Sorsby	discharged for disability, mouth of the Rio Grande, Aug 15, 1846.
William P. Spencer	
William L. Stacy	discharged for disability, Vicksburg, July 10, 1846.
John Stafford	physician, worked in Medical Dept.
Robert J. Steele	
Hugh P. Timmin	discharged for disability, Matamoros, Sept 24, 1846.
G. E. Upson	discharged for disability, Matamoros, Oct 6, 1846.
William Wade	discharged for disability, mouth of the Rio Grande, Aug 15, 1846.
John Waldrop	discharged for disability, Matamoros, Sept 21, 1846.
James Walsh	
James Ward	
James Waugh	wounded, Battle of Buena Vista, Feb 23.
James W. Williams	discharged for disability, Matamoros, Sept 24, 1846.
John N. Williams	
John R. Williams	discharged for disability, mouth of the Rio Grande, Aug 15, 1846.

Company F: Lafayette Guards

Haney C. Ater	
James N. Bigby	wounded, Battle of Buena Vista, Feb 23, left arm amputated.
James W. Blakely	promoted Cpl., killed, Battle of Buena Vista, Feb 23.
James Boyd	deserted Oct 22, 1846, Cerralvo, owes

	U. S. for two rifles, having lost one prior.
Thomas Bragg	discharged for disability, Cerralvo, Oct 26, 1846.
D. A. Brittain	discharged for disabilities, Cerralvo, Oct 26, 1846.
William H. Broach	died, Matamoros, Oct 12, 1846.
William N. Brown	elected 1st Lieut.
Andrew G. Browning	discharged for disabilities, mouth of Rio Grande, Aug 2, 1846.
J. C. Browning	
Thomas Buie	discharged for disabilities, Monterey, Mar 15, 1847.
Andrew T. Burks	discharged for disabilities, Matamoros, Sept 12, 1846.
D. L. Butler	killed, Battle of Buena Vista, Feb 23.
James Campbell	died, Cerralvo, Oct 19, 1846.
Jacob H. Carger	Cpl.
M. D. C. Carloss	Sgt., died Oct 3, 1846, Matamoros.
M. H. Carr	discharged for disability, Matamoros, Sept 28, 1846.
William A. Carr Jr.	died, Cerralvo, Oct 23, 1846.
Jacob R. Chester	musician until Oct 20, transferred to Q. M., wagoner.
James M. Childers	discharged for disability, mouth of the Rio Grande, Aug 8, 1846.
William G. Cloak	
Thomas Coatney	severely wounded in left arm, Battle of Buena Vista, Feb 23.
John Connor	
Thomas A. Davis	discharged for disability, mouth of the Rio Grande, Aug 20, 1846.
Waller Davis	discharged for disability, mouth of the Rio Grande, Aug 24, 1846.
William Delay	Capt.
A. S. Dixon	3rd Sgt., promoted to 1st Sgt, June 1846.

Peter J. Dunevant	killed, Battle of Buena Vista, Feb 23.
W. W. Eaton	discharged for disability, mouth of the Rio Grande, Aug 24, 1846.
D. M. Gardner	discharged for disability, Monterey, Dec 8, 1846.
Enos Garrott	killed, Battle of Buena Vista, Feb 23.
William H. Gee	discharged for disability, mouth of the Rio Grande, Aug 9, 1846.
Crawford Goodwin	
George Goodwin	discharged for disability, Cerralvo, Oct 26, 1846.
J. A. G. Hancock	discharged for disability, Monterey, Nov 23, 1846.
James A. Henderson	discharged for disability, Matamoros, Sept 28, 1846.
Rufus Henry	discharged for disability, Matamoros, Sept 12, 1846.
R. C. Higginbottom	discharged for disability, mouth of the Rio Grande, Aug 20, 1846.
Joseph P. Hobbs	discharged for disability, Matamoros, Sept 8, 1846, Cpl.
Benjamin Hagany	promoted Sgt., Sept 8, killed in Battle of Buena Vista, Feb 23, 1847.
J. K. Holcomb	died, Matamoros, date unknown.
William Holt	transfer to Tenn. Vols., Nov 10, 1846.
W. R. Humphries	assassinated by Mexicans near Monterey, Dec 7, 1846.
S. D. Hunter	discharged for disability, Matamoros, Oct 1, 1846.
David R. Jimerson	discharged for disability, mouth of the Rio Grande, Aug 8, 1846.
Benjamin F. Joiner	died, Matamoros, Oct 23, 1846.
Stephen Jones	killed, Battle of Buena Vista, Feb 23.
Thomas L. Jones	died, Vicksburg, July 12, 1846.
William H. Jones	discharged for disability, mouth of the Rio Grande, Aug 8, 1846.
Absolem Knight	died, Cerralvo, Sept 26, 1846.

Charles Lawson	died, Vicksburg, July 8, 1846.
Charles A. Lewers	discharged for disability, mouth of the Rio Grande, Aug 8, 1846.
A. M. Liles	assassinated by Mexicans, Cerralvo, Oct 11, 1846.
John Livingston	discharged for disability, mouth of the Rio Grande, Aug 8, 1846.
Mathew F. Locke	promoted Cpl., Feb 24, 1847.
John C. Lowe	discharged for disability, Matamoros, Sept 28, 1846.
John Luckett	
Samuel Luckett	
Fredrich J. Malone	2nd Lieut., resigned, Oct 31, reenlisted Jan 15, 1847 as Pvt.
Levi Maya	discharged for disability, mouth of the Rio Grande, Aug 24, 1846.
Alexander B. McFarland	died, Vicksburg, June 24, 1946.
Green McKie	died, Matamoros, date unknown.
Levi M. Meadows	died, Matamoros, Oct 7, 1846.
Charles Moon	
J. T. Morris	discharged for disability, mouth of the Rio Grande, Aug 6, 1846.
Joseph W. Morris	wounded in left wrist, Battle of Buena Vista, Feb 23.
James P. Mullinax	died, Matamoros, Oct 1, 1846.
William H. Owens	
W. S. Parker	died, Cerralvo, Nov 17, 1846.
D. E. Patterson	died, Cerralvo, Nov 2, 1846.
G. Peaterson	discharged for disability, Matamoros, Oct 28, 1846.
James L. Powell	discharged for disability, mouth of the Rio Grande, Aug 20, 1846.
William W. Redding	elected 2nd Lieut., July 1.
Robert J. Shaw	promoted to Sgt., Dec 1, 1846.
William Shuhorn	died, Cerralvo, Oct 10, 1846.
T. L. Simpson	wounded severely in left leg, Battle of

	Buena Vista, Feb 23, died, Apl 13, 1847.
Arthur St. John	discharged for disability, Cerralvo, Oct 26, 1846.
John P. Stockard	elected 2nd Lieut., Jan 29, 1847, slightly wounded, Battle of Buena Vista.
Joseph C. Stockard	discharged for disability, mouth of the Rio Grande, Aug 24, 1846.
John Strong	discharged for disability, Cerralvo, Oct 26, 1846.
William Strong	discharged for disability, Matamoros, Sept 28, 1846.
Thomas Swann	Sgt.
Josephus J. Tatum	Sgt., elected 2nd Lieut., Nov 16, died, Linares, Jan 20, 1847.
Wilson Taylor	discharged for disability, Matamoros, Oct 1, 1846.
William Thompson	promoted Sgt., Sept 8, 1846.
J. H. Tucker	discharged for disability, Monterey, Jan 30, 1847.
John E. Turnbull	
J. H. Turner	discharged for disability, Matamoros, Sept 28, 1846.
William G. Vaughn	discharged for disability, Matamoros, Oct 1, 1846.
E. D. Wallace	
John Webb	died, Cerralvo, Nov 3, 1846.
F. S. Welch	
C. S. Word	discharged for disability, Matamoros, Sept 28, 1846.
Oscar M. Zollicoffer	discharged for disability, Monterey, Nov 23, 1846.

Company G: Raymond Fencibles

W. D. Ainsworth	discharged for disabilities at Cerralvo, Nov 30, 1846.

J. M. Alexander	killed, Battle of Buena Vista Feb 23, 1847.
Jefferson L. Anderson	wounded in abdomen, Battle of Monterey, discharged Oct 14, 1846.
Thomas J. Anderson	discharged for disabilities at mouth of Rio Grande, Aug 11, 1846.
Asa B. Atkinson	wounded left thigh, Battle of Buena Vista, Feb 23, 1847.
George J. W. Bird	discharged for disabilities at mouth of Rio Grande, Aug 20, 1846.
Joseph E. Bond	killed at Buena Vista, Feb 23.
Robert Bowen	wounded in right arm, Monterey, Sept 21 1846, lost rifle when wounded, discharged. Oct 22, 1846.
James Boyd	died Sept 9, 1846, Camargo.
Thomas Bradley	
James S. Brown	discharged for disabilities, Monterey, Nov 12, 1846.
Charles M. Burland	discharged for disabilities, Monterey, Dec 5, 1846.
Philip Burnett	wounded, left elbow and hand, Battle of Buena Vista, Feb 23.
V. S. Burnett	discharged for disabilities, mouth of the Rio Grande, Aug 2, 1846.
Sidney S. Champion	discharged for disability, Matamoros, Sept 25, 1846.
John A. Chapman	
Theodore C. Chapman	promoted to Cpl., Mar 1, 1847.
E. F. Charlton	
Edward S. Charlton	Cpl., promoted to Sgt., Sept 6, 1846, transferred to 1st Tenn. Regt, Oct 8, 1846.
Watson E. Clark	died in hospital, Matamoros, Sept 15, 1846.
Jeptha Conger	transferred to Co. A, Sept 14, 1846.
Louis A. Cooper	killed, Battle of Buena Vista, Feb 23.
William G. Cooper	

Lewis Coorpender	discharged for disability, Monterey, Oct 22, 1846.
W. F. Coorpender	discharged for disability, Matamoros, Sept 16, 1846.
Reuben N. Downing	Capt., severely wounded in right arm, Monterey, Sept 21.
Elijah Dunlap	died in hospital, Monterey, Dec 3, 1846.
Benjamin F. Edwards	severely wounded on right thigh, Battle of Buena Vista, Feb 23.
Leon Eilbott	died in hospital, Monterey, Dec 22, 1846.
Joseph Fairchild	rifle stolen at Camp Allen, Monterey.
Robert Felts	killed, Battle of Buena Vista, Feb 23, rifle lost in battle, taken by enemy.
Samuel R. Fondren	discharged for disability, mouth of the Rio Grande, Aug 19, 1846.
William B. Gallman	discharged for disability, mouth of the Rio Grande, Aug 4, 1846.
Charles H. Gibbs	
James H. Graves	killed, Battle of Buena Vista, Feb 23.
Stephen A. D. Greaves	1st Lieut.
Peter O. D. Griffith	
Job Hammond	slightly wounded, left leg, Battle of Buena Vista, Feb 23.
William Henry Hampton	2nd Lieut.
George W. Harrison	3rd Cpl., slightly wounded in right shoulder and neck, Battle of Buena Vista, Feb 23.
J. C. Hays	3rd Sgt., discharged for disability, mouth of the Rio Grande, Aug 11, 1846.
May Hays	
Kemp Holland	Asst. Commissary.
William F. Hutchinson	transferred to Co. A., Sept 14, 1846.
Newton Ingram	

Daniel B. Johnston	discharged for disability, Matamoros, Sept 12, 1846.
David Jones	discharged for disability, Matamoros, Sept 28, 1846.
Daniel F. Kenner	died, mouth of the Rio Grande, Aug 9, 1846.
Albert M. Key	transferred to Co. A., Sept 13, 1846.
William Lindsey	musician, transferred Co. A., Sept 13, 1846.
William Maben	discharged for disability, Matamoros, Sept 25, 1846.
Thomas F. Mabry	discharged for disability, Matamoros, Sept 25, 1846.
J. H. Mallett	
L. J. Mapp	discharged for disability, mouth of the Rio Grande, Aug 20, 1846.
John A. Martin	transferred to Co. A, Sept 13, 1846, promoted to Cpl.
Malcolm McGinnis	
Francis McNulty	Sgt., elected 2nd Lieut., Sept 6, 1846, killed, Battle of Buena Vista, Feb 23.
Francis A. Mellon	Sgt., discharged for disability, mouth of the Rio Grande, Aug 12, 1846.
John R. Miller	discharged for disability, mouth of the Rio Grande, Aug 11, 1846.
John P. Moseley	
Jesse Odoms	slightly wounded in left hip, Battle of Buena Vista, Feb 23.
Richard E. Parr	killed, Battle of Buena Vista, Feb 23.
Alfred Patton	discharged for disability, Camargo, Sept 6, 1846.
Samuel Potts	killed, Battle of Monterey, Sept 21, 1846.
Milton Pyles	transferred to Co. C., Sept 14, 1846.
John F. Rimes	discharged for disability, Matamoros, Sept 28, 1846.
Nathan L. Rimes	lost one brass band percussion rifle.
Hiram D. Ripley	

William E. Ripley	
Joseph M. Roberts	Sgt.
Reuben Russell	transferred to Co. G, Sept 14, 1846, discharged for disability, Dec 5, 1846.
Romulus M. Saunders	
Thaddeus W. Saunders	slightly grazed in the throat, Battle of Buena Vista, Feb 23.
William Seay	killed, Battle of Buena Vista, Feb 23.
Eli Sellman	died, Aug 17, 1846, mouth of the Rio Grande.
Thomas Sellman	discharged for disability, mouth of the Rio Grande, Aug 11, 1846.
R. W. Shields	discharged for disability, Matamoros, Oct 8, 1846.
Peter Sinclair	Cpl., promoted Sgt., March 1, 1847, slightly wounded, right hand, Battle of Buena Vista, Feb 23.
E. W. Smith	discharged for disability, mouth of the Rio Grande, Aug 11, 1846.
T. C. Smith	discharged for disability, mouth of the Rio Grande, Aug 19, 1846.
S. D. Sojourner	discharged for disability, Monterey, Oct 2, 1846.
Stephen B. Stafford	discharged for disability, mouth of the Rio Grande, Aug 20, 1846.
John H. Stewart	Sgt.
Joshua Stone	promoted Sgt., Aug 11, 1846.
Thomas L. Sumrall	
Samuel B. Thomas	elected 2nd Lieut., March 6, 1847.
Joseph H. Thompson	promoted Cpl., March 1, 1847.
Thomas J. Ussrey	
A. M. Waddill	discharged for disability, Matamoros, Sept 16, 1846.
Wilson Ware	transferred to Co. A, Sept 13, 1846.
James M. Watson	discharged for disability, Matamoros, Sept 16, 1846.
J. J. Watts	transferred from Co. A, Dec 5, 1846.

James Williamson	wounded, Battle of Monterey, discharged, Monterey, Oct 22, 1846.
Samuel D. Wooldridge	Cpl., discharged for disability, mouth of the Rio Grande, Aug 11, 1846.
R. H. Wright	discharged for disability, Matamoros, Oct 1, 1846.

Company H: Vicksburg Volunteers

Edward C. Allen	promoted to Corporal, Feb 29, 1847.
Ervin Barefield	
Daniel S. Bird	sick at Camargo, Sept 1, 1846.
John J. Bobb	elected 2nd Lieut., resigned for illnesses, Sept 6, 1846.
Simeon Brown	
Richard S. Burney	
Stephen D. Carson	a physician, left at Camargo to tend to the sick, Sept 6, 1846, discharged Mar 6, 1847.
William Chaffin	
John S. Clendenin	Cpl., elected Capt., Jan 29, 1847.
Thomas J. Coe	
Edward Cox	deserted July 21, 1846, New Orleans.
George A. Crump	Capt., resigned Dec 21, 1846, Victoria.
John Dart	
Thomas J. Davidson	discharged for disability, Monterey, Feb 1, 1847.
James C. Davis	discharged for disability, mouth of the Rio Grande, Aug 20, 1846.
Daniel Dunlap	
Edward Dunn	discharged for disability, mouth of the Rio Grande, Aug 11, 1846.
James H. Dupree	discharged for disability, Monterey, Feb 1, 1847.
Samuel M. Edwards	wounded, Battle of Buena Vista, Feb 23.
Samuel Ferguson	discharged for disability, Monterey, Sept 18, 1846.

John Finch	discharged for disability, Matamoros, Oct 8, 1846.
Robert Gregg	wounded, Battle of Monterey, Sept 21.
Benjamin L. Groves	
George Hackler	discharged for disability, Matamoros, Sept 25, 1846.
James Hackler	discharged for disability, mouth of the Rio Grande, Aug 20, 1846.
Charles T. Harlan	Sgt., appointed Sgt. Maj., Aug 23, 1846, discharged, Oct 24, 1846.
John A. Harris	
William D. Harrison	killed, Battle of Buena Vista, Feb 23.
William H. Harvey	
Benjamin Hatton	
Sanford H. Hill	
George W. Hise	dishonorably discharged, Dec 12, 1846.
Richard Hopkins	elected 2nd Lieut., date unknown.
Isaac Johnston	
Andrew Kramer	
Henry H. Lauell	promoted Cpl., Nov 4, 1846, wounded, Battle of Buena Vista, Feb 23.
John J. Locke	killed, Battle of Buena Vista, Feb 23.
John J. Luckin	
Armstrong Lyttle	promoted Cpl., Nov 15, 1846.
Hugh M. Markham	2nd Lieut., resigned Oct 19, 1846.
Humphrey Marshall	appointed Sgt. Maj., July 24, discharged for disabilities, Monterey, Oct 8, 1846.
Francis M. Martin	discharged for disability, mouth of the Rio Grande, Aug 11, 1846.
Joseph Martin	
Robert M. Martin	Cpl., discharged, Oct 11, 1846.
Frederick Mathews	wounded, Battle of Monterey, Sept 21, discharged, Monterey, Jan 29, 1847.
John F. Mattingly	discharged for disability, Matamoros, Oct 3, 1846.
David H. McClure	discharged for disability, Matamoros, Sept 25, 1846.

Thomas H. McGaughey	discharged, Monterey, Oct 5, 1846.
William H. McKinney	promoted Cpl., March 31, 1847.
Theodore McMorrough	musician.
Moses McMurray	discharged for disability, mouth of the Rio Grande, Aug 11, 1846.
Robert McNair	musician.
Adam McWillie	
Horace H. Miller	Sgt., appointed Sgt. Maj., Jan 8, 1847.
Robert L. Moore	1st Lieut., killed, Battle of Buena Vista, Feb 23.
William M. Moore	discharged for disability, mouth of the Rio Grande, Aug 11, 1846.
Philip Muldoon	
Andrew J. Neely	
Albert M. Newman	
Avery Noland	wounded, Battle of Monterey, Sept 21.
William Norworthy	deserted, Vicksburg, July 12, 1846.
Elijah A. Peyton	discharged, Monterey, Dec 2, 1846.
John C. Peyton	died, Matamoros, Sept 24, 1846.
John J. Poindexter	Cpl., elected Lieut., Jan 29, 1846.
William C. Porter	Sgt.
Henry F. Raim	discharged for disability, Camargo, Sept 6, 1846.
Patrick Reardon	killed, Battle of Buena Vista, Feb 23.
Hugh Riley	
Benjamin F. Roberts	wounded Battle of Monterey, Sept 21, discharged, Monterey, Oct 24, 1846.
Mitchell M. Roberts	
William D. Robinson	discharged for disability, mouth of the Rio Grande, Aug 20, 1846.
John Ross	discharged for disability, Matamoros, Sept 16, 1846.
Revenna Ross	
Benjamin F. Sanders	promoted Sgt., Feb 29, 1847.

Joseph Schmaling	Cpl., promoted to Sgt., Oct 10, 1846.
Richard D. Shackelford	
George W. Shaifer	discharged for disability, mouth of the Rio Grande, Aug 11, 1846.
Joseph Shannon	
Samuel Shaw	
Joseph Sillers	discharged for disability, Monterey, Oct 11, 1846.
Charles E. Smedes	discharged for disability, Monterey, Sept 28, 1846.
John Smith	
James W. Stevenson	
James E. Stewart	promoted Cpl., Oct 12, 1846, wounded and taken prisoner, Battle of Buena Vista, Feb 23, exchanged, March 2, 1847, elected Lieut., March 6, 1847.
John Straughn	discharged for disability, Monterey, Oct 12, 1846.
Charles Strouse	discharged for disability, Matamoros, Oct 9, 1846.
James J. V. Steele	discharged for disability, mouth of the Rio Grande, Aug 11, 1846.
Joseph P. Tunnell	killed, Battle of Monterey, Sept 21, 1846.
John E. Vandivure	died, Monterey, Nov 10, 1846.
William W. Wadsworth	discharged for disability, mouth of the Rio Grande, Aug 20, 1846.
Thomas White	died from wounds, Battle of Buena Vista, Feb 23.
John M. Williams	died, Cerralvo, Oct 5, 1846.
Rufus R. Williamson	discharged for disability, Matamoros, Sept 17, 1846.
William Winans	
Augustus Wood	

Appendix A

Company I: Holly Springs Guards

Albert L. Abston	discharged for disabilities at mouth of the Rio Grande, Aug 21, 1846.
Garland Anderson	promoted sergent Nov 3, 1846, killed Battle of Buena Vista, Feb 23, 1847.
Samuel M. Allen	discharged, Monterey, March 10, 1847.
John E. Bass	
Berry O. Best	discharged for disabilities at Matamoros, Nov 3, 1846.
John L. Branch	killed, Battle of Buena Vista, Feb 23.
Joseph Bridges	
Leonidas Brown	discharged for disabilities, Matamoros, Oct 21, 1846.
Andrew Burton	discharged for disabilities, Camargo, Sept 7, 1846.
W. Thomas Byars	appointed 1st Sgt., Aug 26, 1846.
Andrew J. Cole	discharged for disability, Matamoros, Sept 12, 1846.
Saul M. Cole	discharged for disability, Matamoros, Sept 21, 1846.
Addison Collingsworth	killed, Battle of Buena Vista, Feb 23.
Charles F. Cotton	wounded in leg, Monterey, Sept 21, discharged, Nov 21, 1846.
William H. Craft	
John H. Crawford	discharged for disability, Monterey, Mar 5, 1847.
Spotswood H. Davis	died, Aug 22, 1846, mouth of the Rio Grande.
Alfred Delap	musician, drummer, discharged Sept 21, for disability.
J. Dickerson	discharged for disability, Matamoros, Sept 21, 1846.
Samuel H. Dill	2nd Lieut.
Perry Dormand	
Joseph A. Downing	killed, Battle of Monterey, Sept 21, 1846.

Daniel D. Dubose	killed, Battle of Monterey, Sept 23, 1846.
Robert I. Eddings	
Charles Edmonson	discharged for disability, Matamoros, Sept 21, 1846.
William E. Eppes	elected 2nd Lieut., June 25, 1846.
Joseph Evans	discharged for disability, Monterey, Nov 5, 1846.
George W. Floyd	enlisted Feb 1, 1847.
Andrew Forman	Cpl., discharged for disability, Matamoros, Sept 12, 1846.
Dr. J. W. Glenn	transferred to Ark. Vols., Aug 21, 1846, appointed Asst. Surgeon that Regt.
Elkanatz Greer	promoted Sgt., Feb 24, 1847.
Vincent S. Greer	promoted Cpl., Sept 22, 1846.
William H. Grisham	promoted Cpl., killed Sept 21, advancing on 3rd fort, Monterey, He was in advance of everyone when he fell.
Samuel S. Hall	
Wiley Hamilton	
Joseph B. Heaton	killed gallantly charging 1st fort, Battle of Monterey, Sept 21, 1846.
John L. Henderson	died, Vicksburg, July 1, 1846.
William Hobbs	
Howard D. Holderway	
John M. Holland	Sgt., discharged for disability, mouth of the Rio Grande, Aug 20, 1846.
William H. Hoskins	
John Hudspeth	wounded, Battle of Buena Vista, Feb 23.
Joseph A. Hughes	
Meridian Jolly	wagoner.
Robert Josselyn	discharged by the Commissary Dept., Monterey, Oct 7, 1846.
David H. Keeling	discharged, Victoria, Jan 15, 1847.
Jerome B. Kerr	
John M. Kincaid	

Andrew J. King	
William Kinnest	supposed to have been killed in New Orleans in July.
Edward Kinnis	deserted, New Orleans, July 13, 1846.
Felix G. Lamen	discharged for disability, mouth of the Rio Grande, Aug 21, 1846.
James Langston	died, Brazos Santiago, July 20, 1846.
Patrick Lee	promoted Cpl., Aug 14, 1846.
John P. Lemay	
John Long	promoted Sgt., Nov 1, 1846.
Robert H. Malone	promoted Cpl., Aug 14, 1846.
James S. Marr	died, Matamoros, Oct 4, 1846.
Plummer M. Martin	promoted Sgt., Nov 25, 1846, wounded, Battle of Buena Vista, Feb 23.
William A. Martin	died, mouth of the Rio Grande, Aug 27, 1846.
Nat Massie	
Thadeus O. McClanahan	wounded, Battle of Buena Vista, Feb 23.
Charles McGimpsey	
Isaac Milam	discharged for disability, Matamoros, Sept 12, 1846.
James P. Moore	discharged for disability, Monterey, Nov 5, 1846.
Christopher H. Mott	1st Lieut.
Elgin A. Mullins	musician.
Leonard H. Murphrie	
Montgomery Nail	discharged for disability, Matamoros, Nov 3, 1846.
Jesse Oldham	
V. B. Orr	discharged for disability, Matamoros, Sept 21, 1846.
John Peace	killed, Battle of Buena Vista, Feb 23.
Rufus E. Philips	discharged for disability, Monterey, Oct 21, 1846.
John Pitman	
Harris I. W. Proctor	

Thadeus D. Randolph	wounded, Battle of Buena Vista, Feb 23, promoted, Sgt, April 12, 1847.
John H. C. Reynolds	died, Matamoros, Sept 10, 1846.
Isaac N. Shelby	discharged for disability, mouth of the Rio Grande, Aug 21, 1846.
Bing L. Shrives	died, Matamoros, Sept 28, 1846.
John H. Smith	discharged for disability, Monterey, Feb 1, 1847.
John B. Smoot	discharged for disability, mouth of the Rio Grande, Aug 21, 1846.
William B. Spinks	commissary Sgt., Oct 27, 1846.
S. B. Stallions	discharged for disability, Matamoros, Sept 21, 1846.
George Taylor	
James H. K. Taylor	Capt.
Walter A. Thompson	
Henry G. Trotter	killed, Battle of Buena Vista, Feb 23.
William D. Tucker	commissary dept., Apl 1, 1847.
James W. Vinson	taken prisoner, Battle of Buena Vista, Feb 23, exchanged, March 4, discharged, March 11, 1847.
Thomas T. Wilkerson	
Gideon Williams	wounded, Battle of Monterey, Sept 21, discharged, Monterey, Nov 21, 1846.
John Williams	discharged for disability, Matamoros, Sept 15, 1846.
Francis A. Wolf	wounded, Battle of Monterey, Sept 21, discharged, Nov 2, 1846.
Joseph Yancey	Cpl., promoted Sgt., Aug 14, 1846, discharged, Nov 24, 1846.
Simon B. Yancey	
Thomas M. Yancey	discharged for disability, mouth of the Rio Grande, Aug 21, 1846.

Company K: Tombigbee Guards

Robert J. Allen	
Thomas G. Ames	discharged for disability at Monterey, Jan 29, 1847.

Samuel C. Astin	detached service, hospital.
James L. Bartee	promoted Corp. Feb 1, 1847.
Richard Bell	left sick at Camargo, Sept 6, 1846.
William H. Bell	Sgt., wounded in arm at Monterey, Sept 21, 1846, discharged, Nov 1, 1846.
John Brand	died at Matamoros, Nov 1846.
Edward E. Brazeale	
George W. Broom	
George W. Campbell	
Green B. Carey	arrested by civil authorities, New Orleans, larceny, July 22, 1846, dropped from rolls.
John A. Cason	discharged for disability, mouth of the Rio Grande, Aug 19, 1846.
Henry M. Cook	
Joseph L. Covington	3rd Sgt., appointed 1st Sgt., Jan 1847.
John E. Cravens	discharged for disability, Monterey, Oct 27, 1846.
William Creight	discharged for disability, mouth of the Rio Grande, Aug 21, 1846.
John W. Cummings	discharged for disability, mouth of the Rio Grande, Aug 8, 1846.
Benjamin F. Davis	
Charles F. Davis	
John E. Day	discharged for disability, mouth of the Rio Grande, Aug 11, 1846.
Tolbert Dockery	discharged for disability, mouth of the Rio Grande, Aug 8, 1846.
Fielding L. Dowsing	discharged for disability, Matamoros, Sept 17, 1846.
John H. Dunn	
Moses D. Echols	
James A. Evans	discharged for disability, Matamoros, Sept 24, 1846.
Jacob Feltman	
George Fisher	promoted to Corp., Feb 1, 1847.
James Flanagan	

William Flanagan	discharged for disability, mouth of the Rio Grande, Aug 8, 1846.
Carman Frazer	
J. P. Gillian	Corp., discharged for disability, New Orleans, July 22, 1846.
Edward H. Gregory	discharged, Dec 12, 1846, Monterey, procured substitute, H. P. Lyon.
Benjamin F. Grughett	promoted Sgt.
James M. Hale	
Thomas Harrison	discharged for disability, Monterey, Oct 9, 1846.
John W. Hartman	musician.
Ely J. Henry	discharged for disability, mouth of the Rio Grande, Aug 11, 1846.
John D. Higgason	discharged for disability, mouth of the Rio Grande, Aug 8, 1846.
John J. Hindsley	
Harrison L. Howard	discharged for disability, Matamoros, Oct 8, 1846.
George Hunt	
Nap Johnson	
Thomas L. Jones	Corp., discharged for disability, Matamoras, Oct 8, 1846.
William Julian	promoted to Sgt., discharged, Dec 12, 1846, procured a substitute, C. T. Valentine.
Milton H. Kelly	died, Matamoros, date unknown.
Argyle A. Kerr	promoted Cpl., Oct 1, 1846.
Thomas L. Kerven	discharged for disability, mouth of the Rio Grande, Aug 19, 1846.
John Langham	
Daniel B. Lewis	wounded in arm, Monterey, Sept 21, discharged, Monterey, Oct 27, 1846.
Edward B. Lewis	wounded in face, Monterey, Sept 21, discharged, Monterey, Nov 23, 1846.
William D. Longstreet	

Henry Lyon	mustered in at Monterey, Dec 12, 1846, substitute for Edward H. Gregory.
William Mallett	died, Matamoros, Oct 8, 1846.
Charles Martin	wounded in leg, Battle of Monterey, Sept 21, discharged, Monterey, Nov 23.
William S. McDuffie	discharged for disability, Matamoros, Nov 6, 1846.
John E. C. McGuin	
John D. McNorris	
Archibald W. Miller	died, Matamoros, Sept 21, 1846.
Alexander Mitchell	
William Moore	
Robert G. Mosby	
William O'Rourke	
Horatio Overton	
Joel T. Parrish	discharged for disability, Monterey, Oct 9, 1846.
Wm. H. H. Patterson	1st Lieut.
Bryant Perry	
James O. Ragsdale	discharged for disability, mouth of the Rio Grande, Aug 11, 1846.
Hugh M. Reese	
James G. Reese	Cpl., promoted Sgt., Dec 1, 1846.
John Renneau	died, Camargo, date unknown.
William P. Rogers	Capt.
James A. Sharman	
Allen Skidmore	died, Cerralvo, Oct 27, 1846.
Platt Snedicor	died from wounds, Battle of Monterey, Sept 23.
David P. Steadman	Sgt., discharged for disability, Monterey, Jan 29, 1847.
Adkinson Stewart	discharged for disability, mouth of the Rio Grande, Aug 7, 1846.
John Stewart	
James Tanner	
John L. Thompson	

James Thompson	wounded in the elbow, Battle of Monterey, Sept 21, 1846.
Robert E. Thompson	
Richard Tierce	discharged for disability, Matamoros, Sept 25, 1846.
Henry Tindall	Sgt., discharged for disability, Matamoros, Nov 10, 1846.
Calvin T. Tinsley	discharged for disability, Matamoros, Sept 17, 1846.
William P. Townsend	2nd Lieut.
John M. Tyree	killed, Battle of Monterey, Sept 23.
Job Umphlett	
Charles T. Valentine	Sgt., Joined as substitute for Sgt. Julian, Dec 12, 1846.
William B. Wade	elected 2nd Lieut., June 26, 1846.
William K. Walker	discharged for disability, Matamoros, Sept 28, 1846.
Thomas Washer	
Morgan Watson	
John Westbrooks	promoted Cpl., Feb 1, 1847.
Archibald H. White	
John C. Willett	discharged for disability, Matamoros, Sept 28, 1846.
William Woodliff	discharged for disability, Matamoros, Sept 28, 1846.

APPENDIX B

A Brief Roster of the Mississippi Riflemen Who Served in the War Between the States

This roster of the men of the Mississippi Regiment known to have served their country during the War Between the States was compiled from *The Papers of Jefferson Davis*, Vol. 3. It is probably incomplete.

Charles M. Bradford (1825–1867)	Lt. Col, 15th Louisiana Infantry; brief service
William N. Brown (1827?–1887)	Capt. 20th Mississippi Infantry; captured, Fort Donelson; captured, Vicksburg; wounded, Franklin, Tennessee
Douglas Hancock Cooper (1815–1879)	Confederate Superintendent of Indian Affairs; Brig. General

William Delay (1814–1871)	Capt. Co. C, 9th Mississippi Infantry
Crawford Fletcher (1824?–1876)	1855–61, Capt. 9th Infantry, U. S.; resigned "not willing to bear arms against country"
Richard Griffith (1814–1862)	Brig. Gen. CSA; mortally wounded at Savage Station, Virginia
Samuel R. Harrison (1819–1867)	Col. 1st Louisiana Infantry; appointed Major of Commissary in Brigade of Joseph R. Davis
Warren Huffman (1823–1864)	Sgt. Mississippi Light Artillery; killed in action, 1864
Thomas J. Kyle (1820–1873)	Capt. Co. G, 3rd Mississippi Infantry, state militia
Evander McNair (1820–1902)	Col. 4th Arkansas Infantry; promoted to Brig. Gen.; wounded at Chickamauga
Frederick James Malone (1826–1891)	commanded Texas State Cavalry Company
George Edward Metcalf (1829–1900)	served in 10th Mississippi Infantry
Horace H. Miller (1826?–1877)	Lt. Col. 20th Mississippi Infantry; captured at Fort Donelson; Col. 9th Mississippi Cavalry
Christopher Haynes Mott (1826–1862)	Col. 19th Mississippi Infantry; mortally wounded near Williamsburg, Va.
Avery Noland (1828–1883)	served as officer; unit unknown
Carnot Posey (1818–1863)	Col. 16th Mississippi Infantry; Brig. Gen., fatally wounded at Briscoe Station, Virginia

William P. Rogers (1819–1862)	Col. 2nd Texas Infantry; killed at Corinth, Mississippi, leading attack on federal fort
Daniel Russell (1820–?)	Col. 20th Mississippi Infantry; resigned 1863, poor health
Romulus M. Sanders (1825–?)	served in Confederate Army; unit unknown
William Henry Scott (1823?–1861)	served briefly as Capt., 1st Louisiana Infantry
James Somerville (1822–1877)	militia officer, Mississippi
James H. R. Taylor (1820–67)	Lt. Col. 15th Tennessee Infantry; brief service
William Purnell Townsend (1822–1882)	Maj. 4th Texas Infantry; wounded
William B. Wade (1824?–?)	Capt. 10th Mississippi Infantry; killed after war by federal troops
Francis A. Wolff (1824–?)	Capt. 3rd Mississippi Infantry

NOTES

CHAPTER 1: MISSISSIPPI ON THE EVE OF THE MEXICAN WAR

1. Nathan C. Brooks, *A Complete History of the Mexican War 1846–1848* (Chicago: The Rio Grande Press Inc., 1965), pp. 1–13, 50–90.
2. Dunbar Rowland, ed., *Mississippi*, Vol. 1 (Atlanta: Southern Historical Publishing Association, 1907), p. 227.
3. Lynda J. Lasswell. "The First Regiment of Mississippi Infantry in the Mexican War and Letters of Jefferson Davis Concerning the War." M. A. thesis, Rice University, Houston, 1969.
4. Rowland, *Mississippi*, Vol. 1, p. 228.
5. *Mississippi Free Trader and Natchez Gazette*, May 26, 1846, quoted in Robert A. Brent, "Mississippi and the Mexican War," *Journal of Mississippi History*, Vol. 31, 1969, p. 206.
6. Vicksburg *Intelligencer*, May 25, 1846, quoted in Brent, "Mississippi and the Mexican War," p. 206.
7. James B. Ranck, *Albert Gallatin Brown: Radical Southern Nationalist* (New York: Appleton-Century, 1937).
8. Rowland, *Mississippi*, Vol. 1, p. 229.
9. Natchez *Courier*, June 24, 1846, quoted in Brent, "Mississippi and the Mexican War", p. 206.
10. James T. McIntosh, ed., *The Papers of Jefferson Davis*, Vol. 2 (Baton Rouge: Louisiana State University Press, 1974), p. 36, footnote 2.

CHAPTER 2: ON TO MEXICO, HURRAH FOR THE VOLUNTEER!

1. William E. Estes, "Something About the First Mississippi Rifles," undated newspaper article, newspaper unknown, Mexican War Subject File, Mississippi Department of Archives and History, Jackson, Mississippi.

2. *The Southron,* Jackson, Mississippi, June 10, 1846.

3. Ibid.

4. Henry W. Barton, *Texas Volunteers in the Mexican War* (Waco: The Texian press, 1970), pp. 27, 49–50. Alexander Lander, *A Trip to the Wars, Comprising the History of the Galveston Riflemen, Formed April 28, 1846, at Galveston, Texas; Together with the History of the Battle of Monterey: Also, Descriptions of Mexico and Its People* (Monmouth, Ill.: Atlas Office, 1847), pp. 1–33. Charles D. Spurlin, *Texas Veterans in the Mexican War* (Nacogdoches, Tex.: Erickson Books, 1984), pp. 70, 71.

5. Estes, "First Mississippi Rifles."

6. Lynda J. Lasswell, "The First Regiment of Mississippi Infantry in the Mexican War and Letters of Jefferson Davis Concerning the War," M. A. thesis, Rice University, Houston, 1968.

7. *Vicksburg Whig,* Vicksburg, Mississippi, June 20, 1846.

8. Samuel Chamberlain, *Recollections of a Rogue* (London: Museum Press Limited, 1957), pp. 30, 31.

9. Robert McElroy, *Jefferson Davis, the Unreal and the Real* (New York: Harper & Brothers Publishers, 1937), p. 32.

10. Brainerd Dyer, *Zachary Taylor* (Baton Rouge: Louisiana State University Press, 1946), pp. 96–98.

11. McElroy, *Jefferson Davis,* p. 33.

12. "To the people of Mississippi," July 13, 1846, in James T. McIntosh, Lynda L. Crist, and Mary S. Dix, eds., *The Papers of Jefferson Davis, July 1846–December 1848,* Vol. 3 (Baton Rouge: Louisiana State University Press, 1981), p. 9.

13. *National Cyclopedia of American Biography,* Vol. III (New York: James T. White and Company, 1906), p. 212.

14. Penix, Joe. "McClung—Death's Ramrod," *Clarion-Ledger,* Jackson, Mississippi, April 3, 1955. This is the first in a three-article series on the life of McClung, the other two appearing on April 10 and April 17, 1955. These articles present undocumented accounts of the life of a very private man, but they agree with the essential facts about McClung's life that appear in more standard sources, such as above note 14.

Stories—even legends—have sprung up about McClung and a character modeled after him, Keith Alexander, appeared in James Street's novel *Tap Roots* (Garden City, N.Y.: Sun Dial Press, 1943). The legends have it that McClung killed six brothers of the slain John Menifee when they challenged him to duels after John's death. McClung was also supposed to have joined forces with the famous duelist

James Bowie in an action that rid a riverboat of several unsavory gamblers.

15. Dunbar Rowland, ed., *Mississippi*, Vol. 2 (Atlanta: Southern Historical Publishing Association, 1907), pp. 184–85.

16. Dunbar Rowland, "Political and Parliamentary Orators and Oratory of Mississippi," *Publications of the Mississippi Historical Society*, Vol. IV, 1901.

17. A Mississippian, "Sketches of Our Volunteer Officers: Alexander Keith McClung," *Southern Literary Messenger*, Vol. XXI (1855), p. 2.

18. Quoted in Rowland, *Mississippi*, Vol. 2, pp. 184–185.

19. Ibid., Vol. 1, p. 286.

20. *Port Gibson Correspondent*, June 24, 1846; *Mississippi Free Trader & Natchez Gazette*, June 23, 1846.

21. "Anecdote of General Bradford," in *The Southron*, Jackson, Mississippi, July 2, 1847.

22. Cadmus M. Wilcox, *History of the Mexican War* (Washington: Church News, 1892), pp. 75–76.

23. Downing, R. L. "Infantry Weapons of the Mexican War," *Antiques*, November 1940, pp. 228–230. Lars Matthew Sexton Merk, "The Interchangeable Eli Whitney," Letters to the Editor, *The Wall Street Journal*, April 6, 1989. As early as 1801, Eli Whitney demonstrated the idea of interchangeable parts for firearms by producing ten different lock mechanisms that could be manufactured to fit the same musket.

24. David Niven, *The Mexican War*, (Alexandria, Va.: Time-Life Books, 1978), 27, as quoted from *Personal Memoirs of U. S. Grant* (New York: Charles L. Webster & Co., 1894).

25. "Autobiography of Jefferson Davis," in T. McIntosh, ed., *The Papers of Jefferson Davis*, Vol. 1 (Baton Rouge: Louisiana State University Press, 1974), p. liv.

26. Chamberlain, *Recollections*, pp. 122–123. At the Battle of Buena Vista retreating Mexican soldiers reportedly shouted at the advancing Mississippians, "*Diablos—camisa[s] coloradas!*"

27. Estes, "First Mississippi Rifles."

28. Vicksburg *Sentinel & Expositor*, July 14, 1846.

29. Editorial note. *The Papers of Jefferson Davis*, Vol. 3, p. 11.

30. *Vicksburg Whig*, July 30, 1846.

31. Ibid.

32. Ibid.

33. *The Papers of Jefferson Davis*, Vol. 3, pp. 12–13, footnotes 1 and 4.

CHAPTER 3: ARMY LIFE ON THE RIO GRANDE

1. *Vicksburg Whig,* August 18, 1846.

2. Rufus Arthur was not the only observer to note this activity at Point Isabel. The *Vicksburg Whig,* January 1, 1847, reported Brazos Harbor still crowded with shippers and many vessels still being wrecked on the bar.

3. *Vicksburg Whig,* August 18, 1846.

4. Entry for August 16 in Eleanor D. Pace, "The Diary and Letters of William P. Rogers, 1846–1862," *The Southwestern Historical Quarterly,* Vol. XXXII (April 1929), p. 261.

5. Hudson Strode, *Jefferson Davis: American Patriot 1808–1861* (New York: Harcourt, Brace & Company, 1955), p. 161. *The Papers of Jefferson Davis,* Vol. 3, pp. 95, 165. Jim Green, also known as Big Jim, was a slave of Joseph Davis, sent to serve Jefferson Davis as a body servant. Jim Green served the Davis family loyally throughout his life, and died in 1867 at Joseph Davis's plantation, Hurricane.

6. "To Robert J. Walker," in James T. McIntosh, ed., *The Papers of Jefferson Davis,* Vol. 3 (Baton Rouge; Louisiana State University Press, 1974), p. 11.

7. "From Zachary Taylor," *The Papers of Jefferson Davis,* Vol. 3, p. 14.

8. McElroy, *Jefferson Davis, the Unreal and the Real,* Vol. 1 (New York: Harper & Brothers Publishers, 1937), p. 55.

9. *The Papers of Jefferson Davis,* Vol. 2, p. 614. On May 28, 1846, Rep. Jefferson Davis spoke in support of a Congressional joint resolution of thanks to Zachary Taylor and his army for their victories of May 8–9, on the Rio Grande.

10. Samuel C. Reid, *The Scouting Expeditions of McCulloch's Texas Rangers: or The Summer and Fall Campaigns of the Army of the United States in Mexico—1846* (Philadelphia: J. W. Bradley, 1860), pp. 43–46. The Texas Rangers, under Capt. Ben McCulloch, scouted the route to Linares using a map found in General Arista's abandoned personal effects after the Battle of Resaca de la Palma.

11. Brainerd Dyer, *Zachary Taylor* (Baton Rouge: Louisiana State University Press, 1946), pp. 188–89. Erna Risch, *Quartermaster Support of the Army: A History of the Corps, 1775–1939* (Washington: Office of the Quartermaster General, 1962), pp. 258–263.

12. Thomas B. Thorpe, *Our Army on the Rio Grande* (Philadelphia: Carey & Hart, 1846), p. 26.

13. *The Papers of Jefferson Davis,* Vol. 3, p. 15, footnote 1.

14. *Vicksburg Whig,* August 25, 1846.
15. *Vicksburg Whig,* September 24, 1846.
16. Entry for August 16 in Pace, "Diary of William P. Rogers," p. 261.
17. *The Papers of Jefferson Davis,* Vol. 3, p. 19, footnote 9.
18. "To Robert J. Walker," August 24, 1846. *The Papers of Jefferson Davis,* Vol. 3, p. 19.
19. *Holly Springs Gazette,* August 14, 1846.
20. "To Robert J. Walker," August 24, 1846. *The Papers of Jefferson Davis,* Vol. 3, p. 19.
21. Ibid, p. 16.
22. *New Orleans Times Democrat,* December 6, 1889, quoted in *The Papers of Jefferson Davis,* Vol. 3, p. 16, footnote 3.
23. Private communication, Jon Harrison, McAllen, Texas.
24. *The Vicksburg Whig,* September 24, 1846.
25. *The Papers of Jefferson Davis,* Vol. 3, p. 19, footnote 1.
26. Entry for August 31, 1846, Franklin E. Smith Diary, private manuscript, Mississippi Department of Archives and History, Jackson, Mississippi.
27. Entries for August 28–31, 1846, Franklin E. Smith Diary; entry for August 31 in Pace, "Diary of William P. Rogers," p. 262.
28. Entry for August 16, 1846, diary of S. K. Chamberlin, quoted in John P. Bloom, "With the American Army into Mexico, 1846–1848," Ph. D. dissertation, Emory University, Atlanta, 1956, p. 50.
29. Letter from S. R. Curtis to his brother, February 17, 1847, quoted in Bloom, "With the American Army," p. 49.
30. David Nevin, *The Mexican War* (Alexandria: Time-Life Books Inc., 1978), p. 62. The soldiers referred to Camargo as "the graveyard." In August 1980, Hurricane Allen caused extensive flooding on the Rio San Juan in the Camargo area. the resulting erosion of the banks unearthed many graves of American soldiers, readily identified by the local people, "because they were buried in wooden coffins."—presumably those buried before the Americans ran out of lumber. Souvenir hunters collected coffin nails, uniform buttons, and even the bones of the Gringos.
31. John B. Robertson, *Reminiscences of a Campaign in Mexico by a Member of "The Bloody-First* [1st Tennessee Regiment]" (Nashville: John York, 1849).
32. Entry for November 15, 1846, Franklin E. Smith, Diary.
33. Alfred H. Bill, *Rehearsal for Conflict* (New York: Alfred A. Knopf, 1947), p. 131.

34. *Holly Springs Gazette,* August 14, 1846.

35. Robert H. Ferrell, ed., *Monterrey Is Ours! The Mexican War Letters of Lieutenant Dana 1845–1847,* (Lexington: The University Press of Kentucky, 1990), pp. 142, 144–145.

36. J. P. Brock to his parents, March 24, and to John Y. Harris, July 22, John P. Brock Letters, William and Mary College, quoted in Bloom, "With the American," p. 272.

37. Franklin E. Smith Diary. Entry for November 15, 1846.

38. Letter from F. A. Hardy to his brother, December 14, 1846, J. A. Rayner Collection, quoted in Bloom, "With the American Army." p. 278.

39. Milton Jamieson, *Journal and Notes of a Campaign in Mexico* . . . (Cincinnati, 1849).

40. Entry for September 18, 1846, in Pace, "Diary of William P. Rogers," p. 262.

41. Quoted from Dyer, *Zachary Taylor,* pg. 184.

42. Tom Owen, *Anecdotes of Zachary Taylor and the Mexican War* (New York: D. Appleton & Company, 1848), pp. 52–53. Thomas Bangs Thorpe, a war correspondent for the New Orleans *Daily Tropic,* wrote under the pseudonym "Tom Owen" and after the war published this collection of stories recorded on the Rio Grande.

43. Nathan C. Brooks, *A Complete History of the Mexican War* (Philadelphia: Grigg, Elliott & Co., 1849), pp. 165–166.

44. Zadoc K. Judd Autobiography, typescript, Brigham Young University, quoted in Bloom, "With the American Army," pp. 20–21.

45. Entry for September 18, 1846, in Pace, "The Diary of William P. Rogers," p. 263.

46. Benjamin F. Scribner, *A Campaign in Mexico* (Philadelphia: Grigg, Elliot & Co., 1847), p. 49.

CHAPTER 4: THE CAPTURE OF MONTERREY

1. Rhoda V. T. Doubleday, ed., *The Journals of Major Phillip Norbourne Barbour and his Wife Martha Isabella Hopkins Barbour* (New York: G. P. Putnam's Sons, 1936), p. 105.

2. Ibid, p. 106.

3. Ibid, p. 107.

4. Justin H. Smith, *The War with Mexico* Vol. 1, New York: The Macmillan Company, 1919), p. 233.

5. John R. Kenly, *Memoirs of a Maryland Volunteer, War with Mex-*

ico, in the Years 1846–7–8 (Philadelphia: J. B. Lippincott & Co., 1873), pp. 99, 101.

6. Manuel Balbontin, "The Siege of Monterey, Memoirs of Lieutenant Manuel Balboutin [sic], Retired Colonel of Artillery of the Mexican Army," translated by John Strating, *Journal of the Military Service Institution of the United States*, Vol. 8 (1887), p. 336. This article is translated from the book written by Manuel Balbontin, *La Invasion Americana 1846 a 1847. Apuntes del Subteniente de Artilleria Manuel Balbontin* (Mexico: Gonzalo A. Estera, 1883).

7. Electus Backus, "A Brief Sketch of the Battle of Monterey; with Details of That Portion of It, Which Took Place at the Eastern Extremity of the City," *Historical Magazine*, Vol. 10 (1866), pp. 207–213.

8. Guillermo Vigil y Robles, *La Invasion de Mexico por los Estados Unidos en los Anos de 1846, 1847, y 1848* (Mexico: Tip. E. Correcional, 1923), pp. 20–21. Also see Ramòn Alcaraz, *The Other Side: Notes for the History of the War Between Mexico and the United States*. Translated from the Spanish and edited by Albert Ramsey (New York: John Wiley, 1850), p. 64.

9. Alcaraz, *The Other Side*, p. 65.

10. J. H. Smith, *War with Mexico*, Vol. 1, p. 230.

11. Alcaraz, *The Other Side*, p. 77.

12. Doubleday, *Journal of Major Barbour*, p. 108.

13. Eleanor D. Pace, "The Diary and Letters of William P. Rogers, 1846–1862," *The Southwestern Historical Quarterly*, Vol. XXXII (April 1929) p. 263.

14. Kenly, *Maryland Volunteer*, p. 119.

15. Backus, "Battle of Monterey," pp. 208–209.

16. Grady and Sue McWhiney, *To Mexico with Taylor and Scott 1845–1847* (Waltham: Blaisdell Publishing Co., 1969), p. 57.

17. Backus, "Battle of Monterey," pp. 209–210.

18. "From Daniel Russell," September 26, 1846, in James T. McIntosh, ed. *The Papers of Jefferson Davis*, Vol. 3 (Baton Rouge: Louisiana State University Press, 1974), p. 47.

19. "Colonel W. B. Campbell to D. C.," July 3, 1846, Governor Davis Campbell Collection, The J. H. Smith Transcripts, Latin American Collection, The University of Texas, Austin.

20. *Vicksburg Whig*, October 29, 1846.

21. "From John L. McManus," October 18, 1846, *The Papers of Jefferson Davis*, Vol. 3, p. 67.

22. Pace, "The Diary of William P. Rogers," p. 265.

23. *The Southron,* Jackson, Mississippi, January 1, 1847.

24. "From Daniel R. Russell," September 26, 1846, *The Papers of Jefferson Davis,* Vol. 3, p. 47. The words "Damn it" were marked for deletion on this document by someone. Since this phrase does not appear on Varina Davis's copy of the document, perhaps Mrs. Davis wished to purify her husband's language.

25. Depending upon whom you believe, the fort was being abandoned by Mexican troops, because (a) The Regulars' version: "Backus . . . shot down the enemy at their guns, firing through the open gorge of the work [Fort Tenería]. . . . The greater part of the enemy had been driven from the work before it was taken possession of by the command of General Quitman." McWhiney and McWhiney, *To Mexico with Taylor and Scott,* pp. 58–59. (b) Davis's version: "The sharp crack of our rifles within point blank distance, soon made it no holiday work for the Mexicans to stand to their guns. Their fire grew slack, and a panic and dread of our deadly aim were evidently coming over them." "Speech at Vicksburg," November 10, 1846, *The Papers of Jefferson Davis,* Vol. 3, p. 81. (c) A Mexican version: "The assault was plain, but a reinforcement came up, sending to the Lieut.-Colonel of the 3d Light to sally forth and charge the enemy. The word to handle the bayonet was answered by enthusiastic vivas, to form columns and then. . . . The parties say . . . that[,] rushing out through the gorget of the work, he [the commanding officer] threw himself into the river, taking to flight among cries of indignation and scorn. By the desertion of the chief of the Light, the enemy took the Tenería." Alcaraz, *The Other Side,* p. 73.

26. A Mississippian, "Sketches of Our Volunteer Officers: Alexander Keith McClung," *Southern Literary Messenger,* Vol. XXI, p. 9.

27. Ibid, p. 10.

28. Hudson Strode, *Jefferson Davis: American Patriot, 1808–1861* (New York: Harcourt, Brace & Company, 1955), p. 172. Davis, like most aristocratic Southerners of his time, loved fine animals. Strode relates that at a later time, when Tartar was to be loaded from a lighter to a steamboat at Brazos Island to be transported, "the sailors could not force him on the ship. They struck him sharply to make him leap. Unused to blows, the enraged Tartar snorted and reared. Finally Davis commanded the sailors to let him alone. Then at the ship's edge, holding the bridle, Davis called the horse's name gently with persuasive assurance. Tartar crouched and waited for the moment the lighter and the ship were on the same level; then he sprang over the intervening water to his master's side."

29. Balbontin, "The Siege of Monterey," p. 340. Christopher Losson, *Tennessee's Forgotten Warriors, Frank Cheatham and His Confederate Division* (Knoxville: The University of Tennessee Press, 1989), p. 9. The banner of the 1st Tennessee Regiment was known as the Eagle Blue Banner and was "a flag depicting an eagle on an azure background with the motto 'Weeping in solitude for the fallen brave is better than the presence of men too timid to fight for their country'."

30. "Sketches of Our Volunteer Officers: Alexander Keith McClung," p. 10.

31. "From Daniel R. Russell," October 18, 1846, *The Papers of Jefferson Davis,* Vol. 3, pp. 70–73.

32. "To John A. Quitman," September 26, 1846, *The Papers of Jefferson Davis,* Vol. 3, pp. 70–73.

33. "From Daniel R. Russell," October 18, 1846, *The Papers of Jefferson Davis,* Vol. 3, pp. 70–73.

34. Tom Owen, *Anecdotes of Zachary Taylor and the Mexican War* (New York: D. Appleton & Company, 1848), p. 76.

35. Nathan C. Brooks, *A Complete History of the Mexican War* (Philadelphia: Grigg, Elliott & Co., 1849), p. 80.

36. Luther Giddings, *Sketches of the Campaign in Northern Mexico in Eighteen Hundred Forty-Six and Seven,* (New York: George P. Putnam, 1853), pp. 180–181.

37. Charles Roland, *Albert Sidney Johnston, Soldier of Three Republics* (Austin: University of Texas Press, 1964), p. 135.

38. *The Papers of Jefferson Davis,* Vol. 3, p. 32, fn 23.

39. Roland, *Albert Sidney Johnston,* p. 136.

40. "From Daniel R. Russell," October 18, 1846, *The Papers of Jefferson Davis,* Vol. 3, pp. 70–73.

41. "Sketches of Our Volunteer Officers: Alexander Keith McClung," p. 10.

42. Report by Gen. J. A. Quitman on battle of Monterey, quoted in Thorpe, *Our Army at Monterey,* pp. 168–172.

43. "From Alexander B. Bradford," September 26, 1846, *The Papers of Jefferson Davis,* Vol. 3, pp. 40–42.

44. *Vicksburg Whig,* October 29, 1846.

45. "To John A. Quitman," September 26, 1846, *The Papers of Jefferson Davis,* Vol. 3, pp. 35–36.

46. Ibid, p. 39, footnote 21.

47. "From Stephen A. D. Greaves," October 18, 1846, *The Papers of Jefferson Davis,* Vol. 3, pp. 64–66.

48. Ibid, p. 66, footnote 9.
49. Kenly, *Maryland Volunteer,* pp. 134–135.

CHAPTER 5: VICTORY IN MONTERREY—CENSURE IN WASHINGTON

1. John R. Kenly, *memoirs of a Maryland Volunteer, War with Mexico, in the Years 1846–7–8* (Philadelphia: J. B. Lippincott & Co., 1873), p. 131.
2. Ibid, p. 144.
3. Entry for October 3, in Eleanor D. Pace, "The Diary and Letters of William P. Rogers, 1846–1862," *The Southwestern Historical Quarterly,* Vol. XXXII (April 1929), p. 263.
4. Kenly, *Maryland Volunteer,* p. 144.
5. Manuel Balbontin, "The Siege of Monterey, Memoirs of Lieutenant Manuel Balboutin [sic], Retired Colonel of Artillery of the Mexican Army," translated by John A. Strother, *Journal of the Military Service Institution of the United States,* Vol. 8 (1887), pp. 352–53.
6. *Vicksburg Whig,* October 27, 1846.
7. B. S. Roberts Diary, November 26, 1846, J. H. Smith Transcripts, Latin American Collection, University of Texas, Austin.
8. Ibid.
9. *Vicksburg Whig,* October 27, 1846.
10. *The Southron,* October 28, 1846.
11. Laurier McDonald, private correspondence. All of these cemeteries as well as the forts on the eastern side of the city have been lost in the urban sprawl of this large and modern city. In 1965 an extensive urban renewal project razed the sites occupied by Tenería, Rincón del Diablo, Purisima Bridge, and the Citadel. The beautiful cathedral remains on the principal square (Zaragosa Square), and the Obispada (Bishop's Palace) on the south side of the city houses a fine museum. Parts of the Obispada are crumbling, and the facade is literally dissolving from the effects of acid rain in this highly industrialized city.
12. *Vicksburg Whig,* November 5, 1846.
13. *The Southron,* October 28, 1846. William Low was eventually discharged for health reasons and returned to Mississippi, where he died on May 12, 1847. McManus, in town on furlough, attended the funeral to "shed a soldier's tear over the grave of his deliverer."
14. *Vicksburg Whig,* November 5, 1846; *The Southron,* July 2, 1847.
15. *Vicksburg Whig,* October 27, 1846.
16. *Mississippi Free Trader and Natchez Gazette,* December 31, 1846.

17. A Mississippian, "Sketches of Our Volunteer Officers: Alexander Keith McClung." *Southern Literary Messengers,* Vol. XXI p. 11.
18. *Vicksburg Whig,* April 1, 1847.
19. *Vicksburg Whig,* February 18, 1847.
20. Tom Owen, *Anecdotes of Zachary Taylor and the Mexican War* (New York: D. Appleton & Company, 1848), p. 100.
21. *Vicksburg Whig,* October 29, 1846.
22. For more on the controversy between the 1st Mississippi Regiment and the 1st Tennessee Regiment as to the capture of Fort Tenería, see James T. McIntosh, ed., *The Papers of Jefferson Davis,* Vol. 3, 25–91, 100–113, 401–406. Christopher Losson, *Tennessee's Forgotten Warriors: Frank Cheatham and His Confederate Division* (Knoxville: The University of Tennessee Press, 1989) p. 14.
23. Gov. David Collection, J. H. Smith Transcripts, Latin American Collection, University of Texas, Austin, p. 31.
24. Ibid.
25. S. Compton Smith, *Chile Con Carne or The Camp and the Field* (New York: Miller & Curtis, 1857), pp. 66–68.
26. Ibid.
27. Ibid. pp. 61–75.
28. *Vicksburg Whig,* September 24, 1846.
29. Balbontin, "The Siege of Monterey," p. 344.
30. *The Papers of Jefferson Davis,* Vol. 3, pp. 21–23.
31. Allan Nevins, *Polk, The Diary of a President 1845–1849* (London: Longmans, Green & Co., 1952), p. 155.
32. "W. B. Campbell to D. C.," November 2, 1846, J. H. Smith Transcripts, The Latin American Collection, University of Texas, Austin.

Chapter 6: The Expedition to Victoria

1. "Worth to Capt. S.," Saltillo, November 20, 1846. Gen. William J. Worth Papers, J. H. Smith Transcripts, Latin American Collection, University of Texas, Austin.
2. Diary of Sgt. James Mullan Jr., September 18, 1846, J. H. Smith Transcripts, Latin American Collection, University of Texas, Austin.
3. Justin H. Smith, *The War with Mexico,* Vol. 1, (New York: The Macmillan Company, 1919), p. 359. Manuel Balbontin, "The Battle of Angostura (Buena Vista)," translated by Capt. F. H. Hardie, *Journal of the Military Service Institution of the United States,* Vol. 8 (1887), pp. 127–128. This article came from Balbontin, *La Invasion Americana*

1846 a 1847. Apuntes del Subteniente de Artilleria Manuel Balbontin (Mexico: Gonzalo A. Estera, 1883).

4. John F. H. Claiborne, *Life and Correspondence of John A. Quitman* (New York: Harper & Brothers Publishers, 1860), p. 281.

5. Eleanor D. Pace, "Diary and Letters of William P. Rogers, 1846–1862," *The Southwestern Historical Quarterly,* Vol. XXXII (April 1929), pp. 265, 270, .

6. Ibid, letter to wife, October 8, 1846.

7. John R. Kenly, *Memoirs of a Maryland Volunteer, War with Mexico in the Years 1846–7–8* (Philadelphia: J. B. Lippincott 86, 1873) pp. 182–83.

8. Claiborne, *John A. Quitman,* p. 284.

9. Kenly, *Maryland Volunteer,* p. 186.

10. Ibid, p. 188.

11. Tom Owen, *Anecdotes of Zachary Taylor and the Mexican War* (New York: D. Appleton & Company, 1848), p. 102.

12. Claiborne, *John A. Quitman,* p. 287.

13. *Vicksburg Whig,* January 27, 1847.

14. Samuel G. French, *Two Wars: An Autobiography* (Nashville: Confederate Veteran, 1901), p. 70.

15. *Vicksburg Whig,* Jan 27, 1847.

16. Claiborne, *John A. Quitman,* p. 288.

17. Entry for January 3, 1847, Franklin E. Smith Diary Mississippi Archives, Jackson, Mississippi.

18. French, *Two Wars,* p. 71.

19. Ibid, p. 71. French intimates that the stolen dispatches intended for Taylor were of great value to Santa Anna in making his decision to march on Saltillo. "This was told by Col. Iturbide, a son of the last emperor of Mexico, whom I met after the war."

20. Ibid, p. 71.

21. Ibid, pp. 72–73.

22. Justin H. Smith, *War with Mexico,* Vol. 1, p. 374.

23. Balbontin, "The Battle of Angostura," pp. 129–134.

24. "To Varina Howell Davis," February 8, 1847. James T. McIntosh, ed. *The Papers of Jefferson Davis,* Vol. 3 (Baton Rouge: Louisiana State University Press, 1974), p. 118.

CHAPTER 7: THE BATTLE OF BUENA VISTA

1. The battle site is described as seen during a personal visit, February 23, 1987. Pines have been planted in rows along the plateaus in an

attempt to slow the effects of soil erosion, and these pines appeared to be flourishing. The battle site may soon become a forest.

2. Justin H. Smith, *The War with Mexico* Vol. 1. (New York: The Macmillan Company, 1919), pp. 371–72. Samuel Chamberlain, *Recollections of a Rogue* (London: Museum Press Limited, 1957) pp. 93–97.

3. J. H. Smith, Vol. 1, *War with Mexico,* p. 383.

4. James H. Carleton, *The Battle of Buena Vista with the Operations of the "Army of Occupation" for One Month* (New York: Harper & Brothers, 1848), p. 19.

5. Chamberlain, *Recollections,* p. 112.

6. Manuel Balbontin, "The Battle of Angostura (Buena Vista)," translated by Capt. F. H. Hardie, *Journal of the Military Service Institution of the United States,* Vol. 8 (1887), pp. 135–36.

7. John S. D. Eisenhower, *So Far from God: The U. S. War with Mexico 1846–1848* (New York: Random House, 1989), p. 183.

8. Carleton, *Battle of Buena Vista,* pp. 30–31.

9. Ibid, pp. 33–34.

10. *The Southron,* April 16, 1847.

11. James C. Browning Diary, Entry for February 21, 1846, Private Manuscript Collection, Mississippi Department of Archives and History, Jackson.

12. Capt. Albert Pike, "Sketch of the Battle of Buena Vista," *Arkansas State Gazette,* Little Rock, April 24, 1847.

13. Ibid.

14. Chamberlain, *Recollections,* p. 129. To Chamberlain their mournful voice sounded like "the dirge of souls in bondage, the cry of an oppressed race."

15. Carleton, *The Battle of Buena Vista,* pp. 45–47.

16. Chamberlain, *Recollections,* p. 118.

17. "Dear Matt," March 2, 1847, in Eleanor D. Pace, "Diary and Letters of William P. Rogers, 1846–1862," *The Southwestern Historical Quarterly,* Vol. XXXII (April 1929), p. 276.

18. Balbontin, "The Battle of Angostura," pp. 142–43.

19. Benjamin F. Scribner, *Camp Life of a Volunteer* (Philadelphia: Grigg, Elliot & Co., 1847), pp. 60–61.

20. Balbontin, "The Battle of Angostura," p. 142. Balbontin reported that, "In vain many Americans, flinging away their arms, showed to our soldiers the rosaries with which they had been provided, crying out that they were Christians."

21. Scribner, *Camp Life of a Volunteer,* p. 62; James T. McIntosh, ed., *The Papers of Jefferson Davis,* Vol. 3 (Baton Rouge: Louisiana

State University Press, 1974) pp. 146, 151, 166–67. S. Compton Smith, *Chile Con Carne*, or *The Camp and the Field* (New York: Miller & Curtis, 1857), p. 299. The 2d Indiana was commanded by Col. William A. Bowles, a physician and former Indiana state legislator. He was personally brave but appeared to have had no military training or experience. After his regiment fled, he took up a musket and fought bravely with the Mississippians during the remainder of the day.

22. Chamberlain, *Recollections*, p. 121.

23. Henry W. Benham, "A Little More Grape," Benham, a member of General Taylor's staff at Buena Vista, wrote this account of the battle in a letter to the editors.

24. Pike, "A Sketch of the Battle of Buena Vista."

25. Balbontin, "The Battle of Angostura," p. 145.

26. Pike, "A Sketch of the Battle of Buena Vista."

27. *The Papers of Jefferson Davis* Vol. 3, pp. 124, 135, 140, 152, 162, 166–67.

28. "To William W. S. Bliss," March 2, 1847, *The Papers of Jefferson Davis*, Vol. 3, p. 144.

29. Ibid.

30. Chamberlain, *Recollections*, p. 126.

31. Pike, "A Sketch of the Battle of Buena Vista."

32. Chamberlain, *Recollections*, p. 55.

33. Pike, "A Sketch of the Battle of Buena Vista." After reviewing the casualty lists for Buena Vista, President Polk wrote in his diary for April 1, 1847: "Many valuable officers and men fell, among them my old esteemed friend, Col. Archibald Yell of the Arkansas Mounted Regiment. I deeply deplore his loss. He was a brave and good man, and among the best friends I had on earth, and had been so for twenty-five years. His eldest, and perhaps his only son, is now at college at Georgetown, and as my impression is that Col. Yell died poor, I will in that event educate the boy, and shall take great interest in him." All on Nevins, *Polk, The Diary of a President 1845–1849* (London: Longmans, Green & Co., 1952), p. 208.

34. A Russell Buchanan, "George Washington Trahern: Texas Cowboy Soldier from Mier to Buena Vista," *The Southwestern Historical Quarterly*. Vol. 58, no. 1 (1954), pp. 84–85. Florence S. Johnson, *Old Rough and Ready on the Rio Grande* (Waco: The Texian Press, 1969), pp. 166–69. Chamberlain, *Recollections*, pp. 202, 241–42, 256.

35. "To William W. S. Bliss," March 2, 1847, *The Papers of Jefferson Davis*, Vol. 3, p. 142.

36. Ibid, p. 142.

37. Justin H. Smith, Vol. 1, *War with Mexico,* p. 393.

38. *The Papers of Jefferson Davis,* Vol. 3, p. 183, footnote 5. The elder Clay was severely grieved over the loss of his namesake. The younger Clay and Jefferson Davis had both attended Transylvania University and West Point at the same time, and were friends. Davis and Henry Clay, Sr., served together in the Senate after the Mexican War—Davis as a Democrat from Mississippi and the elder Clay as a Whig from Kentucky. But Davis fondly remembered that "his eldest son was killed with me in Mexico, and he always associated me with that boy."

39. Ibid, p. 148, footnote 26.

40. "Reuben N. Downing to Richard Griffith," March 1, 1847, *The Papers of Jefferson Davis,* Vol. 3, p. 136.

41. "To William W. S. Bliss," March 2, 1847, *The Papers of Jefferson Davis,* Vol. 3, p. 143.

Chapter 8: A Review of the Battle of Buena Vista

1. "Dear Matt," March 2, 1847, in Eleanor D. Pace, "The Diary and Letters of William P. Rogers, 1846–1862," *The Southwestern Historical Quarterly,* Vol. XXXII (April 1929), p. 277.

2. James H. Carleton, *The Battle of Buena Vista with the Operation of the "Army of Occupation" for One Month* (New York: Harper and Brothers, 1848), p. 121.

3. Samuel G. French, *Two Wars: An Autobiography* (Nashville: Confederate Veteran, 1901), p. 82.

4. Samuel Chamberlain, *Recollections of a Rogue* (London: Museum Press Limited, 1957), p. 120.

5. Justin H. Smith, Vol. 1, *The War with Mexico,* Vol. 1 (New York: The Macmillan Company, 1919) p. 120.

6. Close to Rinconada, the "corner" formed by two intersecting chains of mountains is the famous Paso de los Muertos. In the past, many highwaymen lived in this area to rob travelers passing through the narrow high-walled pass, and crosses were placed on the side of the road to memorialize those slain. Crosses placed in memory of victims of automobile accidents line the modern highway through this pass today.

7. Capt. Albert Pike, "A Sketch of the Battle of Buena Vista," *Arkansas State Gazette,* Little Rock, April 24, 1847.

8. John Connor, "The Maurice Kavanaugh Simons Diary," private manuscript in the possession of the Simons family, Houston, Texas.

General Taylor wrote to Thomas Simons, the young man's father, "He saved the army." Although General Taylor had offered a cash reward of $500 for the service, Simons refused it, saying that it was "a duty required of a soldier and not an act performed for pecuniary reward."

9. *Vicksburg Whig,* March 31, 1847.

10. *Vicksburg Whig,* April 2, 1847.

11. *The Southron,* April 16, 1847.

12. Pike, "A Sketch of the Battle of Buena Vista."

13. Henry Wø. Benham, "A Little More Grape," Letter to the editors, *The Vedette,* Vol. 2, no. 4 (January 1881).

14. Carleton, *Buena Vista,* pp. 104–105. Tom Owen, *Anecdotes of Zachary Taylor and the Mexican War* (New York: D. Appleton & Company, 1848), p. 109.

15. Manuel Balbontin, "The Battle of Angostura," (Buena Vista)," translated by Capt. F. H. Hardie, *Journal of the Military Service Institution of the United States,* Vol. 8 (1887), p. 144.

16. Entry for February 25, in Pace, "Diary of William P. Rogers," p. 275. Not a speaker of Spanish, Rogers probably incorrectly transcribed the utterances of the feeble Mexican soldier. It is conjectured that the soldier said something corresponding to "Quiteme la vida, senor," meaning "take my life, sir."

17. Carleton, *Buena Vista,* p. 127.

18. *Vicksburg Whig,* March 31, 1847.

19. Laurier McDonald, private communication. There are no markers to commemorate the battle dead at either cemetary, but there is one at the site of the battle itself.

20. Robert L. Duncan, *Reluctant General, The Life and Times of Albert Pike* (New York: E. P. Dutton and Co., 1961), p. 129. Duncan wrote, "As the company prepared to leave Mexico, a special detail went to Saltillo to look for Archibald Yell's grave. It was not hard to find because the famous Sante Fe traveller Josiah Gregg had supervised the burial and erected a cross bearing Yell's name. The men dug up the tin coffin and took it by wagon to the port where it was loaded on a ship to be taken back to Little Rock."

21. Benham, "A Little More Grape." *The Vedette:* Owen, *Anecdotes of Zachary Taylor,* pp. 96–97, 130. George Lincoln was popular with the army, and his passing was mourned, and his wedding ring and a lock of his hair sent home to his wife. Lincoln's body was laid out and enshrouded by one of his many admirers, Sarah Bourginnis, who cooked for him at Jefferson Barracks six years earlier.

22. *Vicksburg Whig,* April 6, 1847. French, *Two Wars,* p. 76. Moore's

body was interred in Vicksburg on June 5, 1847, (*Vicksburg Whig*, June 8, 1847), in a solemn ceremony. A line of mourners extended the length of seven squares, and businesses were closed during the day. His epitaph was "honored are the dead who die for their country".

23. J. H. Smith, *War with Mexico*, Vol. 1, pp. 375–79.

24. Two of these cannon were later recaptured by Scott's forces at the Battle of Contreras.

25. "To the Editors of the *Independiente*," April 10, 1847, Carleton, *Buena Vista*, Appendix I, p. 217.

26. Brainerd Dyer, *Zachary Taylor* (Baton Rouge: Louisiana State University Press, 1946), p. 216. The order was received by Taylor on November, 12, 1846, just before he departed Monterrey to capture Victoria.

27. Lester R. Dillon, *American Artillery in the Mexican War 1846–47* (Austin: Presidial Press, 1975), pp. 19–20, 63.

28. "B. Bragg to Duncan," April 4, 1847, Justin Smith Transcripts, Latin American Collection, University of Texas, Austin.

29. Maurice G. Fulton, *Diary and Letters of Josiah Gregg*, 2 vols. (Norman: University of Oklahoma Press, 1944), p. 311. Gregg personally disliked General Wool because of a misunderstanding about the conditions of Gregg's employment as a translator for the army.

30. Duncan, *Reluctant General*, p. 118. Privately Wool referred to the regiment as "the mounted devils." When an orderly attempted to remove one of the regiment from the general's tent by gunpoint, the irate Rackensacker leveled his musket at the General and said, "Old horse, damn your soul, if you give such orders I will shoot you for certain." Another regimental member told one of Wool's staff, "Tell Johnny Wool to kiss our ______."

31. Wool to Brig. Gen. R. Jones, January 1847, Wool Papers, Justin Smith Transcripts, Latin American Collection, University of Texas, Austin.

32. Chamberlain, *Recollections*, pp. 87–90, 91–92, 112. K. Jack Bauer, *The Mexican War 1846–1848* (New York: The Macmillan Company, 1974), pp. 208–209.

33. Duncan, *Reluctant General*, pp. 129–31. Another officer of the Arkansas Mounted Regiment, John Selden Roane, was so angered by Pike's letter that he challenged him to a duel. On July 29, 1847, the two men met on a sandbar in the Arkansas River near Fort Smith and exchanged shots. Neither was injured, but they agreed that honor had been satisfied.

However, other men of the regiment felt much as Pike did. When the men returned to Little Rock to be mustered out, a member of the welcome-home crowd shouted, "I hear you all fought like hell at Buena Vista." J. D. Adams shouted back, "We ran like hell at Buena Vista."

34. Robert S. Henry, *The Story of the Mexican War* (New York: The Bobbs-Merrill Company, 1950, pp. 176–77, 202–204. Justin Smith, *War with Mexico,* Vol. 2, pp. 218–20, 455–56. Gen. Winfield Scott, however, did not hesitate to punish criminals in his theater of command. Risking censure from Congress and the American public, he extended military justice system to crimes against Mexican civilians. For the physical abuse of a Mexican woman in Vera Cruz, one soldier was spread-eagled over a wagon wheel and given twelve lashes with a mule whip, and then sent to prison for the remainder of the war. A rapist was promptly and publicly hanged, the same punishment prescribed for such a crime in the United States.

35. *The Southron,* September 23, 1846.

36. "From Joseph E. Davis," October 7, 1846, in James T. McIntosh, ed., *The Papers of Jefferson Davis,* Vol. 3, (Baton Rouge: Louisiana State University Press, 1974), pp. 55–56.

37. Hudson Strode, *Jefferson Davis, American Patriot,* (New York: Harcourt, Brace & Company, 1925). p. 162.

38. Vicksburg Whig, December 25, 1846.

39. Strode, *Jefferson Davis: Private Letters,* 1823–1889 (New York: Harcourt, Brace & World, Inc., 1966), pp. 43–44.

40. Nichols, *Zach Taylor's Little Army,* 16–17.

41. Entry for March 20, 1847, Gov. David Campbell Diary, Justin Smith Transcripts, Latin American Collection, University of Texas, Austin.

CHAPTER 9: FINAL MUSTER

1. *Vicksburg Whig,* April 3, 1847.

2. Justin H. Smith, *The War with Mexico,* Vol. 2. (New York: The Macmillan Company, 1919), p. 169.

3. Entry of March 7, 1847, in Eleanor D. Pace, "Diary and Letters of William P. Rogers, 1846–1862," *The Southwestern Historical Quarterly,* Vol. XXXII (April 1929), p. 278.

4. Justin J. H. Smith, *War with Mexico,* Vol. 2, p. 170.

5. Samuel Chamberlain, *Recollections of a Rogue,* (London: Museum Press, Limited, 1919), pp. 176–77.

6. "The Citizen Mariano Salas . . . to my fellow citizens," April 21,

1847, City of Mexico, Justin Smith Transcripts, Latin American Collection, The University of Texas, Austin.

7. Justin H. Smith, War with Mexico, Vol. 2., p. 169.

8. Ibid, p. 450.

9. [Luther Giddings,] *Sketches of the Campaign in Northern Mexico by an Officer of the First Regiment of Ohio Volunteers* (New York: George P. Putnam & Co., 1853), pp. 334–35.

10. S. Compton Smith, *Chile Con Carne or the Camp and the Field* (New York: Miller & Curtis, 1857), pp. 315–19.

11. Chamberlain, *Recollections,* p. 69. Chamberlain reported what the rancheros could do to a straggler: "Woe to the unfortunate soldier who straggled behind. He was lassoed, stripped naked, and dragged through clumps of cactus until his body was full of needle-like thorns; then, his privates cut off and crammed into his mouth, he was left to die. . . ."

12. Service Record, William Henry Harrison Patterson. General Quitman had rated Patterson as "an active and enterprising officer of the 1st Mississippi Regiment," and Col. Jefferson Davis had praised his services.

13. John Conner, "The Maurice Kavanaugh Simons Diary," private manuscript in the possession of the Simons family, Houston, Texas, pp. 13–15. In an undated letter from Mrs. M. K. Simons to Virginia McChesney, "On the day of April 27, 1847, he and Wash [George Washington Trahern] were riding together when Mexican Guerrillas fired on them. Maurice's horse ran into a thicket and fell dead, and he fell from him. This was 10 o'clock in the morning and no relief came until sundown. . . . When the surgeon saw how badly he was hurt, he said there was no chance to save his life but to take off his leg. Maurice said he would rather die, and the Dr. gave it up for he said he didn't think he could live anyway, but after Wash had begged him to have it taken off he consented. The surgeon said he had no surgical instruments and Maurice told him to saw it off with a butcher saw which he did. He cut flesh with a butcher knife and the bone with a meat saw. When the operation was done he fainted, and they all thought he was dead, and they went and sat around the camp fire. After a while Wash went to look at him, thinking he was dead. He took his hand and pressed it as if to say 'Good-bye', and your uncle returned the pressure gently. Wash called the Dr. and he bound up the wound and gave him restoratives . . . mexican women nursed him, but it was 18 months before he was able to come home." Simons recovered from his wounds,

thanks to the kind people of the village of Papagallos. This remarkable man served with distinction during the War Between the States as a Major in the 2nd Texas Infantry, probably the only one-legged man to serve in the infantry.

14. William E. Estes, "Something About the First Mississippi Rifles," undated newspaper article, newspaper unknown, Mississippi Department of Archives and History, Jackson, Mississippi. Mexican War Subject File.

15. Robert McElroy, *Jefferson Davis, the Unreal and the Real,* Vol. 1. (New York: Harper & Brothers Publishers, 1937), p. 94.

16. John P. Bloom, "With the American Army into Mexico 1846–1848," Ph.D. dissertation, Emory University, Atlanta, 1956, p. 145.

17. Ibid, p. 145, note 47.

18. James T. McIntosh, ed., *The Papers of Jefferson Davis,* Vol. 3 (Baton Rouge: Louisiana State University Press, 1974), p. 178, notes 1 and 2.

19. "Speech at New Orleans," June 10, 1847. *The Papers of Jefferson Davis,* Vol. 3, p. 181.

20. Estes, "Something About the First Mississippi Rifles"

21. "Speech at Natchez," June 14, 1847. *The Papers of Jefferson Davis,* Vol. 3, p. 183.

22. *Vicksburg Whig,* June 15, 1847.

23. Ibid.

24. *The Papers of Jefferson Davis,* Vol. 3, p. 175, note 3.

25. "To George Talcott," November 7, 1847, *The Papers of Jefferson Davis,* Vol. 3, p. 245.

26. Ibid, p. 246.

27. Ibid, p. 250.

28. *Clarion Ledger Jackson Daily News,* Jackson, Mississippi, April 17, 1955.

29. Robert E. May, *John A. Quitman—Old South Crusader* (Baton Rouge: Louisiana State University Press, 1985), p. 290.

30. Reuben Davis, *Recollections of Mississippi and Mississippians* (Jackson: University and College Press of Mississippi, 1972), pp. 215–18.

31. Invocation to Death
by Alexander Keith McClung

Swiftly speed o'er the wastes of time
Spirit of Death!
In the manhood's morn, in youthful prime
I woo thy breath!

For the glittering hues of hope are fled
  Like the dolphin's light,
And dark are the clouds above my head
  As the starless night.
O! Vainly the mariner sighs for rest
  Of the peaceful haven
The pilgrim saint for the shrines of the blest,
  The calm of heaven;
The galley slave for the night wind's breath,
  At burning noon;
But more gladly I'd spring to thy arms,
  O, Death!

32. Mississippi Department of Archives and History, correspondence from Mary Lohrenz to the author, June 6, 1985.

BIBLIOGRAPHY

The word "acct." following an entry indicates a firsthand account, memoir, or diary written by Americans participating in the campaign in northern Mexico. Especially interesting eyewitness descriptions of the battle for Monterrey and the Battle of Buena Vista can be found in *The Papers of Jefferson Davis*, Vol. 3.

Books

Alcarez, Ramon. *The Other Side or Notes for the History of the War Between Mexico and the United States*. Reprint. New York: Burt Franklin, 1850, 1970.

Allsopp, Fred W. *Albert Pike: A Biography*. Little Rock: Parke-Harper Company, 1928.

Balbontin, Manuel. *La Invasion Americana, 1846 a 1848*. Mexico: Gonzalo A. Esteva, 1883.

Barton, Henry. *Texas Volunteers in the Mexican War*. Waco: The Texian Press, 1970. acct.

Bauer, K. Jack. *The Mexican War 1846–1848*. New York: The Macmillan Co., 1974.

_____. Zachary Taylor—Soldier, Planter, Statesman of the Old Southwest. Baton Rouge: Louisiana State University Press, 1985.

Bill, Alfred H. *Rehearsal for Conflict*. New York: Alfred A. Knopf, 1947.

Biographical and Historical Memoirs of Mississippi. Chicago: The Goodspeed Publishing Company, 1891. acct.

Brooks, Nathan. *A Complete History of the Mexican War 1846–1848*. Reprint. Chicago. The Rio Grande Press Inc., 1849, 1965.

Buhoup, Jonathan W. *Narratives of the Central Division, or, Army of Chihuahua, Commanded by Brigadier General Wool . . .* Pittsburgh: M. P. Morse, 1847.

Carleton, James Henry. *The Battle of Buena Vista, with the Operations of the "Army of Occupation" for One Month.* New York: Harper & Brothers, 1848. acct.

Chamberlain, Samuel E. *Recollections of a Rogue.* London: Museum Press Limited, 1957. acct.

Chance, Joseph E. *The Second Texas Infantry.* Austin: Eakin Publications, 1984, acct.

Claiborne, J. F. H. *Life and Correspondence of John A. Quitman.* New York: Harper & Brothers, 1860.

Copley, James S. *The Sign of the Eagle.* San Diego: The Copley Press, Inc., 1970.

Crawford, Ann Fears. *The Eagle: The Autobiography of Santa Anna.* Austin: The Pemberton Press, 1967.

Davis, Reuben. *Recollections of Mississippi and Mississippians.* Oxford, Miss.: University and College Press of Mississippi, 1972.

Diccionairio Porrúa Historia, Biografia, Y Geografia de Mexico. 2d ed. Mexico City: Editorial Porrua, 1965.

Dillon, Lester R. *American Artillery in the Mexican War 1846–1847.* Austin: Presidial Press, 1975.

Dole, Nathan H. *Poems of John Greenleaf Whittier.* New York: Thomas Y. Crowell Company, 1893.

Doubleday, Rhoda V. T., ed., *Journals of the Late Brevet Major Philip Norbourne Barbour, Captain in the 3rd Regiment, United States Infantry, and his Wife, Martha Isabella Hopkins Barbour.* New York: G. P. Putnam's Sons, 1936.

Duncan, Robert Lipscomb. *Reluctant General: The Life and Times of Albert Pike.* New York: E. P. Dutton & Co., 1961.

Dyer, Brainerd. *Zachary Taylor.* Baton Rouge: Louisiana State University Press, 1946.

Eisenhower, John S. D. *So Far from God—The U. S. War with Mexico 1846–1848.* New York: Random House, 1989.

Robert H. Ferrell, ed. *Monterrey Is Ours! The Mexican War Letters of Lieutenant Dana 1845–1847.* Lexington, Ky.: The University Press of Kentucky, 1990.

French, Samuel G. *Two Wars: An Autobiography of Gen. Samuel G. French.* Nashville: Confederate Veteran, 1901.

Frost, John. *Pictorial History of Mexico and the Mexican War.* Philadelphia: Thomas, Copperwait & Co., for James A. Bill, 1848.

[Giddings, Luther.] *Sketches of the Campaign in Northern Mexico in Eighteen Hundred Forty-Six and Seven.* New York: George P. Putnam, 1853. acct.

Fulton, Maurice G. *Diary and Letters of Josiah Gregg*. 2 vols. Norman: University of Oklahoma Press, 1944.

Grant, Ulysses S. *Personal Memoirs of U. S. Grant*. New York: Charles L. Webster & Co., 1894.

Green, Thomas J. *Journal of the Texian Expedition Against Mier*. Austin: The Steck Co., 1935.

Greer, James K. *Colonel Jack Hays*. New York: E. P. Dutton and Co., 1952.

———. *A Texas Ranger and Frontiersman: The Days of Buck Barry in Texas in 1845–1906*. Dallas: The Southwest Press, 1932. acct.

Heitman, Francis B. *Historical Register and Dictionary of the United States Army, from Its Organization September 29, 1789, to March 2, 1903*. 2 vols. Reprint. Urbana: University of Illinois Press, 1965.

Henry, Robert S. *The Story of the Mexican War*. New York: The Bobbs-Merrill Company, 1950.

Henry, William S. *Campaign Sketches of the War in Mexico*. New York: Harper & Brothers, 1847.

Horgan, Paul. *Great River: The Rio Grande in North American History*. 2 vols. New York: Holt, Rinehart, & Winston, 1968.

Johannsen, Robert W. *To the Halls of the Montezumas*. New York: Oxford University Press, 1985.

Johnson, Florence Scott. *Old Rough and Ready on the Rio Grande*. Waco: The Texian Press, 1969.

Kenley, John R. *Memoirs of a Maryland Volunteer*. Philadelphia: J. B. Lippincott & Co., 1873.

Lander, Alexander. *A Trip to Texas Comprising the History of the Galveston Riflemen, Formed April 28, 1846, at Galveston, Texas; Together with the History of the Battle of Monterey; Also Descriptions of Mexico and Its People*. Monmouth, Ill.: Printed at the "Atlas Office," for the Publisher, 1847. acct.

Lavender, David. *Climax at Buena Vista: The American Campaign in Northeastern Mexico*. Philadelphia: J. B. Lippincott Co., 1966.

Lea, Tom. *The King Ranch*, Vol. 1. Boston: Little, Brown & Company, 1957.

Losson, Christopher. *Tennessee's Forgotten Warriors: Frank Cheatham and His Confederate Division*. Knoxville: The University of Tennessee Press, 1989.

Lynch, James D. *The Bench and Bar of Mississippi*. New York: E. J. Hale, 1881. acct.

Lytle, William M. *Merchant Steam Vessels of the United States, 1807–*

1868. Edited by Forrest R. Holdcamper. Mystic, Conn.: Steamship Historical Society of America, 1952.

McAfee, Ward, and J. Cordell Robinson. *Origins of the Mexican War—A Documentary Source Book*. 2 vols. Salisbury, N. C.: Documentary Publications, 1982.

McCutchan, Joseph D. *Mier Expedition Diary*. Edited by Joseph Milton Nance. Austin: University of Texas Press, 1978.

McElroy, Robert. *Jefferson Davis, the Unreal and the Real*. New York and London: Harper & Brothers Publishers, 1937.

McIntosh, James T., ed., *The Papers of Jefferson Davis*, Vol. 2, *June 1841–July 1846*. Baton Rouge: Louisiana State University Press, 1974. acct.

———. *The Papers of Jefferson Davis*, Vol. 3, *July 1846–December 1848*. Baton Rouge: Louisiana State University Press, 1981. acct.

McWhiney, Grady, and Perry Jamieson. *Attack and Die—Civil War Military Tactics and the Southern Heritage*. University, Ala.: The University of Alabama Press, 1982.

McWhiney, Grady and Sue McWhiney. *To Mexico with Taylor and Scott 1845–1847*. Waltham, Mass.: Blaisdell Publishing Co., 1969. acct.

Malone, Dumas. *Dictionary of American Biography*. New York: Charles Scribners' Sons, 1933.

May, Robert E. *John A. Quitman—Old South Crusader*. Baton Rouge: Louisiana State University Press, 1985.

Meade, George. *The Life and Letters of George Gordon Meade, Major General, United States Army*. Vol. 1. New York: Charles Scribner's Sons, 1913. acct.

The Mexican War. Alexandria, Va.: Time-Life Books Inc., 1978.

Myers, William Starr. *The Mexican War Diary of George B. McClennan*. Princeton: Princeton University Press, 1917. acct.

Nance, Joseph Milton. *After San Jacinto*. Austin: University of Texas Press, 1963.

National Cyclopedia of American Biography. New York: James T. White & Co., 1906.

Nevins, Allan. *Polk: The Diary of a President 1845–1849*. New York: Longmans, Green, & Co., 1952.

Nichols, Edward. *Zach Taylor's Little Army*. Garden City, N.Y. Doubleday & Company Inc., 1963.

Owen, Tom. *Anecdotes of Zachary Taylor and The Mexican War*. New York: D. Appleton & Company, 1848.

Perry, Oran. *Indiana in the Mexican War*. Indianapolis: Wm. B. Burford, 1908.

Ranck, James B. *Albert Gallatin Brown: Radical Southern Nationalist*. New York: 1937.

Reid, Samuel C. *The Scouting Expeditions of McCullough's Texas Rangers*. Reprint. New York: Books for Libraries Press, 1847, 1970. acct.

Risch, Erna. *Quarter Master Support of the Army: A History of the Corps 1775–1939*. Washington: QM Historian's Office, Office of the QM General, 1962.

Robinson, Fayette. *Mexico and Her Military Chieftains*. Glorieta, NM: The Rio Grande Press, Inc., 1970.

Robinson, John B. *Reminiscences of a Campaign in Mexico*. Nashville: 1849. acct.

Roland, Charles. *Albert Sidney Johnston: Soldier of Three Republics*. Austin: University of Texas Press, 1964.

Roller, David C. and Robert W. Twyman. *The Encyclopedia of Southern History*. Baton Rouge: Louisiana State University Press, 1979.

Rowland, Dunbar. *Mississippi*. Spartanburg, S.C.: The Reprint Co. Publishers, 1976. acct.

Samson, William H. *Letters of Zachary Taylor from the Battlefields of the Mexican War*. Rochester, NY: privately printed, 1908.

Scribner, Benjamin Franklin. *Camp Life of a Volunteer: A Campaign in Mexico or a Glimpse at Life in Camp by "One Who Has Seen the Elephant."* Philadelphia: Grigg, Elliot & Co., 1847. acct.

Simon, John Y. *The Papers of Ulysses S. Grant*, Vol. 1: *1837–1861*. Carbondale: Southern Illinois University Press, 1967.

Singletary, Otis A. *The Mexican War*. Chicago: The University of Chicago Press, 1960.

Smith, H. Compton. *Chile con Carne*. New York: Miller & Curtis, 1857. acct.

Smith, George W., and Charles Judah. *Chronicles of the Gringos*. Albuquerque: The University of New Mexico Press, 1968. acct.

Smith, Justin. *The War with Mexico*. 2 vols. New York: The Macmillan Company, 1919.

Sowell, Andrew Jackson. *Early Settlers and Indian Fighters of Southwest Texas*. New York: Argosy-Antiquarian Ltd., 1964. acct.

Spurlin, Charles D. *Texas Veterans in the Mexican War*. Nacogdoches, Tex.: Erickson Books, 1984.

Stambaugh, J. Lee, and Lillian J. Stambaugh. *The Lower Rio Grande Valley of Texas*. Austin: The Jenkins Publishing Co., 1974.

Strode, Hudson. *Jefferson Davis, American Patriot 1808–1861*. New York: Harcourt, Brace & Company, 1955.

———. *Jefferson Davis: Private Letters, 1823–1889*. New York: Harcourt, Brace & World, Inc., 1966.

Tennery, Thomas D. *The Mexican War Diary of Thomas D. Tennery*. Norman: University of Oklahoma Press, 1970.

Thompson, Jerry. *Sabers on the Rio Grande*. Austin: Presidial Press, 1975.

Thorpe, Thomas B. *Our Army at Monterey*. Philadelphia: 1848.

Viele, Teresa Griffin. *Following the Drum*. Lincoln: University of Nebraska Press, 1984.

Vigil y Robles, Guillermo. *La Invasion de Mexico por Los Estados Unidos en Los Anos de 1846, 1847, y 1848*. Mexico: 1923.

Wallace, Edward. *Destiny and Glory*. New York: Coward-McCann, Inc., 1957.

Webb, Walter P. *The Handbook of Texas*. Austin: The Texas State Historical Association, 1952.

Who's Who in America Historical Volume 1607–1896. Chicago: The A. N. Marquis Co., 1963.

Wilcox, Cadmus. *History of the Mexican War*. Washington: Church News Publishing Company, 1892.

Government Documents

Executive Document No. 65, 31st Congress. "Message from The President of the United States communicating the report of Lieutenant Webster of a survey of the gulf coast at the mouth of the Rio Grande," July 27, 1850.

Executive Document No. 13, 31st Congress. "Letter from The Secretary of War, transmitting a report on the route of General Patterson's division from Matamoros to Victoria," December 19, 1850.

Manuscripts and Collections

Bloom, John Porter. "With the American Army into Mexico, 1846–1848." Dissertation, Emory University, Atlanta, 1956.

Conner, John. "Maurice Kavanaugh Simons." Texas A & I University, undated.

Lasswell, Lynda Jane. "The First Regiment of Mississippi Infantry in the Mexican War and Letters of Jefferson Davis Concerning the War." M. A. Thesis, Rice University, Houston, 1969.

McDonald, Laurier B., Private correspondence.
National Archives (DNA). Microfilm Series M-863, Records of the Adjutant General's Office, Compiled Service Records, Mexican War.
Spurlin, Charles D., Manuscript on the Mexican War, unpublished.
The Mexican War Diary of James C. Browning, handwritten manuscript, Mexican War Collection, Mississippi Archives, Jackson, Mississippi.
The Mexican War Diary of Franklin Smith, handwritten manuscript, Mexican War Collection, Mississippi Archives, Jackson, Mississippi.
The Justin Smith Transcripts, Latin American Collection, University of Texas at Austin, Austin, Texas.

Newspapers

Arkansas State Gazette, Little Rock, April 24, 1847.
Clarion Ledger, Jackson, Mississippi. acct.
Holly Springs Gazette, Holly Springs, Mississippi. 1846–1947. acct.
Mississippi Free Trader and Natchez Gazette, Natchez, Mississippi, June 23, 1846.
Natchez Courier, Natchez, Mississippi. June 24, 1846.
Port Gibson Correspondent, Port Gibson, Mississippi, June 24, 1846.
Sentinel and Expositor, Vicksburg, Mississippi, July 14, 1846.
The Picket Guard, Saltillo, Mexico, April 19, May 10, 1847. acct.
The Southron, Jackson, Mississippi. 1846–1847. acct.
The Vicksburg Whig, Vicksburg, Mississippi. 1846–1847. acct.
The Wall Street Journal, New York City, April 6, 1989.

Articles

A Mississippian. "Sketches of Our Volunteer Officers: Alexander Keith McClung." *Southern Literary Messenger,* Vol. XXI, 1855.
Backus, Electus. "Details of the Controversy Between the Regulars and Volunteers, in Relation to the Part Taken By Each in the Capture of Battery No. 1 and Other Works at the East End of the City of Monterey, on the 21st of September, 1846." *Historical Magazine,* Vol. 10 (1866). acct.
______. "A Brief Sketch of the Battle of Monterey; with details of That Portion of it, Which Took Place at the Eastern Extremity of the City." *Historical Magazine,* Vol. 10 (1866). acct.
Balboutin [sic], Manuel. "The Siege of Monterey." *Journal of the Military Service Institution of the United States*. Vol. 8, (1887). acct.

———. "The Battle of Angostura Pass (Buena Vista)." *Journal of the Military Service Institution of the United States*, Vol. 8 (1887). acct.

Bauer, K. Jack. "General John E. Wool's Memoranda of the Battle of Buena Vista." *Southwestern Historical Quarterly*, Vol. LXXVII, No. 1 (1973).

Benham, H. W. "A Little More Grape." *The Vedette*. Vol. 2, No. 4 (January 1881). acct.

Brent, Robert A. "Mississippi and the Mexican War," *Journal of Mississippi History*, Vol. 31 (1969).

Buchanan, A. Russell. "George Washington Trahern: Texan Cowboy Soldier from Mier to Buena Vista." *The Southwestern Historical Quarterly*, Vol. LVIII (1954). acct.

Downing, R. L. "Infantry Weapons of the Mexican War," *Antiques*, November 1940.

Estes, William E. "Something About the First Mississippi Rifles." Undated newspaper article, Mexican War Documents, Mississippi Archives, Jackson, Mississippi.

Henderson, Alfred J. "A Morgan County Volunteer in the Mexican War." *Journal of the Illinois State Historical Society*, Vol. 41 (1948).

Jacobs, Wm. H. "Interesting Letters from an Officer on the Rio Grande." *The Vedette*, December 1888.

O'Neal, H. F. "Aleck McClung and Jefferson Davis at Monterey." *The Vedette*, Vol. 5, No. 1 (January 1884).

Pace, Eleanor D. "The Diary and Letters of William P. Rogers, 1846–1862," *The Southwestern Historical Quarterly*, Volume XXXII (1929). acct.

Penix, Joe. "McClung—Death's Ramrod," *Clarion-Ledger*, Jackson, Mississippi, April 3, April 10, April 17, 1955.

Phillips, George. "A Little More Grape, Captain Bragg." *The Vedette*, Vol. 3, No. 9 (June 1882).

Pike, Albert. "A Sketch of the Battle of Buena Vista," *Arkansas State Gazette*, Little Rock Arkansas, April 24, 1847.

Rowland, Dunbar. "Political and Parliamentary Orators and Orations of Mississippi." *Publications of the Mississippi Historical Society*, Vol. IV (1901).

———. "Badge Members of the National Association of Veterans of the Mexican War." *The Vedette*, Vol. 3, No. 8 (May 1882).

———. "Death of a Mississippi Rifleman." *The Vedette*. Vol. 3, No. 12 (December 1882).

INDEX